ROY WILLIAMS

HARD WORK

A LIFE ON AND OFF THE COURT

WITH TIM CROTHERS

ALGONQUIN BOOKS OF CHAPEL HILL 2011

Published by
ALGONQUIN BOOKS OF CHAPEL HILL
Post Office Box 2225
Chapel Hill, North Carolina 27515-2225

a division of
WORKMAN PUBLISHING
225 Varick Street
New York, New York 10014

First paperback edition, Algonquin Books of Chapel Hill, October 2011.
Originally published by Algonquin Books of Chapel Hill in 2009.
Printed in the United States of America.
Published simultaneously in Canada by Thomas Allen & Son Limited.
Design by Anne Winslow.
All photos courtesy of the Williams family unless otherwise indicated.

The Library of Congress has cataloged the hardcover edition of this title as follows:
Williams, Roy, [date]
    Hard work : a life on and off the court / Roy Williams with
Tim Crothers. — 1st ed.
        p. cm.
    ISBN 978-1-56512-959-7 (HC)
    1. Williams, Roy, [date]   2. Basketball coaches — United
States — Biography.   3. North Carolina Tar Heels (Basketball
team)   I. Crothers, Tim.   II. Title.
    GV884.W58A3 2009
    796.323092 — dc22
    [B]   2009036970

ISBN 978-1-61620-107-4 (PB)

10 9 8 7 6 5 4 3 2 1
First Paperback Edition

To WANDA, who has helped me with everything,
including this book, and is the greatest mom in the world
To Scott and Kimberly, who are my heroes
And to my mother, my father, and my sister, who
I wish were here to read these pages

Contents

Foreword

BY JOHN GRISHAM

IT IS SAFE TO ASSUME that Roy Williams's early years were not filled with great expectations. Look at his ancestors. Few people could (or would) lay claim to the same genealogy that produced the feuding McCoys in Kentucky and the murderous Dalton gang, eventually gunned down somewhere in Kansas. Growing up in the mountains of North Carolina, Roy had an abusive, alcoholic father who abandoned the family, leaving Roy's mother and her two small children with no support and no place to live. They moved from motels to trailers to rooms offered by relatives. His mother labored in factories and ironed clothes for the wealthy to pay the bills and put food on the table. As kids, Roy and his sister hustled part-time jobs and learned that survival depended on hard work.

Life was often unpleasant. When he was eight years old he bounced his first basketball, and the game soon became his outlet, his escape. He loved to play alone, to shoot for hours on dirt courts and in local gyms, often when they were closed and he was not supposed to be there. The game consumed him, and his constant practice turned him into a noticeable high school player. He wasn't tall and he wasn't fast, but his deadly aim was perfected by hours of hard work.

It would be easy at this point to say, "And the rest is history." But not so fast.

Nothing ever came easy for Roy Williams.

As an athlete, he was good but far from great. He realized his limitations as a player, and by the time he finished high school Roy had decided to become a college coach. All roads led to the University of North Carolina and Dean Smith. He tried out for the freshman team, primarily as a means of wiggling his way into the program. He juggled part-time jobs to pay for school, slept little, studied hard, got one degree and then another, and managed to land a volunteer position as a statistician for the varsity. From the bleachers, he watched every practice and every game and took endless notes. His hard work did not go unnoticed.

Dean Smith hired him as an assistant coach, and offered him a salary of $2,700, an amount far less than Roy needed to support his young family. No problem. He hustled dozens of part-time jobs and paid his bills. For 10 seasons he worked under Coach Smith— watching, studying, absorbing every aspect of the game. He learned to teach, to coach, and to win. By the time he left for Kansas in 1988, no coach worked harder than Roy Williams.

When he returned to Chapel Hill 15 years later, he had few peers. And no coach worked harder than Roy Williams.

I met him a few years ago. My daughter enrolled at UNC, and I found myself spending a lot of time in Chapel Hill. It's not unusual to see him jogging the leafy streets around the campus, waving at students and chatting with the neighbors. He loves baseball and is a regular at Tar Heel games in the spring, graciously signing autographs while never missing a pitch. I once bumped into him in a hotel lobby during an ACC basketball tournament, and he was immediately concerned with my ticket situation. I got the impression he had a pocketful and wanted to make sure his friends were covered. I send him a copy of each new book, a small gesture that's always appreciated. I was in St. Louis with my wife and daughter for the Final Four in 2005 when Roy won his first national title. As the final seconds ticked away and Tar Heel Nation was ready to explode, I shared an enormous sense of pride in the fact that we consider each other friends. There was also a mighty sense of relief in knowing that he would no longer be dogged by the second-place finish.

Today, his salary is not an issue. With two national titles, he has silenced those who said he couldn't win the Big One. He has filled the legendary shoes of Dean Smith, and with the same class and grace. The grind of recruiting is somewhat easier since the great players call him. He is still disarmingly warm, affable, genuine, and accessible.

But success has not changed him. The perfect gentleman with the easy grin still burns the candle at both ends so he can bury you in March.

Introduction

THE FACT THAT YOU are reading this book is more surprising to me than to anyone else in the entire world. I never thought I would be writing about myself and what has happened in my life. I have been approached several times about writing a book and I have always said no, but I was finally convinced to do so. I hope I can give you a story that you will enjoy reading and might help you to understand Roy Williams a little better.

There are some things that I need to say that are easier to express in an introduction than in the book itself. I was very fortunate as a young assistant coach to be mentored not only by Dean Smith but also by Bill Guthridge, Eddie Fogler, and Dick Harp. All of those people played an extraordinary role in my development. To this day, I have never called Coach Smith or Coach Guthridge anything other than "Coach." That is the way it will always be with me. Dick Harp coached alongside me for only a couple of years, but I learned a great deal from him about Kansas and the tradition, all of which was very important to me. Eddie Fogler taught me so much about coaching and recruiting, and I still follow many of his suggestions today.

In a book like this, it is impossible to say enough about how lucky I've been to work with all of the assistant coaches I have had during my career. I can only tell you that I have the best staff in America, and it's not even close. A lot of coaches can say that, but none can say it with the conviction that I do. Joe Holladay, Steve Robinson, C.B. McGrath, and Jerod Haase have all been with me for at least 11 years. They make my job so much easier, and they all have tremendous pride in the success that we have had together. I hope they know how important they have been and continue to be. I have also been very fortunate in the past to have had excellent assistant coaches like Jerry Green, Kevin Stallings, Mark Turgeon, Neil Dougherty, Matt Doherty, and Ben Miller. There is no way we could have enjoyed the success we have had over the years if I didn't say "we"; everyone has contributed to that greatly and they all have meant so much to me personally as well. When you hire an assistant coach, you are putting a part of your life and career in his hands. With all of these people, I realized I was in good hands.

In the appendices of the book is a listing of all of the players I have ever coached as a head coach. I would have loved to mention all of these players in the course of the book and what each one meant to me. I want every player to know how appreciative I am of the time I had with them.

To my wife, Wanda, and my children, Scott and Kimberly: during my entire career, I have always hoped that I wasn't embarrassing you. I hope this book does not embarrass you; it was the hardest thing that I have ever attempted to do, but the most positive aspect of it was when I could describe the three of you and how much you mean to me and the fact that you are my life.

In the book there is also a section on my "foxhole buddies." Yes, I know you all think you should be getting even more credit for taking care of me, but I want to keep your heads at a decent size.

I could never write enough in the following pages to give all of these people the recognition they deserve.

In this book are parts of my life that I never thought I would share with anyone. That has been extremely hard. So many times it brought an emptiness to my stomach and tears to my eyes. But I hope you will see, as I came to see, that we never need to be pushed by our problems but led by our dreams.

Roy Williams
November 2009

CHAPTER 1

Stress

ONE OCTOBER NIGHT it got so bad that I woke up at 4 a.m. and went for a walk in the neighborhood. It was a little spooky, and I wondered if anybody else was awake and if they were thinking, "Who is that guy walking around at this hour?" So I didn't walk on the sidewalk. I walked right down the middle of the street, because I didn't want anybody to think I was a burglar and shoot my rear end.

I just couldn't sleep.

I never sleep very well in the preseason, but I got less sleep during the 2009 preseason than any year I have ever coached. From the start of practice, an average night's sleep for me was about four hours. So many things were running through my mind. I keep a little notepad and pen on my nightstand and a lot of times I come up with an idea and turn the light on and write it down and then try to go back to sleep. But during the '09 preseason there was never any going back to sleep. In all my years of coaching I have never felt more pressure.

It was all because of what I wanted for one kid. I so badly wanted Tyler Hansbrough to reach his dream. This was his last chance to win a national championship. I can never remember wanting something so much for one of my players.

I think part of it was because Tyler didn't come back for his senior year at North Carolina to improve his stock for the NBA draft. He came back because he enjoyed college and he wanted to win a national title. A very physical, no-nonsense kid from Poplar Bluff, Missouri, who had been the centerpiece of our team for three seasons, Tyler had received so many individual awards, but he never cared about any of them. All he ever really wanted was the big team prize. It felt like Tyler was carrying all of what is good about college basketball on his shoulders. I know it sounds corny, but I really felt it was only right for him to win a national championship.

During the preseason, I had tried to tell Tyler not to let a championship be his only goal, because odds were that it was not going to happen. He looked me square in the eye. "Coach," he said, "I want to win it so bad."

I remember it was the very end of August when I first heard that Tyler had a problem with his shin. He told the trainers he thought he got kicked, and they put some ice on it. When our preseason conditioning started in the middle of September, his leg was still bothering him, and it hurt more and more as we got closer to the start of the season. So we did an MRI and a bone scan and the problem was diagnosed as a stress reaction condition. The bone was weakened, leading to the possibility of a stress fracture or worse.

It's the kind of injury where nobody really knows what's going to happen next. Our doctors told me that in two weeks we might see some improvement or we might not. At four weeks we might see some improvement or we might not. I could let him have six weeks off and then he could come back to practice for five minutes and break his leg. Tyler was worried he might miss the whole season. I told our doctors, "You know what they call the guy who finished last in medical school? Doctor. You know what they call the guy who finishes last in coaching? Ex-coach." Every day I jokingly threatened to fire them, but I wanted them to understand how serious this really was.

I had no choice but to let Tyler sit out as long as he needed to, which was hard because he was the returning National Player of the Year and a guy that's going to get 20 points and 10 rebounds every game. That's a pretty big security blanket for a coach.

Tyler sat out of practice for two weeks and then we started working him back in a little bit at a time. That was the toughest part. We'd be doing a drill that was 12 minutes long and I planned to let Tyler do half of that, but we'd get nearly through half and I'd think, "Gosh, I wonder if I should take him out?" I always knew that if I let him go one more play, he could possibly hurt himself. Every time he jumped, I worried that he might come down and snap his leg. I was thinking every play could be his last. Every day at practice before I went out on the court, I'd say a little prayer: "Let this team play well. Let me help this team and let no one get hurt, especially Tyler." In every drill, instead of coaching my team, I was peeking at Tyler with one eye and my watch with the other, wondering if I should pull him out. I finished every practice with a splitting headache. I was so worried I might end the guy's career.

On top of all that were the expectations. While Tyler had never seriously considered leaving UNC early for the NBA, three other underclassmen—Ty Lawson, our lightning-quick point guard; Wayne Ellington, our deadly outside shooter; and Danny Green, an excellent all-around player on the wing—had all submitted their names for the NBA draft. In June, when those three guys opted to pull their names out of the draft to improve their stock with another college season, I read a story in the newspaper that said North Carolina could have one of the greatest teams ever. Then, in the summertime when I was recruiting, other coaches would say to me, "The good news is you're going to have a great team. The bad news is that everybody's going to expect you to win a national title. And if you don't win it, everybody will say your season wasn't a success." As much as I hated to admit it, I knew what they were saying was true.

The Associated Press preseason poll came out and we were unanimously voted No. 1. The *Sporting News* printed a story titled "They Just Can't Lose" and said that we might be the best college team in 30 years, with a chance to be the first undefeated team since 1976, when Bobby Knight did it with Indiana. What scared me was reading that and knowing my players were hearing about it and, even more, that their families were buying into it. I knew that somewhere in the back of their minds, those guys who had considered leaving early for the pros were going to be thinking about what the NBA player personnel people had told them they should do to improve their draft positions, and they'd have their parents reminding them about it. I don't care how good a parent you are, if you're not careful you can really hurt a child by just focusing on what he needs to accomplish. That will also undermine his team. So I was trying to control what my team heard, but I couldn't control what their parents told them. I couldn't control their classmates saying, "We can't wait until basketball season starts. We're going to kill everybody!"

I have never coached any team that had so much pressure put on it. The year before we'd gone 36–3, won our conference regular season and tournament championships, and then lost in the Final Four. Some people thought the season was a failure. Now we were supposed to go undefeated in a time of parity in college basketball when there are so many more high-quality teams that it just doesn't happen anymore. I knew that every game we played was going to be overanalyzed so that if we won by 25, people were going to say we should have won by 30. It was never going to be enough. That's an uncomfortable feeling when you can't be excited about winning.

Every day I said to the team, "I want you all to realize that our goal to win a national title is realistic, but also understand that the only people you've got to please are me and yourselves. That's it. Don't be concerned about what anybody else is saying. Those other people have nothing invested in it. You're the ones who are sweating in the weight room. You're the ones who are running yourselves half to death at the end of practice."

I told them to ignore the expectations and I think they tried to put them out of their minds. I knew I'd be fighting all year to try to keep that weight off my team. I still thought it was something that we could never rest on. We had to attack it every single day. I knew I'd have to keep reminding them to enjoy the ride. But in the back of my mind, I also knew it would always be there. I felt the worst stress of my entire life.

That night as I walked down the middle of my street at 4 o'clock in the morning, I was thinking, "How can I live with myself if I don't get Tyler and the rest of these guys back to the Final Four?"

I HELD TYLER out of the first two games of the season. That was a hard decision because we'd also lost Marcus Ginyard, a senior and our best defensive player, after he'd injured his foot in the preseason, and we didn't have any idea when he was coming back. Then freshman Tyler Zeller broke his wrist in our second game against Kentucky, and we thought he could be out for the whole season.

In our third game, we went to UC Santa Barbara and Tyler felt much better, so I let him play. I could tell he was pressing. He missed some shots that he normally makes. He also sprained his ankle early in that game, which added another question mark as to whether he was healthy enough to play.

Then we went to Hawaii for the Maui Invitational and I didn't play Tyler in the opener of the tournament against Chaminade. He played all right in the next game against Oregon, but we limited his minutes. He proved that the ankle was not a problem, but I was still concerned. I couldn't decide whether to play him the next night in the championship game against Notre Dame. I knew he'd be so fired up to play against a Top 10 team and against Luke Harangody, another big guy who was supposed to be pretty good. I talked to Tyler in warm-ups and I said, "Big fella, how do you feel?"

Tyler said, "Coach, I'm fine."

"No, Tyl—"

"Coach, I'm fine!"

"I just want to make sure I'm—"

"Coach, I'm fine!"

I thought I was going to have to fight him.

"Okay," I said, "I'll start you, but if I don't like what I see, I'm taking you out of the game and you won't play anymore."

I didn't really mean that, but I was just trying to remind him that I was the head coach. So I started him and he was sensational. He scored 34 points and we won.

A week later we went to Detroit to play Michigan State at Ford Field, where the Final Four would be played. Michigan State had been through a tough travel schedule leading up to that game and they had a couple of guys hurt, so we tried to establish a quick tempo right from the start. It was a close game for a while, but right before the half I noticed that the Michigan State players were not sprinting back on defense and seemed to be tiring. I turned to my assistants and said, "They're done. If we keep the hammer down, this one is going to be over with early in the second half."

We were up by 14 points at halftime, but early in the second half we pushed the tempo even higher. Michigan State started coming up short on open shots. We took away their second shots and kept running our break, and they hit the wall. It felt like a snowball rolling down the hill getting bigger and bigger. We won by 35. After the game I said, "Guys, we were really good today, but that other team helped us. They lost their legs. Say good things about them, because we may play them again down the line."

Then I added, "If we keep playing our tails off, we might even have a chance to come back here."

A week before Christmas, Tyler broke the UNC scoring record against Evansville, but he was still saying that his shin ached and throbbed after games, so we did another MRI and bone scan. The doctors found no fracture lines, and the bone was healing, so I told him, "Tyler, your leg is okay. You're driving yourself crazy and you're driving us crazy. We need to put this to rest." After that meeting he was fine. I don't think he mentioned his shin again the rest of the year.

We won our first 13 games of the season. Tyler recovered to lead our team in scoring in the last six of those games, establishing himself again as the focal point of our offense. Ty was playing brilliantly at the point, rarely turning the ball over and making three-point shots whenever he was given an opening. Then in our Atlantic Coast Conference opener at home against Boston College, we got beat. We were so fat and happy and I think we were surprised by how emotional Boston College was. Rakim Sanders came into that game shooting under 30 percent from three-point range for them and he made four against us. Tyrese Rice scored 25 points and made shots even when we had fingers in his nostrils. Boston College made plays they had not made the whole season. It was one of those games when the people in our locker room understood that we had to give Boston College some credit even when the people outside of our locker room would be saying that we screwed it up. We didn't play great by any means, but they had played really well and we had to accept that. That doesn't mean the media accepted it. They blasted Ty. They said he wasn't quick enough to defend Rice and that it was a mismatch. I had to handle that. I had to make sure that everybody knew that Ty wasn't the only reason we lost that game, and that it was just one game.

But the loss was a shock to everybody on our team—not just the fact that we lost but that we lost to an unranked team at home. It shook our confidence. A coach can see that right away. In our next practice there was no laughing and trash-talking between drills. It was deadly serious. We'd move the ball three times to a guy with a wide-open shot, and then he'd pass it up to a teammate with the same kind of shot. Our guys just weren't sure of themselves.

Our next game was a non-conference game against College of Charleston, and in the first half we came out tight. We won that game easily, but it didn't erase the lack of confidence that we felt, because we all knew we didn't play great. I knew that our problems could linger.

Four days later, we played our second ACC game at Wake Forest, an undefeated team that was ranked in the Top 5. It turned out to be one of those nights when everything felt like it was going in their favor. Their mojo was right, their cycle of the moon was right, their biorhythms were right—and we were struggling. Jeff Teague went absolutely bonkers from the perimeter and scored 34 points for them.

Tyler made only three of his 12 shots and Ty turned the ball over four times, the most turnovers he'd had all season.

That game was the first time that I saw my team have serious doubts. Our shot selection, our patience, our poise, our resolve—we lacked everything that helps you win a tough game. I tell our kids all the time that in every close game somebody's going to give in and let's not let it be us. But that night it was us. We panicked. We didn't defend. We didn't run back on defense. When our guys came over to the sideline for timeouts, they had a beaten look. They were not walking up on their toes, carrying themselves like they were going to win. They were shuffling around with their heads down and their shoulders slumped. None of them had the confidence that their teammates could get it done, so they didn't play as a team. Each of them was thinking, "I've got to make the shot. I've got to get us out of this mess."

We lost that game by three points. When we left the court, the crowd was chanting, "Over-rated! Over-rated!" I clearly remember walking into the tunnel and hearing one guy yell down at me, "That's right, Williams, your team sucks!"

Our locker room was split into two rooms. The players sat in one room, and I walked into the other to think about what to tell them. I never prepare what I'm going to say at the end of a game that we lose, because I'm always dumb enough to think we're going to pull it out at the end. So after losses I always give myself a little more time to collect my thoughts. I know they're more likely to remember what I say to them after a loss because that's when I have everybody's attention.

I paced around that room for about three minutes. I knew we were dealing with a lot of negatives. We'd lost our first two conference games. I knew that the media was going to go after Ty and say that he'd been outplayed badly by Rice and then Teague. After the Boston

College game there had been a sense of doom from the press and that had carried over to the public. I'd already seen people jumping ship, and now I knew everybody was going to say that we were sinking. All around us that night there was panic.

In basketball, no matter how good your team is, you're always one step away from falling off a cliff. If the players' confidence isn't restored quickly, a team that has lost two in a row can all of a sudden lose four straight, and then it gets to be five out of six, and then it's six out of eight, and there is nothing to grab onto, nothing to slow you down. You just keep falling. I knew our team was standing on the edge of that cliff.

When I walked through the door into the players' locker room, I expected to see some anxiety, but it was a lot worse than that. Some guys were crying. Some guys were really ticked off at themselves. Some guys were really ticked off at other people. Some guys were feeling sorry for themselves. Some of them were just disgusted with the way we'd played. The looks on their faces told me that I couldn't just say, "Hey, Wake had a great night." That wasn't going to work. They needed me to tell them how we were going to be all right.

As I turned to speak to them, I did what I have always done.

I drew from my past.

CHAPTER 2

Angels and Demons

I PROBABLY SHOULDN'T SHARE this because It's not really something to be proud of, but one part of my family tree goes back to the McCoys who feuded with the Hatfields all those years. On the other side of the tree, my mother's side, they changed their name from Dalton to Deyton because they didn't want to be associated with the Dalton Gang, some nasty folks who were killed trying to rob a bank in a small town in Kansas. There are no heroes in my family history, just a bunch of outlaws and fighters.

My dad had 12 brothers and sisters, and my mom had nine, and everybody lived within a few miles of each other in the mountains of Western North Carolina near Asheville, where I was born and raised in the early 1950s. It was a very hardworking family on both sides. My mother quit school in the 10th grade and my father quit school in the sixth grade, both of them to go to work. My mother started working in the cotton mill and my father, as a 13-year-old, started picking cotton before it went to the mill. I was brought up in a very uneducated family.

My grandfather on my mother's side owned a pool hall in Caroleen, North Carolina. Friday night would be the only night he'd drink, but he would drink a lot. He'd drink so much that when somebody brought him home, he couldn't undress himself. He'd come home with the money he'd earned for the whole week and he'd tell my grandmother, "I'll give you $5 if you'll take my shoes and socks off. I'll give you $10 if you take my coat and shirt off." That became Granddaddy's way of giving Granny the grocery money.

My grandmother on my father's side we all called Big Mom because she looked after the whole family. Her husband, Pop, ran his own little sawmill—a shed and a saw is all it really was—and when I was four or five years old, all the cousins and I would bundle kindling for him. Pop would cut logs to make furniture. The leftovers were kindling, so on Friday afternoons Pop and I would go into the African-American section of town and sell kindling to people that still heated and cooked with a woodstove.

My mother's name was Lallage. I thought she was an angel. She was intelligent. She was sweet. She was shy. She appreciated the most simple things in life. She lived by the Golden Rule: treat folks like you'd like to be treated. She enjoyed people and she was polite, but she had a fence around her and she wouldn't let anybody in until you passed her test. Very few people got inside that fence.

Family was all that mattered to my mother. Family was her first priority and second, third, fourth, and fifth. Nothing ever got in the way of that. She always put the rest of the family ahead of herself. All she cared about was providing, having a roof over our head, clothes for us to wear, and food for us to eat. Everywhere we'd go, she packed up my older sister, Frances, and me; it was like the mother duck and her little ducklings.

My mom was stronger than my dad.

My dad was so funny. His name was Mack Clayton Williams, but everybody called him Babe. His mama gave him that nickname because he was her favorite. She treated him like her baby, even though he was somewhere in the middle of all of her kids. Babe would pick on everybody in a jovial way, and they could pick on him. He had this laugh that made his whole body shake. For all of my cousins, he was their favorite uncle. He liked to play tricks, and if a rubber snake showed up somewhere, you knew who was behind it. Everybody loved Babe.

My dad could tell a story a hundred times and he'd laugh just as hard at the end of the hundredth telling as he did at the first. I remember one time a bunch of the Williams family went to a Baptist revival with my uncle Glenn, who was a deacon in his church. When we got back home, my daddy started teasing Glenn by saying, "Glenn is so cheap that when the collection plate came around, he put a five-dollar bill in there and then he reached in and took back four ones. Isn't he supposed to be setting a good example for the rest of us?"

He was giggling about it and Glenn swore that he didn't do it, but Daddy was never one to let the true facts get in the way of a good story. He was always kidding people. In fact, that was his life. He wanted to have fun, and sometimes having fun got in the way of some of his responsibilities as a husband and a father.

My dad was an alcoholic. He smoked. He cursed like a sailor. Every vice you could have, he had. He didn't play any sports; he just worked and worked and worked. I remember somebody once asked him about running. "The only time I'm running," he said, "is if I'm real afraid of the guy that's chasing me."

My dad was a good man, but alcohol changed him. When I was a kid, I enjoyed being around him if he was not drinking and I hated being around him if he was. Drinking put him on edge. It could make him mean. It made me not even want to talk to him.

My first childhood memories are of having a lot of fun with my cousins playing cowboys and Indians. My favorite picture is of me holding a six-gun poised to shoot, because I remember how happy that made me feel to be a cowboy living in a time when you were either a good guy or a bad guy.

But at around age seven, it wasn't fun anymore. My dad started going to the beat of a different drum. A lot of nights he came home drunk at 2 or 3 o'clock in the morning. One night he came home with two black eyes, because he'd been in a bar and gotten into a brawl. But that was just him.

Lots of people in my family were drinkers and fighters. Every gathering, every reunion, and every family picnic on the Williams side ended up with two of the boys going at it. I remember at five or six years old asking one of my cousins, "Who's going to end up fighting tonight?" There would always be a fistfight over something that somebody said that somebody else didn't like, just because there was so much drinking going on.

There was one little area in Asheville where my grandparents and three of their grown sons lived, all within 100 yards of each other, in little houses along a dirt road. Maybe that's where the Hatfields and McCoys figure in, because there were several times when the boys from over the hill came by and they wanted to play with us, but at the end somebody always drew a line in the sand. That's just what we did. It was the Williams boys against everybody else. I'd bloody a guy's nose and he'd bloody mine, and then two days later I'd be playing and fighting with those same guys. I wasn't a great fighter, but I was never afraid of a scuffle.

One of my uncles, who we called "Hillbilly," once told me the story of a night at a beer joint called the Silver Slipper. A guy came out of the bar and said that my dad and my uncle Gordon were about to get in a fight with some other guys and the other brothers might want to go in there and help them because there were three of theirs and only two of ours. Uncle Hillbilly said, "Naw, they ought to be able to handle that. Let's just see if they're tough enough."

So Hillbilly and the others stood there and watched through the window while my dad and Gordon fought the other three guys. The Williams boys came out and they'd won, but they looked like they lost. That was the only kind of competition I knew. Were you tough enough? And when somebody drew a line in the sand, would you step across?

BETWEEN MY MOTHER and father there was a lot of physical abuse. He would come home drunk and push her around, and Frances and I would try to stop it. I'd try to separate them, but I was too small and my dad would just push me away.

My mother and father split for the first time just after I'd finished first grade. My mother took us away and the three of us lived all summer in a single room at the Shamrock Court Motel, which my aunt Doris owned. My mother would go off to work and Frances was off doing odd jobs for somebody, so I would go around with another of my aunts, Leona, who was a maid at the motel. She paid me 25 cents a day to take off the dirty pillowcases and put on clean ones. At lunch Aunt Doris would fix me a sandwich, and then I'd go and work some more in the afternoon. That was it. There was no ballplaying. Nothing that kids do. It was just survival.

When the school year started, we moved in with another aunt. We lived in her trailer because she had an empty bedroom. I slept on the couch and my mother and sister shared the back bedroom. We lived there for four or five months, and then Dad started coming by and my parents got back together again. That lasted a little while before they broke up again. We left again and lived with another aunt. All of these aunts that put us up were my dad's sisters. They were all mad at Babe because they knew that his drinking and carousing was ruining my family. It was difficult for me to understand why my father was doing this to us. My mom and dad got together and broke up, got together and broke up, and the last time we moved out I was 11 years old.

Frances was four years older than me. She was outgoing but not very goal oriented. She was fun but not the life of the party. She was caring but she didn't dote. Even as a teenager, she was really looking forward to growing up, to moving on with her life. She was anxious to get out of our house and start the kind of family we didn't have. We didn't spend that much time together, didn't play much together, but we had a typical brother-sister rivalry. She would always tell people that when we washed dishes together, she would wash and I would dry but I wouldn't dry the pots and pans because I said they were too heavy. She always thought I was trying to get away with something, but she was a good sister.

I know Frances was also upset by our family situation, but she didn't seem to be as bothered by it as I was. She was older, more mature, and just handled it better. During the tough times, she was keeping an eye on me more than I knew she was, but I just wasn't willing to talk about our mom and dad splitting up. I never really talked to anybody about it. I pretended it wasn't there.

During one of the times when my mother and dad got back together, we lived in a house on Warren Avenue. That was the first and only house we ever owned. My mother, Frances, and I left and came back, and left and came back, and then one day when we were staying with one of my aunts, my dad said, "Why don't you guys come back and stay at the house, and I'll leave and let you guys live there?"

We'd only been back living in that house for two weeks when these two guys pulled up in the driveway. They were wearing dark sportcoats, white shirts, and ties. I was on the porch, but I ran in the house to tell my mom as they came walking up the steps. I remember latching the screen door, and I wouldn't unlatch it to let them in. It turned out that during that seven-month time period that we'd been gone, my dad hadn't paid the mortgage. So they came and foreclosed on the house. They told us we had three days to get out. I went and packed up my stuff, and we moved back to the motel. To this day I still have a negative feeling about people in dark sportcoats, white shirts, and ties.

Every time my parents got back together, there was a lot of fighting. My dad never hit my mother with his fist, but he went as far as he could go without doing that. I tried to run away from home one time because I just wanted to get away. I didn't get very far; I don't know if I wanted to get very far. I just wanted to shock my dad into stopping. I was always feeling like I needed to escape.

ONE OF OUR NEIGHBORS at that house on Warren Avenue had a basketball goal in the backyard. I never had a basketball, but they had one, and when I wanted to get away from what was going on at home, I would just go over there and shoot. The goal was a pole with a plywood backboard, and there was no net, just a bent rim. I'd go over there for hours. If it was raining or snowing, I'd get filthy on the dirt court, but I didn't mind. It was something I could do by myself. All I needed was a basketball and a goal and some sweat and I could lose myself in the game. I was in heaven, like a kid left all night in a candy store. That court was my refuge, the one place where it felt like there were no problems in the world.

When I was 11, we moved to a place on Reed Street. We were 100 yards from Biltmore Elementary School, where there were some asphalt courts. Every day after school, I'd go home, change clothes, and head straight to the courts to play basketball until 6 o'clock.

When I was in the seventh grade, a few other boys and I started sneaking into the Biltmore gym to play. I always played with older guys. One of them had the idea of hiding someone in the bathroom, and then when the head of the physical education department would go home at 4 o'clock, our guy would come out of the bathroom and pop the gym door open and we'd play on the court inside.

One time we were in there playing and one of the guys started clowning around with a fire extinguisher, and it sprayed all over the girls' locker room. That just infuriated me, and that's when I started sneaking in by myself, because I didn't want to be responsible for anybody else. On one outside wall there were some uneven bricks I could climb to get to a second-floor window. I opened the window and dropped down to the balcony inside the gym. I never turned on the lights. There was just an exit sign lighting each end, and I would play in the half dark. I would just shoot and rebound and shoot again. It was peaceful, and at that point the peaceful part of it was more important than getting to be a better player.

I got caught several times. It became a little bit of a challenge for this one policeman to catch me in there and run me off. He came in the gym a couple of times and would find me mopping the floor. He probably thought I was trying to keep it cleaned up, but I was just trying to cover my tracks. I didn't want anybody to know I'd been in there.

Finally, one night he said, "It doesn't look like I'm going to be able to stop you. How do you get in here?"

I was scared to death. It was dark, and I took him outside and showed him how I climbed up the outside of the building. Then he said, "Okay, come on with me."

I had been in the junior deputy sheriff's program, and one day they were taking everybody to the jail and the courthouse just to show them what it was like, and I didn't go that day because they said they were going to fingerprint everybody and that frightened me. So when the policeman put me in the back of the police car, I thought he was taking me to jail. He drove over to Mr. Norton's house. Mr. Norton was the school principal. When we reached his house, the policeman got out of the car and said, "Stay here."

I was about to mess my pants, I was so dadgum scared. He knocked on the door, and when Mr. Norton opened it I could see them talking. After a little while, Mr. Norton went back in the house and then came out to the car. I sat there trying to figure out how I was going to tell my mom that she had to come bail me out of jail. Mr. Norton reached in the window and handed me a key. It was the key to the Biltmore gym.

"I don't want you to kill yourself climbing in the window anymore," Mr. Norton said, "but you are responsible for anyone in there with you."

I never took anyone in there with me. The only time I ever used that key was when I could be by myself.

ONCE MY SISTER got a job working weekends at Kress's five-and-ten store, I was on my own. Really on my own. I was 11 years old. On Saturdays I would get up at 8:30 and my sister and my mother would already be gone to work, so I'd eat my Cheerios alone. It was Cheerios with canned milk and I would dilute that with water. That was my milk, because it was cheaper. Then I would go to Biltmore Elementary School and I would play there all day.

Some Saturdays I would go to the YMCA, riding the bus because we had no car. I played basketball there, too, but also I learned to play Ping-Pong and pool and chess. I learned to swim enough to stay alive. I would stay there until two in the afternoon. Then I would leave and go to Pack Memorial Library. I would sit there for hours reading the different newspaper sports sections and then catch the last bus back home in the evening.

Then, in the seventh grade, I joined a basketball league at the YMCA. In my very first game I remember I came down the court and I passed the ball to the guy on my right and he shot it and missed it. On our next possession, somebody gave me the ball and I passed it to the guy on my left, and he shot it and missed it. The third time I came down the court I shot it and it went in, and I've been shooting ever since.

During that whole time period when I was very unhappy, my mother was so strong and she took such good care of me. When I started going to town by myself, she would always say, "You just do the right thing."

One time, I said, "Mom, how do I know what's right?"

"You'll figure it out," she said. "You just make sure you do the right thing."

And so one Saturday I didn't save a nickel for the bus ride home from the YMCA. I told the bus driver, Mr. Haynes, "I don't have a nickel. Can I ride the bus home and I'll give you back the nickel next week?"

He said, "Come on in here, son."

I got on the bus and rode home. The next Saturday morning I wasn't going to the YMCA until 9, but I knew the first bus would come to my stop at 7:30. I waited out at the bus stop and when it came, I walked up the stairs and gave Mr. Haynes a nickel. "I'll see you in an hour or so," I said. "I'm not riding this bus."

He said, "Why didn't you just wait and bring it to me then?"

"I didn't want you to think I wasn't going to pay you back."

I HEARD MY MOM cry herself to sleep sometimes. I know she worried about how she was going to pay the bills. There were a couple of times she had to ask our landlord's secretary if she could pay the rent a few days late. Sometimes that lady was harsh to her. There were times when my mom didn't know how she was going to get through the next day, but she always found a way.

She had worked for Chakales Hosiery for a long time and then she went to work for Ball's, a place that made jars, and then she went to work for Gerber baby food, but she kept getting laid off. A couple of times my mother had to take unemployment and it embarrassed her. She would fill out 100 job applications to try not to take money she hadn't earned. Eventually, she got a job at Vanderbilt Shirt Factory and she worked there for 25 years.

In my seventh-grade year, my mom started taking in laundry to make extra money. She would do ironing for people, 10 cents for a shirt or a pair of pants. They'd come by to bring the clothes on Friday afternoon and I never wanted to go to the door. I didn't think it was right that she should have to do those kinds of things. It made me feel like people thought my mom was inferior. It was one of those things that really bothered me. So I would just leave.

AFTER SCHOOL MY BUDDIES and I used to go home past Ed's Service Station, which had a vending machine where you could get a Coke for 10 cents. One day my sister said she saw us at Ed's and asked what we were doing there. I told her and my mom that we liked to stop at Ed's after playing basketball and get Coca-Colas to drink while we'd sit there on the sidewalk and talk.

Now my mom knew I loved nothing more than a cold Coca-Cola, but she also knew I didn't have the money to buy one. "What do you do?" she asked me.

I told her, "Oh, they have a nice water fountain. I just get some water."

The next morning I'd gotten myself ready to go to school as usual, because my mom always left earlier to go to work. I walked into the kitchen and sitting on the corner of the table was a dime. My mom didn't have very much money, but she was too proud to allow her son not to have what other kids had. After that, when she cashed her paycheck at the grocery store, she'd get rolls of dimes so that she would be sure to have one there for me every morning.

She did that every day for years.

GROWING UP I ALWAYS knew my dad was wrong. I hated the drinking. I wanted my mom and dad to be together, but I didn't want them to be together if it was going to be that way.

The summer I turned 14, my parents had been apart for a couple of years. My dad hardly ever paid the child support. He'd pay one month and skip seven, then pay another month and skip nine. My mom talked to a lawyer and they served a warrant for my dad's arrest and said he had to catch up on child support. My dad came by the house. He was drunk and angry. It was the worst time I can ever remember. He went after my mom. I pulled him off of her, pushed him down, and grabbed a bottle and put it under his chin. "Get out of here or I'll bust this over your head," I said. "I'll kill you!"

The whole scene was very nasty, but I didn't care. When he got up to leave, I said, "I never want to see you again. I never want you to set foot in my house again for the rest of my life."

My dad never, ever came back to our house again. After that, I rarely saw him, only a couple of times when my sister made me go with her to visit him. Frances was more forgiving, but I was not. I was mad that he'd torn our family apart.

CHAPTER 3

Home Games

I HAD NO DREAMS. No goals. Nothing whatsoever.

My dad worked at a sawmill, my uncles worked at a sawmill, and my grandfather had his own little sawmill. I didn't think about it much, but I guess I figured that would be me.

I wanted to be good in school, though. Some of my older cousins and uncles had trouble reading, and I knew that I didn't want to be like that.

And then, when I was in the third grade, my teacher, Mrs. Cheek, put up a list of the top 10 students in the first grading period. There were only 25 kids in the class, but my name was not on the list. She put it up on this little chalkboard right beside the regular blackboard and I had to go in there every day for six weeks and stare at it, and that really ticked me off.

After that, for the next five grading periods, my name was the first one on the list. To see my mother's reaction when I brought those report cards home was so important to me. She was so proud that she told all of my relatives about my grades.

Whenever anybody asks me how I came to be so competitive, I trace it directly back to that experience. That's the first time I can ever remember any competition at all, except for fighting. And that was the first time that I ever even thought about competition. Now most of my friends think of me as the most competitive person they've ever met.

So I kept trying to be a good student for those two reasons: because I wanted my name on that board and because I thought it would make my mom happy. Not because I saw it taking me anywhere.

My family never had a television until I was six years old. I thought it was a new invention. We got two channels and sometimes a third. Not long after we got the television, one of my grandfathers visited and suggested we watch a baseball game. To this day, one of my favorite numbers is 7, because during the game that day they showed footage of Mickey Mantle hitting a home run left-handed and a home run right-handed. The announcers also talked about how Mantle was the fastest player in all of baseball. I was starstruck.

So baseball was my first love. It was the first sport I played on a real team. In Little League I'd pitch one game and catch the next. Those were my favorite positions because they allowed me to stay the most involved in the game. I played second base and shortstop and pitched in Babe Ruth baseball when I was 15, and we won the district championship. I was one of the best players on my team.

In high school I figured I would play basketball in the winter and then baseball in the spring. In my freshman year I played junior varsity basketball. I was only 5'3" and 104 pounds and I didn't start on the JV team. But at the end of the season, they had a junior varsity tournament for the county schools. In the second game of that tournament, I played almost all of the fourth quarter and I made 10 out of 11 free throws, but we still lost on a last-second shot. I felt really positive about the way my freshman year had ended, but I was still thinking that as a sophomore I'd play on junior varsity again.

That spring some of my friends got to talking to the varsity basketball coach, Buddy Baldwin, after his history class. They asked him what he thought the team's prospects were for the next season. I ran into one of them, Ronnie Slider, later that day, who told me, "Boy, Coach Baldwin had some great things to say about you maybe making the varsity next year."

The next day at school I was walking down the hallway and Coach Baldwin stopped me. "You really finished the season strong," he said. "If you work hard over the summer, you've got a chance to do some big things."

That was one of the best things anyone had ever said to me. It made me feel so good, and at that moment I made the decision that I was going to outwork everybody. I switched almost all of my attention from baseball to basketball. I still played baseball, but I stopped working as hard on it. That spring I'd take 10 swings in batting practice and then I wouldn't take 10 swings again until practice three days later. In the meantime I'd shoot 1,000 jump shots. Over that summer, I played in Babe Ruth baseball games, but as soon as the game was over I'd go straight to the basketball court at Biltmore Elementary, change into some sneakers, and play pickup basketball with my baseball uniform still on. I was so excited about the basketball season starting.

I remember one afternoon I had stayed around to do some extra drills after everybody else left the pickup game. I was absolutely worn out. I was just sitting on the sidewalk before I got up to walk home when I thought, "How good must Coach Baldwin feel to make me feel this good? And I'm not the only person he's done this for. I want to be like Buddy Baldwin. I want to be a coach."

NOT LONG AFTER she graduated from Roberson High School, Frances got married. So once I was in high school, she was gone. Because my mother was always working, I had all these other people who took care of me and just looked after me in general. My friend Walt Stroup's mother worked at Belk's department store in the layaway section, and she told me to come and see her when it was time to get school clothes. She got 25 percent off on all the clothes because she worked there. Every year in high school, I'd get two pairs of blue jeans, two shirts, and a pair of shoes to replace the ones with holes worn in the bottom from the previous year, and we'd put it all on layaway. Before the start of my sophomore year, I bought two pairs of pants and three shirts. When it dawned on me how much money it was, I asked Mrs. Stroup if she could take one of those shirts back because I thought I'd spent too much of my mom's money.

During my senior year, one of the teachers at Roberson, Carl Conley, picked me up and took me to school every day. He was this preppy guy who had just gotten out of Mars Hill College. He gave me some clothes, so for the first time in my life I had sweaters that actually matched my pants. I had a particular outfit that I wore each day and then they all had to be washed on the weekends. I had exactly five outfits, and I hoped nobody noticed.

When I joined the varsity basketball team as a sophomore, Coach Baldwin wanted his players to wear coats and ties to games. I had one sportcoat and I wore it to every game. I had one tie and I wore it to every game. I didn't want anybody to know that, but if you look at all the pictures of me dressed up, it's the same coat and tie every time. My junior year, I got a second tie.

The first steak I ever ate was when I was a junior and they took the basketball team to Buck's restaurant in Asheville. I thought, "Man, this is pretty good food." They collected money from the parents to pay for that dinner. It was $10 per person and somebody came up to Mr. Crandall and I overheard him say, "This is for my son, David, and for Roy. Let me take care of it, and don't say anything to his mom."

I pulled Mr. Crandall over to the side after the meal and thanked him and said that one day I would repay him. But he told me not to worry about it.

In our senior year it looked like David Crandall was not going to graduate because of his grades. David had decided to join the Marines and he'd let his grades slip, but I convinced him that it was important to get his high school diploma. So the last three weeks before final exams I stayed at the Crandall house every night and quizzed David because I wanted him to graduate. I heard that his typing teacher, Mrs. Mathews, wasn't sure she was going to pass David, so I went to see her. She said, "Roy are you here about your grade?"

I said, "No ma'am, I want to talk to you about David's grade."

"Youngsters like you are the reason I'm in teaching," she said. "I'll take care of David. You don't worry yourself about it."

When graduation came around and they gave us our diplomas, Mr. Crandall said, "Roy, do you want half of this, or do you want to let David keep all of it?"

David was a great friend and he and his family helped me in so many ways that it made me feel good to help him. It never bothered me that people were doing nice things for me as long as I had an opportunity to make it square.

ONCE I STARTED PLAYING basketball, gosh, I wanted to be good. It was a passion with me. From the seventh grade until the end of high school, I got a basketball for Christmas every year because I'd worn the last one out.

I would practice basketball in the house. We lived in a four-room house and I made a route from my bedroom and laid the ball up right-handed over that bedroom door, took a left-handed dribble and laid it up left-handed over the kitchen door, laid it up right-handed over the living room door, laid it up left-handed over my mother's bedroom door, and then I'd go back past the bathroom and fake laying it up on one side and then lay it up on the other side of the doorway. Once a week or so, I had to take a washcloth and some soap to clean off the spots over the doors where the dirty basketball had bounced up against it so many times. When she was home, my mother never once told me to put that frickin' ball down, even though it must have driven her crazy.

Just like Coach Baldwin had suspected, I started on the varsity team the first game of my sophomore year. I had a dream the night before the game that our center, David Crandall, got the opening tap, tipped it to me, and I took it down the court and dunked it. I was in my 50s before I ever stopped dreaming about dunking the ball.

The next night the ball was tipped to me and I made a nice pass to Walt Stroup, who scored to put us ahead 2–0. A few minutes later, Coach Baldwin called a timeout because we were down 19–2. We weren't very good that year. Our record was 1–19 and that made me work even harder in the summer. Walt and I would go to the Biltmore courts and work on the screen and roll for hours every day; when more kids would show up, we'd try to execute in a pickup game what we'd been practicing. Walt and I played together so much that we became good teammates because we could read each other's minds on the court.

By my junior year I'd grown to 5'7" and 125 pounds. We weren't really sure how good we were going to be that season, but I got more confident with each game. We raced the ball up and down the floor, and we had three or four guys that averaged in double figures. That was the way I liked to play, as fast as possible. Erwin High was the best team in the county, and they froze the ball against us for most of the fourth quarter because we were too fast for them and they knew that was the only way they could beat us. We lost in the semifinals of the county tournament and then in the semifinals of the district tournament.

I was a good little high school player and I made the All-County team. I had always played with older guys growing up, so I'd learned early to pass the basketball. I became a much better shooter as I got older, but I got as much satisfaction out of passing as I did shooting. In the open court I could really attack people because I could score with either hand. Defensively, I worked extremely hard and I was never afraid to take a charge against anybody. I was limited by my size, but I never played against anybody who I thought was quicker than me. Even though I was a point guard, Coach Baldwin told me he needed me to score.

Coach Baldwin was very demanding. He was not a curser, but he would lose his temper with us at times, and when he did, he'd run us really hard until he thought we got the message. Throughout my high school career, Coach Baldwin preached to me about three things: working on my game, being a team player, and caring about my teammates. Each and every day at practice he reinforced a part of that and he became the most influential male in my life. He was like a big brother who gave me a better idea of how to act in the world. He taught me that when I shook someone's hand, I should do it firmly while I looked them straight in the eye. He was the first person to give me a great deal of confidence. He made me believe I could be somebody.

I was doing all right in the classroom, but Coach Baldwin inspired me to study harder. In his history class, he gave a test on the U.S. Constitution and he told us it was going to be the toughest test we ever took. That was a challenge to me. I really studied and I scored 100 on it and he stopped me after class and said, "I have never had a student make 100 on that test."

I said, "You talked about how tough it was going to be, so then it became a competition, and I wanted to show you I could win it."

In the summer after my junior year, I finally went to Coach Baldwin and told him what I wanted to do with my life. I don't know if I waited so long because I was afraid he'd laugh at me or think I was crazy. I went into our team meeting room one day before practice and I said, "Coach, I know what I want to do. I want to be a coach."

He said, "That doesn't surprise me. I thought you might want to do that."

Coach Baldwin made me believe I could accomplish things that probably nobody in my family thought I could. Nobody in my family had ever gone to college. When I started high school, I didn't even know what college was. One day in the eighth grade, my friend Eddie Payne told me he'd gone to Wake Forest's basketball camp—I had no clue what he was even talking about. I didn't want to say anything because I didn't want to appear stupid, but I didn't even know that world was out there.

Coach Baldwin was the first person to talk to me about college. I realized that if I wanted to be a coach I had to be a teacher, and if I wanted to be a teacher, I had to go to college. I took the SAT, and eventually I had basketball scholarship offers from six smaller colleges in the area: Piedmont College, Asheville-Biltmore, Wofford, Winthrop, Catawba, and Mars Hill. I remember visiting Mars Hill and working out with two other players and then going into the coach's office. The coach set scholarship papers in front of all three of us, and the other two guys signed them. I just pushed mine back to him and said, "I'm not ready to make this decision yet." He got a little mad at me.

By that time Coach Baldwin had started talking to me about going to college at the University of North Carolina if I really wanted to be a coach. He laid out a plan for me to try to make the freshman team and then I could watch Coach Dean Smith run his varsity practice. Coach Smith was not totally established yet, but Coach Baldwin really felt like Coach Smith had turned the corner and was on his way to becoming a big-time coach. Coach Baldwin thought that Coach Smith could be a great role model for me.

I WAS VERY BUSY in high school. Along with playing varsity basketball and baseball, I kept stats at all of the football games. I had gained so much confidence that I also earned the lead role in the senior play and was elected president of the student body. My girlfriend in my junior and senior years, Pam, was a cheerleader. She was also on the square dance team and she nagged me all summer before my senior year to try out for that team. I didn't want to be on the stupid square dance team, but she kept badgering me.

The first night of tryouts I struggled with it, so I got two of my basketball teammates who had been on the square dance team the year before, David Crandall and Rick Scarborough, to help me. They came back to my house and I made them write out every move during the whole dance routine. Those two dummies and I went through the whole dance over and over in my living room for hours, because if I was going to try out, I was going to make the team. I was not going to *not* make the square dance team.

I wasn't very good, but the team sponsor was the home ec teacher, Miss Weir, and she thought the sun rose and set on me. So I was going to make the stupid team.

The first event we ever participated in was the Duke University Folk Festival in the fall of my senior year. I'll never forget the list of performers: Joan Baez, Janis Joplin, B.B. King, and the Roberson High square dance team. We square-danced on the stage at Cameron Indoor Stadium.

The next morning, Miss Weir asked the bus driver to drive us over to Chapel Hill. We walked around a little and talked to some girls from Roberson who were going to UNC. As we got on the bus to go back to the hotel, Miss Weir turned me around to face the campus and she said, "Roy, this is where I want you to go to school. This is where you belong."

THERE WERE SO MANY people like Miss Weir, who made an effort to look out for me. Mrs. Baldwin was the toughest teacher I ever had in high school. I had her for Algebra II as a junior and Advanced Math as a senior. The clock was behind us in the room and it was months into my junior year before I built up enough courage to turn around and see what time it was. She was tiny, but she was so intimidating. On the floor she had marked four little *x*'s and that's where the legs of your desk were supposed to be. No excuses. That's the way she was.

Now, by the time I was a senior, I'd go into her class and tease her a little and say, "Mrs. Baldwin, why are you teaching us logarithms? That junk isn't ever going to help us." I was just agitating her all the time. Her nephew was Coach Baldwin, which might explain why she took such an interest in me succeeding.

One morning before home room, I said to her, "You got a second?"

She said, "I've always got a second for you, Roy."

She knew I was deciding between going to Georgia Tech, where I'd been offered a full scholarship to be an engineer, or going to North Carolina.

I said, "I wanted to tell you before you hear it from somebody else that I'm going to go to North Carolina because I want to be a coach."

"That engineering scholarship would be so much better for you," she said. "I've told you that 100 times. Are you sure this is what you want to do?"

"Yes, ma'am."

So she stood up and I hugged her, and then I left. That morning, in second period, I sat down in her class and said something smart-alecky to her like I always did, and then she announced, "Before we start, I want you kids to listen to me. I want you girls to not mess with Roy, because Roy is going to North Carolina to be a coach instead of going to Georgia Tech on a full scholarship to be an engineer. One of these days Roy is going to come to my house to borrow a loaf of bread."

She told all the girls not to have anything to do with me. A girl named Wanda Jones was sitting in the room at the time.

BEFORE MY SENIOR basketball season, all I thought about was finally getting a chance to play in the state tournament. I had listened to state playoff games on the radio after my sophomore and junior years, and I had dreamed about a moment like that.

But Ken Wilson, our biggest player at 6'3", tore up his knee playing football that fall and couldn't play for basically the whole year. David Crandall was 6'2" and weighed 160 pounds, and he was our center and our only rebounder. We had two 5'11" forwards. I was 5'8"and the other guard was 5'7". We felt like we were undermanned the whole season.

I scored 21 points in the first game of the season, but we lost. I got 26 in the next game, which we won, and then in the third game I got 35 in a win and I broke Walt Stroup's school record for points in a game. Then I had 16 in the fourth game and we lost. The next day before practice, Coach Baldwin said, "Roy, I've got to talk to you. We're 2–2 and I don't think we can keep running the ball like we've been doing."

I said, "Why?"

"Crandall's the only rebounder and if he outlets the ball to you, I'm happy, but if he passes it to Ronnie or Ricky or Boodie, I don't know where they're going to throw the dadgum thing. We need to slow it down. It's what's best for our team."

That decision took away the best part of my game, which was pushing the ball up the floor. Coach Baldwin had a great feel for the game and what kids could do, and it was what was best for that team, but to this day that decision has had a great influence on me. I want to attack people and I want my team to have only one option to receive the outlet pass.

The day after the fourth game, I sprained my ankle badly in practice and I went to the doctor the next morning. Dr. Cappiello told me not to play for the next 10 days. Luckily, there was nobody else in the room to hear that. I soaked my foot in a bucket of ice for three days straight, and I played in our next game. My ankle was killing me. Dr. Cappiello saw my name in the newspaper and he called Coach Baldwin the next day and asked, "Did Roy not tell you what I told him?"

Coach Baldwin pulled me out of class to ask me what the doctor said. "Coach, it's *my* ankle," I said. "I want to play." I was not going to miss a game in my senior year.

I was the team captain that season, and during games I was already thinking like a coach. I was always thinking about what adjustments we should be making. I was a pain in Coach Baldwin's butt a few times, trying to think through the game so much instead of just playing it.

I averaged 17 points a game that year and finished my career as Roberson's all-time leading scorer. We got to the district final, just one win away from the state tournament. In that game, we had the ball out of bounds with five seconds to play and down by one point. Coach Baldwin diagrammed a play for me to throw it in and then for a teammate to pass it back to me. When we broke the huddle, Coach Baldwin looked at me and said, "Take it to the basket and make a play."

I was very comfortable with that. I felt like I could do that better than anybody. I was going to take it to the basket and either make the basket or get fouled and we were going to win the game. I was sure of it. So I threw the ball in to one of my teammates, who dribbled it directly to the corner, jumped up, took a shot . . . and missed. We lost the game and I was so mad at him in the locker room. I was screaming at him, "Why didn't you give me back the ball?" We went to Burger King afterward and I wanted to fight him. I still haven't forgiven him.

MY MOM NEVER MISSED a game. She would bring along a pencil and one of those tiny pads with the spirals at the top. If I scored a field goal, she'd write down 2 and if I made a free throw she'd write down 1, and then at the end of the game she'd know before anybody else how many points I'd scored. She would always show me her little sheet of paper when I got home.

I'll never forget one game when this guy tried to steal the ball from me and I just dribbled it behind my back and made a little bounce pass and we scored. A fan from the other school sitting in front of my mother said, "Oh, big deal, who does he think he is?"

My mother tapped him on the shoulder and said, "That's my son. That's who he is. That's why it's a big deal."

In my senior year, deep in my soul, I thought I was the best basketball player in Western North Carolina. My dad lived eight miles away, but he never came to see me play a game. I put that aside and told myself that it didn't bother me, but it did.

That year we played Enka High School and the game went to five overtimes. One of my cousins came to see the game and I played all right in regulation, but during the five overtimes, I was great. He went home and told my dad what I'd done, and then he told me that Daddy was going to come to the next game. That next game I played my butt off, but later I found out he wasn't there. Every once in a while somebody told me my dad was coming to a game and I always played great, but he was never there.

CHAPTER 4

A Small Fish

I FIRST MET Wanda Jones in ninth-grade algebra class. From the 10th grade on, we had almost every class together and we became friends. While I was president of the student body, Wanda was vice president of the senior class, and she was dating the president of the senior class.

Like me, Wanda decided to come to UNC. I was glad she was there at the start of my freshman year in college because I struggled the first five weeks. We started our college education on Friday, the 13th of September. Roberson was a small high school with only 130 students in our graduating class, and I had been a big fish in a very, very small pond. In college I was nobody. I was a number. The place was so big and I couldn't find my niche. I couldn't find my comfort zone. Wanda was a friendly face, someone to go to dinner with; she loved college from the beginning and I needed to keep hearing that. She provided me some stability.

For my entire life I'd had all of these people helping me out. All of a sudden I was in Chapel Hill and my girlfriend was back home and my mom was struggling because I was gone. I was homesick. My roommate was even more homesick than I was, which only made it worse. I hadn't brought home a schoolbook my entire senior year of high school and suddenly I needed to study two or three hours a night. I was wondering if I shouldn't have taken one of those scholarships to play basketball at a smaller school closer to home.

But then everything changed. On October 15, 1968, I began tryouts for the freshman basketball team. I knew one thing: I had worked harder for those tryouts than anybody. If somebody was going to be giving in, it was not going to be me. Sometimes at a tryout coaches will let you play a little and then run you a lot to see who quits, because no coach enjoys cutting people. So for 10 straight nights before tryouts I had run the steps at my dorm, 10 flights up and down, 10 times every night. A couple of times I thought my heart was going to explode. I was motivated by fear. I didn't know if I was going to make the cuts, but at least I knew that I was in better shape than anybody.

I tried out on Tuesday, Wednesday, and Thursday and made the first cut. I had another practice on Friday. Then my mom called and told me she was going to see a doctor for some tests. She sounded anxious about it, so I asked my coach, Bill Guthridge, if I could leave early on Saturday to go check on my mom. I played through about half of the practice, walked out in front of Carmichael Auditorium, hitchhiked home to Asheville, made sure my mom was all right, and went to the Homecoming football game that night because my girlfriend was cheerleading. Then on Sunday morning I walked back out to the highway and thumbed back for freshman tryouts that night. Seventy-seven guys tried out for the UNC freshman team that year and they were going to keep 15. Seven guys were on scholarship, which meant that 70 guys were trying out for those other eight spots.

When it was time for the final cut, I walked up to the door of the basketball office where they had the list posted. I saw my name up there on the final roster. I didn't yell out because there were people around, but when I walked away my feet were not touching the ground. I was so happy and relieved to have made that team. I called my mother and then Buddy Baldwin and told them I'd made it.

I'd never seen a big-time college basketball game before I played in the preliminary game for one. We played Gaston College in the Charlotte Coliseum before the varsity played Vanderbilt. I only played a few minutes in the game, but I was amazed at my lack of confidence. I was shocked at how much bigger and faster the competition was than in high school. That shook me. In that game I was dribbling the ball down the court in a 4-on-3 fast break—which I'd done hundreds of times—and all of a sudden the frickin' ball was not there. Nobody took it. I just lost control of it. I was thinking, "What is the matter with you? Can't you even dribble?" Later in the game I got fouled and missed a free throw because I was nervous. I had never felt that way in my life. I have never forgotten how nervous I was that night, so as a coach I always try to be prepared for the fact that my freshmen may be feeling the same way. That's why I am always trying to instill confidence in my players, so that they're better prepared than I was for that game.

It had never really been my dream to wear the North Carolina jersey, so what was most memorable to me that night was that the coaches gave us all $3 postgame meal money. Hot dogs in the Charlotte Coliseum were only 25 cents and I thought, "My gosh, why do I need all this money? I'm not going to eat 12 of them."

We had some really talented players on our team. *Basketball Times* picked us as the No. 1 freshman team in the country, so we had our team picture in that magazine. Back then freshman basketball was a big deal. We had 3,300 people in Carmichael Auditorium that year to watch us play Duke and there was no varsity game following us that night.

We finished the season 16–2; we lost one game at North Carolina State and the other at Gardner-Webb; with Artis Gilmore as Gardner-Webb's center, they were the top-ranked junior college in the country. I was one of the last guys off the bench. Every day in practice, I faced a guy named Steve Previs, one of our scholarship players who would become a star on the varsity and play briefly as a professional. It was very humbling for me because Steve was so much more talented than I was. I think that was good for me. It opened up my eyes to what kind of athlete was out there.

I still remember the two baskets I made that season. One of them was in a game when we were beating N.C. State badly in Chapel Hill and I came in for the last minute. In the final seconds of the game, I drove the left baseline, and one of their big guys, Paul Coder, came over to block my shot, but I shifted the ball around and scored over him right before the final buzzer, and the crowd cheered like crazy. Coder was cussing and I just turned around and ran to the locker room. The other basket was a jump shot at Duke. There was another jump shot I took later in that game that hit every part of the rim and bounced out, and I couldn't believe it didn't go in. That could have been my career high.

I also remember one game against Duke when I drove into the lane and shot a floater, and Don Blackman jumped up and caught it with one hand over the rim and outletted it for a fast break basket the other way. It made me so mad. I will always believe that was goaltending.

In high school I'd been the king of the court, but in college I was nothing. I may have been our least talented player, but I cared more than anybody else on the team, so I had to figure out how I could contribute. I thought my job was to work really hard in practice and try to push the guys who played to make them better. During warm-ups before every game, I would walk up to Bill Chamberlain and say something like, "Big fella, I've got to have 18 points and 13 rebounds out of you tonight." Then I'd go to Previs and say, "You need to give us 14 points and nine assists." I said something like that to every starter before every game.

I guess I was already coaching.

Even though I wasn't playing much, I still found ways to compete. Early in that season the coaches took us into the physical education lab and had us run on a treadmill with the incline at 12 degrees. We were supposed to run until we couldn't run anymore and then we'd ask them to stop the treadmill. I knew Previs had run for 5 minutes and 50 seconds and that his was the best time. Chamberlain was right in front of me and he went for just over a minute and nearly collapsed with exhaustion. I had heard from those who'd gone before me that it was hard to get your arms comfortable, so when it was my turn, I kept stretching my arms, and the guy conducting the test came in and asked, "Are you okay?"

I said, "I'm fine."

After a few minutes, he came back in again and said, "Are you sure you're okay?"

"I'm okay."

Then he went out and came back in. "Is everything still all right?"

"I'm fine."

Finally, he came back in the room and told me, "Well, this is all we need. I'm going to go over and cut the machine off."

I'd done 7 minutes and 10 seconds on the treadmill before they stopped it.

Two days later, we were leaving the court after freshman practice while the varsity team was walking on, and one of the varsity players, Joe Brown, said, "Hey, you're the guy who ran so long on the treadmill."

I was so dadgum happy that the word had gotten out to the varsity. I kept walking and I heard someone else say, "Did he really run for more than seven minutes?"

It was all about the competition, and I kept trying to be the best teammate I could possibly be. In our last freshman game we won the Big Four freshman tournament in Fayetteville, and I came into the game at the very end. On the bus ride home that night, I walked up to where Coach Guthridge was sitting and said, "I appreciate you allowing me to be on the team. I really enjoyed it."

He said, "I would have liked to have played you more, but—"

I interrupted him and said, "Coach, you played the right people." And I turned around and walked back to my seat.

Playing on that team had turned my whole world around. I don't know if I would have made it through my freshman year at UNC if it hadn't been for basketball. I found something that I could love. It allowed me to be part of a team again.

AFTER MY FRESHMAN SEASON, I knew that if I wanted to continue playing basketball, it would have to be somewhere other than the University of North Carolina. I had gotten a five-page letter from the coach at Oral Roberts saying that if I was not happy and wanted to play more I should consider transferring there. It was flattering. Piedmont College, Asheville-Biltmore, and Mars Hill all still wanted me to come, too. Each one of them had heard from Buddy

Baldwin that I might be considering leaving North Carolina, but I was never really serious about that.

I knew that when I left the tournament in Fayetteville that night it would be the last organized basketball game I was ever going to play in. By then I knew for certain that playing wasn't my goal. My goal was to learn to be the best coach I could be.

My freshman year I started staying after our team's practices to watch Coach Smith's varsity practices. I tried not to be a pest. I didn't want to be underfoot, getting in everybody's way. I sat high up in the bleachers to keep my distance and also so that I had a good view of everything happening on the court. I had a legal pad and a pencil and I wrote down every drill and diagrammed the alignment of the players. I wrote down whatever Coach Smith said. Whatever Coach Guthridge said. I wrote down what time each drill began and how long it took. I was writing out my own practice plan.

I knew that was what I wanted to learn more about. I only had one worry: would I have enough money to stay in school? That was the driving force behind everything.

I was barely piecing together the tuition payments with a few scholarships that I had received, including a $500 good-citizen scholarship from the Civitan Club in Asheville, but I didn't want to take out any student loans. One of my financial aid checks turned out to be a $200 loan, so I gave it back. I just didn't want to owe anybody any money. When I went to the university cashier to return the check, the lady said, "Son, we don't very often have people come by here to give us money back."

I basically had no money to live on. The night we got back from the Big Four freshman tournament, we were dropped off in front of Woollen Gym. At that moment, my checking account was down to 35 cents, but I wasn't going to call my mom for money. I saw a sign outside the intramural office about a meeting for officials. It was a clinic to teach people how to umpire softball games. I had umpired Little League baseball games in Asheville, so I had some experience. I went in and told the guy who interviewed me that I could really use that money, so he hired me and let me work all four nights of intramurals, Monday through Thursday. From that moment on, I worked 24 hours a week for the rest of my college career. There was a 4–7 p.m. shift and a 7–10 p.m. shift, but I worked both. I made $1.05 an hour. It wasn't much, but it was more than I had.

During the summer before my sophomore year, I worked several jobs to pay for a used Mustang and to have enough money to keep me in school. When I came back to Chapel Hill, I went straight to the intramural office and started refereeing football, soccer, volleyball, basketball, wrestling, horseshoes, and anything else they could find for me. I got to be known as the best referee on campus. By my senior year they'd made me the supervisor of intramural officials, and I had 108 students working under me. My graduate school year I was the assistant director of the intramural program. I was making $200 every two weeks, which at that time was more money than I could have ever imagined.

I was really proud that my five years of college cost my mother only $35. She sent me a $20 check my freshman year and a $15 check my sophomore year, and after that I said, "Mom, I'm okay. Don't send anything else."

WATCHING BASEBALL GAMES on television for many years, I really got interested in following the players' statistics. It got to the point where I knew that if Mickey Mantle went 1-for-4 in a particular game, his batting average had dropped from .340 to .338.

When my dad worked at Chakales Hosiery, he had a friend there who was a big Dodgers fan. When I was in first grade, I visited him at the mill and Daddy started talking to the guy about Mickey Mantle's and Yogi Berra's batting averages. Then he pointed to me and said, "I'll bet you a beer that Roy can tell you exactly what their averages are." They made the bet and the guy went and found a newspaper, and then I said, "Mickey Mantle is hitting .337 and Yogi Berra is hitting .321." My dad won that bet.

I had always enjoyed math and working with numbers. During my senior year at North Carolina, I was still watching as many of Coach Smith's basketball practices as I could squeeze in around working for intramurals. One day one of the varsity team managers came up to me in the bleachers and said, "Coach Smith would like to ask you a question."

I was scared to death, but I walked down to meet Coach Smith.

He said, "If you wouldn't mind, I'd like you to be a statistician for us and keep a points-per-possession chart. I really need somebody to do that who's going to concentrate and do a good job and know what's going on in the basketball game."

I said, "Coach, I would love to."

I was trying my best to act normal, but I couldn't really believe what was happening. It was the first conversation we'd ever had. I think it was Coach Smith's way of challenging me and I took it very seriously. That season I was asked to keep the stats at some preseason scrimmages, and Coach Smith liked what I did. I was precise and he could read my writing. When the season started, I did that for every home game and any of the road games in the state that I could drive to.

My points-per-possession chart was the only thing Coach Smith wanted to see at halftime. He didn't care about getting the regular stat sheet. So I had about 60 seconds after the end of the first half to get that to him. I would go knock on the locker-room door and hand the chart directly to him, and he'd usually say, "Not very good, huh?" or "Pretty good, huh?" I'd always agree with him.

After one of those preseason scrimmage games, the head manager came over and got the chart from me, and I started to leave. Suddenly I heard Coach Smith say, "Roy, hold on a second. How did you list that last play?"

"I thought that we had possession," I said, "so I left it with the white team and not blue."

"That's good."

He started to walk away but then turned back and said, "You really do a nice job."

"Thanks, Coach."

We had two or three little conversations like that, but that was about it.

In the summer of 1973, after my graduate school year, a top high school prospect named Phil Ford decided he was coming to UNC's basketball camp. Apparently at lunch one day, Coach Smith said to Coach Guthridge, "Let's get the best referee we can find and put him in Phil's gym."

Coach Guthridge asked him, "Do you want me to try to get Roy?"

Coach Guthridge knew that I officiated all of the biggest intramural games, so he called me and asked if I'd stop by the basketball office. I hadn't worked at UNC's basketball camp before, but when Coach Smith asked me if I would referee Phil's games, I said I would. He told me that UNC really, really wanted Phil Ford.

Phil Ford enjoyed himself at basketball camp that summer because every time Phil drove to the basket, Phil got fouled. On the defensive end, Phil got the charge call in his favor every time. Phil played great.

Phil came to UNC.

I AM ONE of the few students who ever attended the University of North Carolina and never drank a beer. When I was a kid I saw what alcohol did to my family, and I made a conscious decision that I was not going to drink. I never smoked either. I remember having a sip of beer when I was in high school and I just didn't like the taste. I think I never acquired the taste because I never *wanted* to acquire the taste. The idea that drinking too much could be hereditary scared me away. I used to tell my college buddies, "You have to get drunk to act a fool. I can act a fool without drinking a drop."

I was always so busy that I didn't have much time to go to campus parties. It was nothing for me to work out two or three times a day and then I worked lots of nights with intramurals. I didn't go to the library a lot. I wasn't an exceptional student. I made a 2.235 grade point average in each of my first two semesters, but after that I made the dean's list five of the next six semesters. I found enough time to study and I found time to play.

Intramurals was my athletic outlet. I played every sport you could possibly play and I was voted one of the best intramural athletes on campus. During grad school, we had 16 guys in my Masters of Arts in Teaching Health and Physical Education program. I decided to organize us as a team and try to win a campus championship. We called ourselves the Peacocks because Dr. Bill Peacock ran our program. Just participating in a sport earned you points, so I played everything. I threw horseshoes, played volleyball, basketball, football. In wrestling,

I walked onto the mat the first night and the other guy was just like me, another country bumpkin. So I wrestled him and I won because he wasn't in great shape and the minutes go by really slowly in that sport. The second and third nights I got forfeits, and so all of a sudden I was in the final. This guy came walking in wearing earmuffs and knee pads, and he turned me every which way but loose. He beat me up. He nearly killed me. But that's what I did for points.

I was organizing every team and making sure we had people playing every sport. I recruited Fred Mueller and Pat Earey, two guys on the faculty who were good handball players, to play on our intramural handball team. That ticked off the law school team, but since we were competing in the Graduate and Independent division, anybody could play. David Stroupe, who was getting his doctorate at North Carolina and had played basketball at Wake Forest, was on our volleyball team. Larry Cooper, a chemistry professor, who I knew had played college baseball, was on our fast-pitch softball team. Our pitcher on that team was Steve Partenheimer, and he could windmill it so fast that nobody wanted to catch him, so I was our catcher. Softball was the final event that decided the overall championship and the Peacocks won the softball title and the campus title. I took great satisfaction in that, not just as one of the players on that team but also as the general manager.

My college experience was so different from most of the other students' at that time. I could have done anything I wanted, but I chose to go to the gym, and that's basically where I stayed. It was such a period of unrest. The Black Student Movement protested wages for the food service workers. We had a great football player, Judge Mattocks, who just quit the team one day because he didn't like the establishment. The Kent State shootings happened while I was a sophomore, and we had some protests on campus. Also in my sophomore year they had a Vietnam draft lottery and everybody went to the student union to see what our draft numbers would be, based on our birthdates. Mine came up 111. I remember Dickie Ramsey, a freshman basketball teammate of mine, got 15. He quit school the next day and enlisted in the military. The word at that time was that everybody from around 100 on down was going to be drafted and that even student exemptions might not keep us from getting drafted. I never thought about running off to Canada, and yet I never really thought about fighting in Vietnam, either. I just thought that if those were the cards I was dealt, that's what I would do.

I'll never forget a letter I got from my high school buddy Ronnie Slider who was in Vietnam. His letter told me about his second week over there and how he was scared to death. One night all hell broke loose, and he fired his rifle until it was so hot that he couldn't hold it anymore. He wrote that he never saw the enemy, that he was just shooting out into the dark. Another friend, David Crandall, was over there and got malaria and is still on disability from his Vietnam service.

At first I was such a believer in our country and in our leaders that I thought the war was the right thing to do. By the end, I hated it. I went from being a hawk to someone who wanted us out of there.

I would talk to Wanda a lot about the war. We did lots of things together our first year in college. She would come to some of my freshman games. We would sit together to get varsity basketball tickets and then go to the games together. We would go to dinner once or twice a week. We went to concerts. We'd go out, but we weren't dating. My girlfriend would visit and stay with Wanda, and Wanda's boyfriend would visit and stay with me, and then during the spring semester of freshman year we just decided to get rid of the middle people and that was it. I like to say that I finally slowed down enough for her to catch me.

After that, there was hardly a day that we didn't see each other. She lived in Cobb Dorm for four years and whenever I came over to pick her up for a date, I would whistle for her. I had an extremely loud whistle and after a while, the girls above her and below her would come to their windows and shout, "Hi Roy, are you taking me to dinner tonight?" I made a lot of friends over there, but Wanda was always the one who came out and got in the car.

I moved into a trailer off campus my junior year, and Wanda started doing my laundry for me because it was easier for her to do that in her dorm than for me to do it in a Laundromat. That's when I knew it was serious. It was a very pleasant friendship that turned into courtship. On most Saturday nights Wanda and I would buy sirloin steaks and potatoes and head to my trailer to cook supper. We'd eat our steaks with cold Coca-Colas.

In the final summer of my graduate school year, I needed two more courses to get my degree. One was required and the other I wanted to be really easy. I heard about a guidance counseling course taught by Dr. Perry. I'd heard it had no tests, no papers, and no projects. That was my kind of class. My roommate, Roy Barnes, and I went to find out about it and were told it was full. So I told Roy that we were going to see Dr. Perry at his house. Roy didn't want to go, so he hid behind a bush when I knocked on Dr. Perry's door.

When he opened the door, I said, "Dr. Perry, my name is Roy Williams. I'm in graduate school in health and physical education finishing my master's. I need one more course to graduate. I would like to take your course, but they said the only way I could get in was with professor approval. Dr. Perry, this is it for me. They told me that your course has no tests, no papers, no projects—and I'm being honest with you, that's what I want. I can contribute in class with the best of them. Will you let me in?"

Dr. Perry said, "Son, you have to have mighty big balls to come to my house and say that to me."

"I'm just being honest," I said.

"Is that guy with you?" He pointed at Roy in the bushes.

"That's my roommate," I said. "He's just afraid to come up here."

"I should let you in and not him."

He led us into his home and he showed us all these antiques. A maid brought us some lemonade and we sat down in his living room. Finally, he said, "I've got to give you credit for coming over here."

Then he wrote out a note and handed it to us and said, "Be in that class tomorrow morning at 9 o'clock."

DURING A TRIP HOME to Asheville over Easter break of my graduate school year, I asked Wanda to marry me.

We were in my Mustang going uptown to a movie and I had brought the ring. I didn't want to just pull out the ring box, so I needed to hide it someplace. Because I was always ready for a basketball game, I had my shoes, my shorts, and my jockstrap in the backseat. So I put the gym shorts on top of the little ring box. We were driving along and I said, "Hey, reach back there in the backseat. I've got something for you under the gym shorts."

She fished around in the gym shorts and pulled out the ring box. I never said, "Will you marry me?" I never dropped to a knee. I just said, "Well, what do you think?"

She said, "Sure, why not?"

I know there have been a few people in the world who've had a more romantic proposal. The bottom line is that my future bride found her ring in my jockstrap, and she's always said that she should have known right then what she was getting into. There was no way around the fact that she was going to spend the rest of her life around smelly guys in a gym somewhere.

CHAPTER 5

Being Like Buddy Baldwin

THE DAY AFTER I asked Wanda to marry me, I was cutting my mom's grass right before I left Asheville to come back to school. I ran out of gas so I went around to the back door where I kept a gallon milk jug with gas in it. That's when I heard the phone ring and I stepped inside to answer it. It was Mr. Estes, a former principal at Biltmore Elementary School. We'd been close ever since the day in third grade when a bee had flown onto my Creamsicle while I was eating it and he'd pulled the stinger out of my tongue with some tweezers. He was a big fan of mine when I played basketball at Roberson.

Mr. Estes said, "When are you going back to school?"

"As soon as I finish mowing my mom's grass," I said.

"On your way out of town," he said, "stop by Owen High School and visit with the principal over there, Charlie Lytle."

"Mr. Estes, I don't know if I have time."

"Son, get your butt over there and visit with Charlie Lytle. He wants to hire you as his head basketball coach."

I finished mowing my mom's grass, took a bath, and drove to Owen High School, which was about 10 miles east of Asheville. I went in and talked to Mr. Lytle for 45 minutes. We talked about my basketball career at Roberson and what courses I'd taken at UNC. Then, toward the end of the conversation, Mr. Lytle asked me, "We have won six games or less in basketball for six straight years. What makes you think you could do any better?"

"I just have this feeling I can do it," I said. "I don't have a record or anything that can prove it to you, so you've got to make that decision. But I can do it."

He offered me the job. Mr. Estes had told him, "If you don't hire this boy it's going to be the dumbest thing you ever did. And when you hire him and he beats Buddy Baldwin, I will stand at center court and sing the Owen High School alma mater for you."

Mr. Lytle told me, "I don't know if you're any good, but Bill Estes thinks you're really good and I'm going to hold him to that."

I KNEW THAT being the head basketball coach at Owen High was not a plum job, because if it had been a plum job I would not have gotten it. There weren't 27 guys lined up outside Charlie Lytle's office begging to be interviewed. But it was nice to be home. Wanda was happy to be back in the Asheville area and my mom was not only happy to have me around but pleased that I had any job at all.

That summer of 1973 Mr. Lytle called me in to his office along with our football coach, Jim LeVine. "Roy, I hate to do this to you," Mr. Lytle said. "I know you're already going to be coaching basketball and golf, but we need another assistant football coach. We need you to coach the backs on the freshman team."

"I don't know anything about football," I said.

"You'll be fine," Jim said. "You'll be with Ralph Singleton coaching the varsity for three weeks. You stick with him and you'll be comfortable by the time the freshmen report."

Ralph had been coaching at Owen since the rocks cooled and when I met him I said, "I'll try my best, but I don't know anything about coaching football."

So I showed up at the football field for my very first practice as a coach of any sport and I was totally lost.

I was on the field with my shorts, T-shirt, hat, and whistle and at least I *looked* like a real football coach. We lined up everybody and they hit themselves in the head like football players do, and I started to feel a little more comfortable. I followed Ralph over to coach some of the backs and he picked six guys and said, "Y'all go with Coach Williams and start on the monkey roll."

I had no clue what the monkey roll was. That worried me a little because this was the players' first impression of me as a coach, and I had no idea what to tell them to do. My heart was pumping 150 beats a minute, and my throat was closing up. Finally, I said, "All right, who wants to go first?"

Three guys stepped up and I didn't know what the dickens they were supposed to do, but at least I knew it was going to take three of them to do it. I backed away from those three kids and I got my feet spread about shoulder width apart and my weight evenly distributed on the balls of my feet. I didn't know what they were going to do, but I was going to be ready to move. I said "Go!" and the first guy dropped on the ground and rolled over and the next guy dove over him and rolled over and then the third guy did it, and by that time the first guy was back up and doing it again. That was the monkey roll.

My next problem was that I didn't know when to tell them to stop, so I didn't stop them. All of a sudden Ralph turned around and saw that none of those three kids were getting up anymore. They were just struggling up to one arm and one knee and falling over the other guy because you're only supposed to do that drill for 30 seconds. I'd had those poor guys going at it for four minutes.

The best part was that those three guys went to my basketball players. "Coach Williams is the toughest son of a gun you're ever going to meet," they said. "You guys better get in shape or he's going to kill you."

THE FIRST TIME I walked into Owen High's basketball gym a couple of guys were in there playing one-on-one. I introduced myself and said, "Be back here tomorrow night at 6 o'clock and bring anybody else you know who plays basketball."

Thirteen guys showed up. I watched them play pickup games to see what I had, but before the night was over I was playing with them, because some of the guys were so out of shape they had to stop. It was somewhat discouraging, because I was by far the best player in the gym. On the other hand, I immediately earned their respect on the court, which was important because I was only 22 years old and some of them were 18. At one point the ball was bouncing toward the sideline, and I chased it down, grabbed it with my right hand as I was falling out of bounds, and flung it behind my back to a guy I'd seen breaking up the floor, and he caught it and laid it up. Everybody just went crazy. At that point, they didn't know if I could coach, but they knew I could kick their butts in a pickup game.

Before that first season, the local newspaper wrote an article about me, and I made some ridiculous statements. I talked about how we were going to run a fast break–style offense and we were going to press on defense. Heck, we could barely get the ball up the floor without dribbling it off our own feet.

We didn't have any youth or middle school basketball programs in our area, which meant that the week before the first game I was showing our freshmen which way to face on the opening tap and which spot to stand along the lane when somebody was shooting a free throw. Most of those kids had never played an organized game.

Despite all of that, I was trying to instill the philosophy of UNC basketball. During our preseason conditioning, I told them if they wanted to play they had to meet the same standard as the players at North Carolina by running a mile in seven minutes. I arrived at my first practice holding a minute-by-minute practice schedule just like Coach Smith. I tried to teach them UNC's offense and defense, but I figured out pretty quickly that there were some things that were just not going to work. The UNC passing game required savvy. Our guys did not have a lot of savvy. So we had to make some changes.

I look back and think what a terrible coach I was then. I didn't do a good job of determining who were my best scorers and how we could get them the ball to score. I made up my mind that we were going to play primarily man-to-man defense, even though we weren't athletic enough to play it. But I kept trying to do it anyway. When we played against a tall center, I tried to have our defense front him, and the other team would just throw it up at the rim and their big guy would get the rebound and lay it in. I knew that if we'd played behind their big man at least he'd have to score over us, but I was stubborn. I didn't understand yet that just because something worked in practice, it wouldn't necessarily work in games.

I knew that one of our forwards, Arthur Howard, was a slasher. Arthur could not shoot from the outside and he was not a post player, but I put him in an offense with his back to the basket. I tried to make him something he was not. Bobby Stafford was 6'4" and a solid post player with good touch around the basket, but our offense had so many other people running around in the lane that it was too crowded for Bobby to get the ball. Our point guard, Carl Moore, couldn't shoot very well, but I never told him not to shoot. I thought basketball was all about playing hard and unselfishly, but there were so many tactical things that I screwed up.

I remember a night when we lost by one point and we had the last nine shots of the game. We were 0-for-9. We were playing volleyball with the ball back and forth across the backboard. When that happens, it's up to the coach to figure out something different, because obviously what we were doing wasn't working.

I had two qualities as a young coach. I was very demonstrative and I talked too much. That's a bad combination. I kicked trash cans at halftime because I was livid that my players couldn't do what I told them to do. Once I kicked the door of a bathroom stall and it nearly hit me in the nose on the rebound. Another night I brought the entire team over to our two-room garage apartment for a pregame meal, and we had 14 players piled on top of each other. You are supposed to eat no less than four hours before a game, but because we had to wait until school let out, we ate barely three hours before the game. And we had fried chicken. That night Bobby Stafford, our best player, walked over to our bench early in the second half and said, "Coach, I can't move. I ate too much chicken." As soon as he said it, everybody else admitted that they felt the same way. We lost that game in the second half because everybody had stomachaches.

That first season we finished 2–19; it nearly killed me. The day after the season ended I had a doctor's appointment and I was diagnosed as having a hyperacidic pre-ulcer condition; it lasted for years.

In my second year we were 6–16, and we lost nine games by one or two points. During the county tournament a newspaper article came out that said all the conference coaches agreed that Owen was the most improved team during the season and that our future was bright. Back at Owen, however, I started hearing some jokes from other coaches and teachers that Charlie Lytle must have been crazy to have hired North Carolina's statistician, a kid who was barely older than his players. There were people who thought I should be fired. I'd also heard some grumbling from fans in the stands. The father of one of my players visited Mr. Lytle to ask if he was happy about what was going on with the team. But I was never afraid of getting fired, because by that time Mr. Lytle had more confidence in me than I had in myself.

The next season, I thought we were going to be pretty good, but we started out 1–3. We were awful. Going home after that fourth game, I was miserable, but I tried to hide it. I didn't talk to Wanda much about it except to say that our team stunk and we had to get better. It just wasn't as big a deal to anybody else as it was to me, but that was the first time in my life that I ever had trouble sleeping. I lay awake all night. The next morning I talked to Carl Conley, who was a friend and a coach as well, and I said, "I don't know if I'm made out to do this stuff or not. Since the ninth grade this is all that I've ever wanted to do, but am I doing what I should be doing?" Carl told me to stick with it and that he really believed I was meant to be a coach.

That was the only time I have ever doubted myself. I felt like I was working hard, teaching the right drills, and preaching the right sermons, and I thought that we should be able to win, but the other teams were not cooperating.

I started questioning myself. Why are we not winning? Should we be playing the point zone? Should we be throwing it in to the big guy every time? That was a long weekend of soul searching.

On Monday I told the players to be at practice a half hour early for a meeting. In the meeting I said, "Guys, we're too good to be this bad. We've got too much potential to be doing this, but everybody's got to be willing to buy in. I want people to say whatever is on your mind right now. Let's get everything off our chests."

The little sophomore point guard, Kerner Long, said, "I think I should be able to shoot more. All you ever tell me to do is throw it inside to Bobby."

I said, "That's right, because that's what's going to be best for our team."

Another guy told me he thought he should play more. I had to tell him he didn't play because he wasn't as good as the guys ahead of him. That made him cry, and I almost started crying there with him.

We aired a lot of things that needed to be said, needed to be out in the open, so that I could explain why we were doing what we did. There were some negative and some positive comments, but it established a better relationship among the players and gave them confidence that I would listen to their concerns and not just say, "I'm the coach, shut up and do what I tell you." It made them believe that they could trust me. It was a very emotional meeting, the first time I'd really gotten the kids to be honest with me.

That meeting saved the season and, who knows, maybe saved Roy Williams as well. After that, we won nine games in a row. It restored my faith that I could get everybody to accept their roles and work together for a common goal.

In the next-to-last game of that season we were up by one point with eight seconds to go against Mountain Heritage High, and Rusty Norton was on the free-throw line for us, shooting two. If I could have picked anybody on our team to be shooting those free throws with the game on the line, I'd have picked Rusty. He was also the best player on my golf team, and I felt he was the guy whose nerve I could trust the most. Rusty missed both foul shots, and Mountain Heritage sank a 35-footer at the buzzer to beat us. It cost us the conference championship, but I would still trust Rusty with those two free throws today.

I felt like the program had turned a corner. We were at a level where we could compete with anybody. We weren't a freebie win for even the best teams anymore.

The next two years we finished 13–10 and 10–15. It was a really good time for me to learn. I was evolving as a coach and as a man. In April after my fourth season, my son, Scott, was born and a month later we moved out of the garage apartment and into a house we'd had built. It felt like a natural progression to becoming an adult. I would take Scott to the gym at Owen, and he would sit in his stroller and watch my team practice while the rhythm of the game lulled him to sleep. He took his first step on the basketball court at Owen.

Those days were so crucial to me in realizing how important each of my individual players was and how to build relationships, instead of only being concerned about points and rebounds.

There's no question that even then, as we were raising our first child, I saw coaching basketball as a way to give some kids who needed it the kind of father figure that I never had. Players would come by my office and we would talk more about life than basketball. Bobby Stafford consulted me about every decision that he made. The baseball players and the girls' basketball players would stop by and talk to me about what they wanted to do after graduation. It wasn't unusual for me to have 15 kids in my office before or after school. I was essentially a guidance counselor who just happened to be the basketball coach.

I tried to mentor my players the way Buddy Baldwin had guided me at Roberson. I mandated coats and ties on the road. I joined the players after practice to sweep the floors and wipe down the basketballs, and then I drove many of them home. Wanda made bologna sandwiches to feed the players on the bus back from road trips. We invited them over for cookouts and fed them milk and doughnuts after off-season shootarounds. I wrote personal notes of encouragement to individual players. Before every game I passed out index cards to our top five or six players with what I expected out of them. Sometimes it was just how many points I needed them to score, but other times it was more than that. We had a talented sixth man named Byron Bailey who never started a game for us. One night I wrote him a note: *Don't ever lose faith, because one of these days you're going to be huge for us in a big-time win.* That very night one of our starters got into foul trouble and Byron made 10 free throws in the fourth quarter to clinch a win for us.

On the court, I felt like we played better each season, even if our records didn't always reflect that. We just couldn't quite get over the hump. We didn't have any big guys, or we didn't have any guards, or we had some key player get hurt, or one year, our best player just decided he didn't want to play. We never had the depth of talent that could help us withstand these problems.

During at least half of our practices I'd get out there myself and play somebody one-on-one, first to score three wins, during a water break. I never lost a game. We had great kids, but that says a lot about their skill level. Some of them were really very competitive, and I loved that they kept on trying to beat me—because when I first arrived it didn't make any difference to them. So we established that competitive spirit.

Our team's improvement was never more obvious than in our results against Roberson High, my alma mater. The first time I coached against Buddy Baldwin we lost by 55 points. It was 81–26. Roberson was bigger. They were faster. They were stronger. They could shoot better. Defensively, they were like piranhas. We couldn't get the ball across halfcourt. At Roberson's summer basketball camp I'd taught many of their players the defensive trap that I learned at North Carolina, and it seemed like they stole the ball from us 100 times, so I was wishing I hadn't done that. Then they killed us again, 77–39, playing at Owen. Buddy would tell me after those games that I was doing the right things but that it would take time to see results and that really reassured me.

In my second season we beat Roberson. Bobby Stafford hit a jump shot with just under two minutes left to give us the lead and we won 35–33. I remember it didn't give me any extra satisfaction to beat Buddy. It was just a win. Maybe it was because I knew that a guy who was very important to me wasn't feeling very good. But after the game, I did call Mr. Estes. "I thought you were going to be at the game tonight to sing the alma mater at center court," I said.

"You tell Charlie Lytle that I'll be down there first thing tomorrow morning," Mr. Estes said, "and we'll go down to that gym and I'll sing it just for him."

WHEN I FIRST took the job at Owen High School, I could see myself staying there forever. It gave me a chance to live my dream of being like Buddy Baldwin. After five seasons, I had a 45–68 record, but the program had improved a lot. It had turned around from a program that generated virtually no interest to where little kids walked around saying, "I can't wait until I'm an Owen Warhorse basketball player."

But I had started thinking it might be really good to have just a basketball program to coach, so I wouldn't feel like I was cheating kids in the classroom. Teaching my class in health and physical education was not my interest. Teaching kids about the food groups was not my interest. Certifying kids in a first-aid course was not my interest. Coaching the basketball team was my only interest. There were times when I'd organize my students to play a volleyball game, and while the game was going on, I'd be working on my basketball practice plan. I knew that was not right. So that's when I started thinking about coaching at the college level. It had nothing to do with money or fame. I just wanted to be able to devote my whole day to what I really loved.

Every summer while I was coaching at Owen, I was invited to work at the UNC basketball camp. I used to play a game with the campers. When I first met them on Monday morning, I'd bet all 64 kids that by Tuesday night I would know all of their first and last names, and if I got somebody's name wrong, I would buy them an ice cream cone. I never bought an ice cream cone. Coach Smith liked my energy, my enthusiasm, my organization, and how I had a personal relationship with each kid. I always thought, "This is somebody's son. How would I want him to be treated if he were my son?" After a few summers, they started placing me out in the gym farthest away from campus because they felt they didn't have to check up on me very much.

At the end of every summer, I'd get a handwritten note from Coach Smith saying that I'd moved into the highest echelon of camp coaches and how comfortable he was when he walked into the gym and saw me there. At the closing-night staff party in the summer of 1978, Coach Smith said he wanted to talk to me. We went and sat in a booth by ourselves. He asked me if I was interested in coming back to North Carolina to be his part-time assistant coach.

I was so excited and flattered. I couldn't really believe it. But there was a catch, and I asked Coach Smith if I could think about it and talk to my wife. I went back home and told Wanda that Coach Smith had offered me the job. I said, "Honey, it only pays $2,700 a year."

Wanda thought I was nuts. She said, "That's the stupidest idea I've ever heard. We've just built a house, our son is 15 months old, our friends and family all live here. We're making $30,000 between the two of us and you're asking me to go back to North Carolina for $2,700 a year?"

"Honey, it'll work out."

She looked into my eyes, exhaled, and said, "When do we leave?"

CHAPTER 6

The Best Dadgum Calendar Salesman There Ever Was

I N MY FIRST SEASON as an assistant coach at North Carolina, I didn't say 10 words. I was scared to death. The only sound that came out of my mouth was a whistle. I would referee in practice because I felt that was a way I could contribute.

During games, I kept a chart on the bench of what offenses and defenses we called, the quality of shots taken, and the results of each possession. At halftime I'd give Coach Smith that statistical analysis. I could tell him, for example, that every time our offense ran "Fist," we wound up with a layup, or that we got four turnovers in the six times we called our "Scramble" defense, so our double-teaming was effective. It was the first time Coach Smith had ever had that kind of information and he really liked it. I did it to keep myself busy because I'd get upset at some of the foul calls, but I didn't want to say anything to the referees. I would have had a heart attack if an official had ever called a technical foul on me.

In my third year we were playing at N.C. State and for some reason I turned to Coach Smith on our bench and said, "Coach, what do you think about running 'Biggie'?"

He stood up right away and yelled, "Jimmy, run Biggie!"

My heart jumped into my throat. We ran the play and scored.

The next time we got the ball, Coach Smith asked me, "You want to try Biggie again?"

"Yeah, maybe to the other side," I said.

So we ran it to the other side and we scored again.

After the game, while we were waiting in the parking lot to ride the bus home, I said, "Coach, you really made me nervous. I just threw out that play as a suggestion."

He said, "Let me tell you something. The other coaches throw plays out to me all the time. If you throw one out at me, I know you have thought it through so much that I don't have any worries about going ahead and calling it. I want you to stay that way. If you suggest something, I'm going to do it."

That made me feel really good. In three years, that was the first suggestion of any play I had ever made. I was starting to feel like a real coach.

I USED TO JOKE that in Coach Smith's terminology, my job as part-time assistant coach meant full-time job, part-time pay. It was extremely difficult to survive financially during my first couple of years back in Chapel Hill. I was doing every odd job I could possibly find to feed my family. My day was dominated by two things, coaching and trying to figure out more ways to make some money.

I had five jobs my first year. I ran a little basketball camp for children of the university faculty and staff, and I charged each kid $15 for a week. At the end of each week I made $80 after expenses. I worked for a transport company taking staples out of eight-inch-thick stacks of bills, putting them in numerical order, and then stapling them back together again. I thought, "I've got a dadgum master's degree and now I've got to learn how to count again?"

Every Sunday during the football and basketball seasons, I woke up at 5 o'clock in the morning to drive videotapes of the UNC football and basketball coaches' shows to the local television stations in Greensboro and Asheville. Those drives became so monotonous. I remember timing myself each Sunday, always trying to find a quicker route. In Asheville, I'd have a late breakfast with my mother and then I'd drive right back to Chapel Hill. I drove 504 miles and made $113 per trip, minus the money I spent on gas. That was what I did on my day off. For me, Sunday was not a day of rest. I spent nine hours in the car. I did that for five years.

The hardest job I had was selling calendars. The calendars had pictures of the UNC players on them with room for a company's advertisement at the bottom. The job began with cold calls to businesses that had advertised in the football program, and those calls weren't very successful. One guy said, "Why should I buy calendars? I spent $250 to have an ad in the program and the team only won five stinking games!" During that first year there were days when I would go see 15 people and not sell a single calendar. I hated being told no. It wasn't just the rejection, it was the disdain. It was awful. That summer I drove 9,000 miles, sold 10,500 calendars in nine weeks, and made $2,400.

In the meantime, Coach Smith had helped find Wanda a teaching job at Chapel Hill High School that paid $9,000. She did that for a year, but the second year we decided to go ahead with our plans for a second child because we thought if we waited until we could afford it, it might never happen. So Wanda taught part-time until October when Kimberly was born. I still have our income tax returns from 1980, and our combined income, two 30-year-olds with two kids, was $8,910. It was hard sometimes, but we managed.

I don't know many people who paid a higher price to get started, but I did those kinds of jobs for many years to be able to stay in coaching. There were times when I despised it. It was demeaning. I felt like I was begging. I nearly got to the point of thinking, "I can't do this anymore." But then I remembered that I liked to eat.

BUT THERE WERE definite paybacks to being where I was. I was the first college coach ever to get really excited about Michael Jordan. I always thought that the primary reason Coach Smith hired me at North Carolina was to recruit. The summer before Jordan's senior year of high school in 1980, I was calling high school coaches trying to get them to send their players to our basketball camp. We got Buzz Peterson and we got Lynwood Robinson. And then a guy named Mike Brown, who was the athletic director of the New Hanover County Schools, called us about a kid named Mike Jordan. Coach Guthridge went down to Wilmington to see Jordan play, but when he came back he said, "I don't know how good he is. He's very athletic, but all he did was shoot a lot of long jump shots and he didn't make many of them."

I called the Laney High School coach, Clifton "Pop" Herring, and he told me that he thought Jordan was going to be a star. I convinced him to send Mike to North Carolina's summer camp.

On the afternoon when we were doing camp registration we rounded up the campers to play pickup games in Carmichael Auditorium. The counselors would bring in 30 kids at a time and they would play for 30 minutes and then the next group would come. A group came in and I stood there and watched this one player for a few minutes. I thought, "God almighty, he is really good." We had some solid players at camp, but he was clearly the best of all of them.

After the game I walked up to him and I said, "What's your name?" He said, "Mike Jordan."

I asked him if he wanted to play another session and he did. I watched him the whole 30 minutes and he was great. He walked 15 minutes back to his room and then walked all the way back, because he wanted to play a third session. I was sold.

When we finished up there, I left to go have dinner with another assistant coach, Eddie Fogler.

"Well, did you see anybody you liked?" he said.

I said, "Eddie, I think I just saw the best 6'4" high school basketball player I've ever seen."

"Who the heck is that?"

"Mike Jordan."

"Really?"

"Eddie," I said, "he is phenomenal."

By Tuesday of that week Coach Smith had eaten breakfast with him one day and lunch with him the next, and he offered him a scholarship.

I talked to Pop Herring, and it was decided that Jordan should go to the Five-Star basketball camp that summer, where he'd get some national exposure and top competition. At Five-Star, when Jordan went to one court, I followed him. When he moved to another court, I followed him. It was like there was nobody else there. I watched every step he took. He won the MVP award at the camp all-star game and all five individual awards. *Street & Smith's* preseason magazine had already come out, and Mike Jordan was not listed among the top 500 players in America. The next year, he was a McDonald's All-American and a North Carolina Tar Heel.

The first player I ever helped recruit at North Carolina was James Worthy in 1978. James was so superior to his competition in savvy and athleticism. I would drive down to Gastonia to watch him play in high school. I saw him play seven times, and each time I came back firmly believing that he was a man among boys. The last three schools James was considering were North Carolina, Kentucky, and Michigan State. James had this deep voice and he thought he could mimic people really well, so he put a handkerchief over the phone and called his father during his recruiting visit to Kentucky and pretended he was Coach Smith. He tried to get his dad to say some things to "Coach Smith" about how well James's recruiting was going with North Carolina. When James's dad told me that story, I knew his son was coming to UNC.

One afternoon I was the only coach in the basketball office when the phone rang. It was a UNC fan who ran a gas station near Albany, New York, and he told me about a kid named Sam Perkins, who was a junior in high school up near there. I took down all the information and gave it to Eddie Fogler. We followed up every lead, so Eddie called the high school coach that afternoon. When we started talking about Sam in the office, Coach Smith realized he had seen him play at a USA Basketball event and he asked me to fly up to see Sam play at his high school in Latham, New York. I saw a player who was unbelievably smooth and effortless about his game, the kind of player who at the end of the game you thought he'd done all right, when in fact, he had 30 points and 15 rebounds. He was 6'9" and rail thin with an extraordinary wingspan and the ability to block shots and score on a jump hook. He made doing hard things look easy, and that matched his personality. Sam's nickname was "Big Smooth." But Sam's recruitment was far from smooth. UCLA, San Francisco, and Syracuse were also after him, so I went up to see him a lot. I'd go out with Sam's coaches after every game. We'd stay out until 3 a.m. and then I'd be on a 7 a.m. flight home that same morning.

After the high school season in his senior year, Sam played in the Dapper Dan game in Pittsburgh. Eddie and I stood in the hallway outside the locker room, waiting for him after his game, but Sam never came out. Finally, I asked a guy to go in and check and he said there was nobody in there. I went back to the hotel and I must have walked around the lobby 50 times. I saw every other player, but I could not find Sam. Finally, I spotted Tom Yeager who was part of the NCAA enforcement staff and I said, "Tom, something is going on. Sam Perkins did not come out of the locker room and he is not here. All of the other coaches are here except San Francisco."

By 2 a.m. I finally gave up and went to my hotel room. Not long after that, I got a phone call from Yeager and he told me they'd found Sam. The San Francisco coaches had gone into the locker room and taken Sam out a back door. They had taken him and his girlfriend out to eat, which was illegal. They had taken him to Denny's. A few months later, we got Sam, and San Francisco got nailed with a recruiting violation.

We recruited Brad Daugherty from my old stomping grounds outside Asheville. Brad's oldest brother, Greg, was 7'0" and hated basketball; the middle brother, Steve, was 6'5" and had played for me at Owen. Steve didn't have any great talent, but he loved to play. Brad would eventually grow to 6'11" and he had great skills and desire, but when I left Owen he was still a fat 5'11" eighth-grader. He'd made me mad that summer at my basketball camp by being disruptive during drills, and so I threw him out and told him not to come back. That night I got a call from Brad's father, who asked me if I would stop by his house the next morning on the way to camp to talk about Brad. So I went over there. "Coach," he said, "you didn't have my first boy and I wish you had. You had my second boy and I was glad you did, and now you're going to have Bradley. I'm going to ask you to let Bradley come back to your camp and if he makes you mad, you bust Bradley's ass, and then you call me and then I'll really bust Bradley's ass when he gets home."

Three weeks after that conversation, Coach Smith asked me to come back to North Carolina, so I never coached Brad at Owen. But I did recruit him to North Carolina. On his recruiting visit, Brad, Steve, and their mother came for a football game. Coach Smith, Steve, and I were sitting in the stands when Steve told a story about a recent talk between Brad and his father at the family dinner table. He told us his father had said, "Bradley, you have an opportunity to go play basketball anyplace in America and I think that's great. You get to choose where you want to go. I want you to know that I'm going to be really happy wherever you go . . . as long as you choose that school where Coach Williams is." Brad came to UNC as a 16-year-old, and four years later he was the first pick in the NBA draft.

The reputation of UNC helped a lot in recruiting. I remember recruiting Rick Fox. He lived in Warsaw, Indiana, which was a hard place to get to. I had to take two flights and then drive an hour. Rick didn't play his senior season because he had moved to Indiana from the Bahamas through a church-sponsored program and had been ruled ineligible. So I'd go up there a lot just to watch him practice and play pickup games. When Rick finally announced his decision, he said he'd dreamed about going to UNC ever since he was a little kid. Later I said to him, "Rick, why didn't you tell me that a long time ago? I might have made fewer trips to Warsaw to watch practice."

Another player we tried to recruit during my first season as an assistant was Ralph Sampson. I still believe Ralph was the most gifted high school player I have ever seen. He was 7'4" with the agility of a 6-footer. Opponents were not going to get offensive rebounds and they were not going to guard him with one guy. Ralph changed a game with his size. I was the lowest guy on the North Carolina totem pole, so I made nine trips to Harrisonburg, Virginia, to see him play. Ralph had narrowed his options down to 52 colleges in January of his senior year. His recruitment was during the time period when college coaches could "bump" prospects, which basically meant we could say hello. So after every one of his games, 10 to 15 coaches would line up around the court hoping to bump Ralph and his family. I got tired of hanging around for an hour after every game, so one night I said the heck with it and went to Howard Johnson's for some ice cream. All of a sudden the Sampson family came walking in. I said hello to them, and Mrs. Sampson said, "We come here after every game." So for the next five trips up there I never stayed at the gym after the game. I'd just drive to Howard Johnson's.

Ralph eventually narrowed his decision down to four schools: North Carolina, Kentucky, Virginia, and Virginia Tech. It was wild because he waited until the last day you could sign a letter of intent to make his choice. That morning he didn't know what he was going to do, and before he went out to speak at the press conference, he said, "Mom, I don't want to do this."

She said, "You're going to go out there and make an announcement or I'm going to go out there and tell them you're going to Virginia because that's the closest to home."

So Ralph walked out and said, "Well, I guess I'm going to Virginia."

I'd spent all that time and we'd spent all that money, and the guy said, "I *guess* I'm going to Virginia."

That was a great introduction to recruiting.

WANDA HAD BEEN on the editorial staff of the Roberson
High School yearbook, and a few years after we graduated from there
she told me that during our senior year I had won the class vote for
Most Athletic, Most Likely to Succeed, and Most Dependable. But
apparently the rules stated that you could win only one award, and
because I'd won by the largest majority in the Most Dependable cat-
egory, that was what I got.

When Wanda first told me that, I was disappointed, because I
would have preferred to win Most Athletic. But the more I thought
about it, I realized that Most Dependable meant that people could
trust me and count on me, and that really meant something to me. It
really became more and more important with each stage of my life.
I realized that being dependable would take me further than being
athletic.

I earned my keep early on as an assistant coach at North Carolina
by being dependable. I was willing to do whatever was asked, and
nobody ever had to wonder if it would get done. When I wasn't on
the road recruiting, I would go through 36 newspapers a day to see
if there were articles about recruits or other teams we were playing. I
ran our study hall. I went around to players' dorms every morning to
make sure they had left for class, and then I checked the classrooms
to make sure they'd made it there. I did bed checks on the road trips.
And I coached the junior varsity team.

If I had a glaring weakness as the JV coach, it's that I wasn't very
good at scheduling. We played teams that were all really good, so we
were under .500 my first year. But eventually we got to be more competitive. I felt like we were always going to be undermanned because
most of the teams we played consisted of recruited players, so I was
really tough on our guys. I motivated through fear. I'd run the crap
out of them if we didn't play well in practice. We ran and ran and

ran so we could try to at least get a conditioning advantage on our opponents. I would drill them in the fundamentals and tell them that the game of basketball is a game of mistakes and we've got to make far fewer than the other team to have a chance.

Coach Smith used to watch each of our games for a few minutes and then make suggestions. One time he diagrammed a delay game for me on a paper napkin, and after we'd tested it with the junior varsity, Coach Smith adapted it to his varsity team.

Coaching that team was coaching at its purest. My junior varsity team was fueled so much by emotion; those guys were not going to go to the NBA, and there was nobody in the stands except girlfriends and parents. They were playing basketball because they loved to play and they loved to wear a North Carolina jersey. The only dream I had to sell was that if a spot opened up for a walk on with the varsity, it would go to one of our guys. We did have several players move up during the eight years I coached the team. Those were the only reasons for them to put up with me pushing them as hard as I did.

It was the best coaching experience I could have possibly had because we were always underdogs. I would try different things to cover our flaws, and I didn't have to read in the paper the next day whether it was successful or not, because no media came to the games. There was no shot clock, so I could hold the ball as much as I wanted to. I could change defenses on every possession if I wanted to. We would try to use lots of gimmicks to bother the other team. We won one game when we shot 13 backdoor layups, which makes you wonder why the other team never wised up.

We played Duke four times and we beat them all four times, but one game in particular really ticked them off. We played Coach Smith's "Four Corners" for the whole game; we spread the floor, kept the ball away from them, and ran time off the clock unless we had an open layup. We beat them even though they were much more talented than us that year. I was proud that we never lost to a team that fielded nonrecruited players like we did.

One night we played Fork Union Military Academy, whose center, Melvin Turpin, would go on to be the sixth pick in the NBA draft a couple of years later. Fork Union's players dwarfed us across the front line, but we controlled the tempo the whole game by spreading the floor and holding the ball as long as we could until we got a high-percentage shot. We had the ball out of bounds with three seconds to play, down by just a point. I called a set play, and Walker Worth made the shot at the buzzer, but the officials said he let it go too late. They didn't count the basket and we lost 54–53. Coach Smith was out watching before his game and I remember he walked over and asked the timekeeper if he was sure that he'd started the clock at the correct moment.

I walked into our locker room and I was just devastated. I talked to my players and then I let them go, and I headed out to catch my breath a little bit. I drank a Coca-Cola in about five seconds and sat down on our bench with a few minutes left in the varsity warm-up. Coach Smith was there and he slid down next to me and said, "Show me that play you just ran at the end of the game."

He was really just trying to make me feel better, but we did end up putting that play in with the varsity.

Whenever I coached the JV team and we struggled, I couldn't sleep. I remember the day that one of our varsity players, Jeff Lebo, came back to the trainer's room before their game and found me standing back there with red, puffy eyes. He said something to me, but I was in another world and so I looked up and said, "Let's be ready, Jeff."

He walked away and asked our trainer, "What's the matter with Coach?"

"The JV lost and he is really not happy," the trainer said.

Lebo said, "It's just a JV game."

"Not to Coach Williams."

BEFORE THE 1981 SEASON I went to Coach Smith and said that I thought we needed to have a conditioning program that consisted of more than just running a mile on the first day of practice.

He said, "Okay, you do it."

So I called Indiana and Kentucky and got them to send me their conditioning programs and met with our assistant track coach, Don Lockerbie, and I made up my own program. We did some distance work and we ran some hills, but we focused our workout on running 220-yard sprints. We worked up to a test at the end of four weeks that included 15 220-yard sprints with 90 seconds rest in between. Each guy had a specific time he had to run them in. Every once in a while Don would come out and watch just to reassure me that I wasn't going to kill anybody.

The players met me for conditioning three days a week in the fall, and I tried to exhaust them. I tried to bury them. One of our players, Al Wood, once told me, "Coach, I see that stopwatch in your hand and that whistle around your neck and it makes me feel like you are the most powerful man in the world."

When Michael Jordan first got to UNC, we were sitting at the track one day after conditioning. It was just the two of us. "Coach," he said. "I want to be the best player to ever play here."

"You'll have to work much harder than you did in high school," I said.

"But, Coach, I worked as hard as everybody else."

"Oh, excuse me. I thought you just said you wanted to be the best player to ever play here. Working as hard as everybody else is not even going to come close, son."

That was the end of the conversation.

Two days later, after the next conditioning session, Michael came up to me and we were sitting there alone again. He said, "Coach, I've been thinking about what you said. I'm going to show you. There will never be anyone who will outwork me."

He did that. From that day on, Michael tried to kick everybody's rear end in every drill. We had James Worthy, Sam Perkins, Matt Doherty, and Jimmy Black, and he was trying to destroy all of them. That's when I knew we had something special.

IN MY MIND at the end of the 1982 regular season we were the best team in the country. Coach Smith had taken a lot of criticism from the press about coaching in six Final Fours and never winning a national championship, but I felt there was no way we were not going to win this one. We had reached the NCAA Tournament final the year before and gotten a taste, and in '82 I was sure we were going to win the whole thing.

We were playing Georgetown for the championship and it was a close game throughout. We were down by one point with 32 seconds to play. Coach Smith called timeout and the guys came over to the bench. The negative look on all of their faces scared me to death. It was the first time that night I ever had the thought, "My gosh, we could lose this game."

The players sat down in chairs and the coaches knelt down in front of them, and I can remember it like it was last night. Coach Smith said, "Okay, we're in great shape. We're exactly where we want to be because we're going to determine the outcome of this game."

I pretended to cough so I could look up at the scoreboard just to make sure I had the score right, because he was making me feel like we were ahead.

Then he said, "I'm serious. We're exactly where we want to be. This basketball game is ours. We'll run 'Lineup' in case they're pressing, but I don't think they will be. We'll get it in and let's see what they're doing. I believe they'll stick in a zone. If they are, let's run "2" and look for the lob, but I don't think it will be there. If it's not, don't worry about it, penetrate and then try to pitch on the backside. If we get the shot and it's open, take the shot. James, when you go for the lob, go ahead and get inside position on the weak side. Sam, you get inside position in the middle, so even if we miss the shot, we'll get the rebound and put it back in. If they get the rebound, don't worry about it. Just foul them. There's no way they can make a free throw in this situation. We're going to determine the outcome of this game."

When the team left the huddle, I felt so much better. The look on everybody's face had changed 180 degrees. I saw Coach Smith pat Michael on the back and say, "Michael, if you get it, knock it in."

We went out on the court, ran "Lineup" and they didn't press, so we threw it in; they did stay in a zone, so we looked for the lob, but we didn't get it. We threw it on the backside to Michael and he took the shot and knocked it in and we won the national championship.

I was thrilled, but it was also a moment of relief for me because I was tired of everybody saying Coach Smith couldn't win the big one. I had tears rolling down my face and that was why.

I also learned a little bit about coaching that night.

• • •

DURING THE SPRING after my second season as an assistant coach, I stood outside of our two-bedroom apartment holding Kimberly, and there were mosquitoes all over us because we were living on a flood plain. It was miserable. I walked back into the apartment and I told Wanda that I was going to sell 22,000 calendars that summer and we were going to move into a house.

I was learning some of the tricks of being a salesman. Instead of dealing with businessmen who had no particular love for UNC, I started making my pitch to rabid Tar Heel fans. Instead of pitching to 10 businesses in a town, I realized it was better to go visit three and try to sell them on the idea that there was some snob appeal to saying that they had calendars when other folks didn't. That summer I sold 23,000 calendars and made $9,000 and we moved into a house on Lady Bug Lane with three bedrooms, two baths, and a nice yard with azalea bushes that was all ours.

Three years later, I sold 40,000 calendars and we moved into an even bigger house closer to campus. Three years after that, when I did it for the last time, I drove 3,000 miles over five weeks, sold 55,000 calendars, and made $30,000. I was the best dadgum calendar salesman there ever was.

We weren't the only ones upgrading our living arrangements. With the money I made from selling calendars, I had a house built in Asheville for my mother. It was the first house she had ever really owned. We'd designed it with three bedrooms so that Frances and I could both visit at the same time and have our own bedrooms. The day I moved my mother's stuff into the new house, Frances was there and she said she was going to go pick up Mom and bring her back to the house. I said, "Tell Mom I want fried chicken and biscuits and gravy for supper and I'll be back at 7:30."

Frances said, "Aren't you going to be here when Mom comes in for the first time?"

"No," I said. "I don't want to see her cry. Just tell her to have my supper ready."

I went to the golf course, and when I got back to the house, that was one of the great moments of my life. I walked into the kitchen and saw my mother stirring gravy and she turned around and I could see her drying her eyes with a tissue. We were never very outwardly affectionate toward each other, but she turned around and wiped her hands on her apron and I walked over and hugged her. It was one of those hugs that she didn't want to let go and I knew I was about to cry, so I kind of backed away and said, "Mom, get back to your gravy. I'm starving."

As an assistant coach at North Carolina I always felt like if I did the best job I could, someday the right head coaching job would open up and it would be staring me right in the face. It would be mine and have my name written all over it.

In March 1985 Coach Smith had a conversation with Dick Sheridan, the athletic director at Furman, about their basketball coaching vacancy. I followed that up by calling Dick to tell him I was interested in the job. I liked the fact that Furman was just across the South Carolina border from Asheville, that it was a pretty campus, and that the program had a history of success. I interviewed with Dick and then with the university president, Dr. John Johns. Then I met with the school's search committee, and Dr. Johns asked me, "Would you take the job if we offered it?"

I said, "Dr. Johns, I can't answer that because it hasn't been offered. Right now I'm more interested in my North Carolina team beating Auburn tomorrow night than I am in this job. But you've got to believe that if I do get this job that I'm going to be more interested in Furman winning than any other school."

Dr. Johns wouldn't offer me the job without knowing my answer. North Carolina lost to Villanova a few days later, and on the flight home our sports information director, Rick Brewer, asked me about what was going on with Furman. I said, "Rick, I think I'm going to Furman."

I had done some serious thinking about the job and talked to some people about joining me as assistant coaches. I was cocky enough to think Furman was going to offer me the position, and I'd made up my mind that I would take it if they offered. But when I got home there was a phone message from Dick Sheridan. I called him back, and he told me that Dr. Johns couldn't come to grips with the fact that I wouldn't give him an answer before the job was offered, so he had hired another coach. I wasn't disappointed. I never second-guessed how I'd handled it. I just thought it wasn't meant to be.

Then in August, I was contacted about the job at Tennessee–Chattanooga. It was funny because every day that summer we had been driving by Frank Porter Graham Elementary School, and my daughter, Kimberly, would yell out, "That's where I'm going to school next year." She was so excited and she had just started at that school when Chattanooga fired their coach and they called me for an interview and then offered me the job. I liked the city and the program was one of the best in its conference, but I felt I owed my family some stability. I called Coach Smith and said, "I can't do it. All summer I've been hearing Kimberly saying, 'That's where I'm going to school next year.' It's just not right."

In February of the next season, we played at Georgia Tech, and the next day I flew down to Mississippi State. I arrived there incognito a few hours before I was supposed to meet with their athletic director about that school's coaching job. I got my rental car, drove to campus, and walked around a bit to get a feel for the place. I met two African-American girls sitting on a bench and I asked them how they were doing. They didn't know who I was, but they were very friendly. They gave me the sense that Mississippi State was not the place for me. I was left with a bad impression of what normal students thought about the student athletes. And I didn't like seeing the Confederate flag flying everywhere. That night I went to a Mississippi State basketball game. After the game the athletic director took me to the university president's home and he offered me the job. I told them I'd have to go back and talk to Coach Smith about it.

I had gotten the calendar sales up enough at that point that I was earning an overall salary of about $38,000 a year. Mississippi State was offering me $138,000 a year. I came back and told Coach Smith, "I can't do it. I don't think it would fit me."

"You know there are not many people who would turn down a raise of $100,000," Coach Smith said.

"I've got enough money to feed my family now," I said. "I've got to enjoy what I'm doing." So I turned down Mississippi State.

I tried to get involved at Florida State when the position opened up after the 1986 season. I sent in my résumé, but they said they didn't want to consider any assistants, so I couldn't even get interviewed there.

At the same time, Eddie Fogler left UNC to take the Wichita State coaching job. Coach Smith called me in and said, "Eddie's going to take the Wichita State job and you can go with him, but I'd really like you to stay here. You've done a great job for us."

I said, "If you'll have me, I'd rather stay."

After eight years, I was finally a full-time assistant. We had great teams during the next two years, and I felt like I was getting more responsibility every year.

During the 1987–88 preseason, Coach Smith had some health problems. His nose started bleeding and sometimes he couldn't get it stopped, and on a few occasions he sat up in the stands and let Coach Guthridge and me handle practice. During one practice, when I was teaching how to defend the lateral screen, Coach Smith came to me afterward and said, "Roy, you did a great job today. I've got to let you do more coaching and not dominate things so much."

I told him, "Coach, the way things have been going around here I'd say it's working pretty well the way it is. But I've got to have learned something, you know. I've been here for nine years."

Every day he'd been preparing me to be a head coach, telling me to think like a head coach in every instance.

In the spring of 1988 the equipment manager at George Mason called and said that he'd been talking to the athletic director who wanted to know if I'd come up and talk to them about their coaching opening. The equipment manager's cousin, Steve Garay, worked at our basketball camp, and Steve was always bragging about me. So I flew up to Fairfax, Virginia, on a Thursday and I met with 10 people on their search committee. I walked into a conference room and the athletic director, Jack Kvancz, told me that everybody around the table had questions for me.

I said, "How about let's do this first. Let me tell you what I'm going to do. Let me tell you how I'm going to run the program and then at the end if you have any questions, ask me."

So I talked for 40 minutes about how I was going to run the George Mason basketball program. When I was done, Jack looked around

and said, "Anybody have any questions you want to ask the coach?"
Not one person asked a question. Then he asked one of his assistants
to take me to see the coach's office and the locker room. About 15
minutes later Jack came up to me and said, "You just blew everybody
away. That's a group of very opinionated people and not one of them
could come up with a question to ask you. I want you to be our new
basketball coach."

I said, "Great."

I flew back that night and I couldn't sleep. I told Coach Smith
about it the next day. I was in outer space that whole day. Jack called
on Friday and said, "I'm coming down on Saturday morning. I'll
bring the contract. We'll dot the *i*'s and cross the *t*'s and we'll agree
on everything. You'll sign it. I'll sign it. I'll bring it back and then our
president gets back on Sunday, and we'll fly you up and have the press
conference on Sunday afternoon. It's a done deal, and, Roy, I am so
pleased that this has worked out."

On Friday night I did not sleep at all. I was lying awake feeling
like I was trying to convince myself to take the job and that I would
be taking it just to have the opportunity to be a head coach. I got up
at 6 a.m. and I was going to go for a run, but I stopped dead in the
driveway, went back in the house, called Jack Kvancz, and said, "Jack,
I can't do it. I know your flight is soon. Don't come. I'm not going to
take the job."

I waited until about 10 a.m. because Coach Smith doesn't get up
early, and I called him and said, "Coach, I've got some bad news for
you."

He said, "What's that?"

"I called Jack Kvancz back and told him I'm not going to take the
job."

"How do you feel?"

"Relieved."

"Then you made the right decision. Just be patient. The right job will come along and you will know it."

Two months later, I got that job.

CHAPTER 7

Big-time Ballcoachin'

D RIVING BACK FROM a round of golf on June 13, 1988, I heard on the car radio that Larry Brown had left the University of Kansas to coach the San Antonio Spurs. I got back to the basketball office at about 4 o'clock and Coach Smith came to see me. He said that the athletic director at Kansas, Bob Frederick, had called him and asked if he would be interested in coming back to his alma mater to coach the Jayhawks. Coach Smith told him, "No, they've just named a building after me here and I'm going to stay, but I've got a guy on my staff that you should think about. He's going to be one of the next great coaches."

Coach Smith told me, "Just hang tight. I think you'll have a shot at the end."

I thought Coach had been drinking or something. Everybody knew that Kansas had just won the national championship in April with Danny Manning and the Miracles, and so they would want a big-name coach to replace Larry Brown. I wasn't even a household name in my own house. Kansas is one of the premier programs in the entire country, so I thought there was no way that I'd be the next coach there.

A couple of weeks went by and about every third day Coach Smith told me that he'd heard that Kansas had talked to another coach but that I'd still have a chance. He told me that Dick Harp, a beloved former coach and player at Kansas who was working on our staff at that time, was campaigning hard for me. Then one day Coach Smith came to my office and said, "What are your plans for July 4?"

I said, "Wanda and I are going to Asheville and then the next day we're going on vacation to Bermuda for four days. It's been four years since she and I have had a vacation without the kids or the team."

Ten minutes later, he came back into my office and said, "On your way to Bermuda can you meet with Bob Frederick at the Atlanta airport?"

So Wanda and I flew to Atlanta and I met Bob in the Delta Crown Room and we talked for an hour and a half while Wanda sat about 20 feet away reading a book. Bob interviewed me, but I didn't get the feeling he was recruiting me as much as he was evaluating me. He had a very distinguished, stately, genuine presence about him that made me feel like I could trust him completely. I also liked how much he revered the tradition of Kansas basketball.

We flew to Bermuda and I couldn't sleep. Our second day there, Coach Smith called and said that Kansas wanted me to come back as soon as possible and meet with their search committee.

"Coach," I said, "we've only been here two days. Are you trying to get me divorced?"

"There are not many chances to get the job at Kansas," he said.

Wanda and I went to dinner. "You're here physically," she said, "but you're not really here, so we might as well go."

So Wanda and I packed up and we left and I was torn to pieces about whether this was really the right thing for me to do. The thought of leaving UNC reminded me of leaving Roberson High for college, going from a place where I was totally comfortable to the great unknown. We landed in Atlanta; Wanda flew back to Chapel Hill and I went to Kansas. I arrived there at about 8:30 p.m., where I was met by the assistant athletic director and the sports information director. I was starving, so we stopped at a Hardee's on the turnpike so I could get a hamburger. When we got to Lawrence, they took me into a conference room in Allen Fieldhouse to meet with the committee. It was 10 p.m. by then, and I was thinking about what Coach Smith had told me when he had called me in Bermuda. He'd said, "You're Bob Frederick's choice and the chancellor agrees. So if you do all right with the committee I think you're going to be the new coach at Kansas."

I was telling the committee members what I would do as a head coach and they were asking me a few follow-up questions. But all I could think about was Magnum, P.I., and how he would always talk about that little voice in his head. I had this little voice in the back of my head, too.

Finally, I said, "Guys, let's stop just a second. I'm having a real struggle here. Everything you're saying about the University of Kansas is great. Coach Smith says it's great. I'm not trying to upset you, but I've got this little ol' voice in the back of my head saying, 'Son, why don't you thank these people and apologize for wasting their time and get your rear end back to Chapel Hill?' That's what I'm fighting right now, my love for North Carolina and the thought of leaving there. Chapel Hill has been a dream place for me. It's nothing bad against Kansas, it's just that I love coaching at the University of North Carolina."

By the time I'd finished, I was choking up. One of the people at the meeting was Galen Fiss, who was Coach Smith's college roommate at Kansas and an 11-year All-Pro linebacker for the Cleveland Browns, a no-facemask kind of guy. He had tears in his eyes and suddenly he stood up. He said, "I'd like to address what you just said. Roy, I want you to know that what you said doesn't make me think any less of you. It makes me think more of you. That's the reason I want you to be our coach, because you love the University of North Carolina. I love the University of Kansas. Nobody could love Kansas any more than I do, and I believe that you could love it like that, too. I want somebody here who's going to love this university the way I love this university. I want somebody here who'll love my school like you love your school. Kansas is no different from North Carolina. You have people there you love, and you will have people here you'll love. That's all I've got to say."

When he sat back down there were big tears rolling down his face. I got cold chills. You could have heard a pin drop.

Then Bob Frederick said, "Roy, I've got to ask you. If we offer you the job, will you accept it?"

I took a deep breath and paused for a few seconds until my mind was completely clear. Then I said, "Yes."

It was about midnight when I called Wanda and said, "They offered me the job and I took it."

Wanda said, "Great."

I told her there were three tickets for her and Scott and Kimmie to fly out for the press conference the next day. Then I called my old friend Jerry Green, who was the coach at UNC–Asheville, and asked him to be my assistant. A few days earlier Jerry and I had sat on the front porch at my mother's house and I'd said, "What do you think about the University of Kansas?"

He said, "What am I supposed to think?"

"Jerry, I think they might offer me their coaching job. Would you want to go with me?"

"Hot damn, that is big-time ballcoachin'. Damn right I'm with you."

Then I went in and told my mom about it and she said, "Why are you thinking about leaving North Carolina? Don't you love your job?"

I said, "Well, Mom, there's one difference. Kansas is going to let me be the *head* coach."

"Don't you love your job?" she said.

It didn't make any difference to her whether I was a head coach or not. She was going to miss me.

I WENT BACK to the hotel that first night and lay down on the bed, and I had a scary realization. I said to myself, "My gosh, I just took a job and I have no idea what this place even looks like. I have no idea if it's beautiful like Chapel Hill or if it's desolate or what it is."

I didn't sleep a lot and the next morning I got up early. I called Wanda and I asked her, "What did the kids say?"

It was one of those neat moments in a father's life because she said that Scott, who was then 11 years old, had come into the kitchen as soon as he woke up and said, "Mom, what happened?"

She told him, "Your dad is the new head basketball coach at the University of Kansas."

He pumped his fist and said, "*All right!*"

When she told me what he'd said, before I knew it, I had big tears in my eyes.

As soon as I hung up the phone, I realized my stomach felt just awful. I went into the bathroom and threw up. Then Bob Frederick picked me up and we went to see the Kansas chancellor, Gene Budig. Then Bob took me down to his office and I stepped into the restroom and threw up again. After that, Bob took me to see a booster, and when I came back from that meeting, I threw up again. Then I did the press conference and I went back to the hotel and I threw up again. Then I did an interview with the local media and went back to my room and threw up. When Wanda arrived she said, "Do we need to take you to the hospital?"

During the day Bob Frederick had taken me to a doctor's office and the doctor said, "Well, you do have a little bit of an ear infection and that's probably what's causing it."

I said, "Could stress have something to do with it, too?"

That was my first day as the head basketball coach at Kansas.

DURING ONE OF MY conversations with Coach Smith about the Kansas job, I'd said, "Coach, this is your alma mater. Larry Brown was their coach and they just won a national championship. Are you sure you want me to do this? Are you sure I can do this?"

I'll remember his response until the day I die. Coach Smith got very stern with me and he said, "Let me tell you something. You can be just as good a coach as Larry Brown. Don't you forget that. You just do what you think is right and it'll work out."

It was almost as if I'd insulted him. By this point in my life, I'd gone from being a student who worshipped Coach Smith to a high school coach who called him "the Godfather" to a member of his coaching staff who was still totally in awe of him. He was my teacher and I thought of him as the best coach there's ever been. I believed everything he said as the gospel truth. So once I took the Kansas job, I kept hearing Coach Smith's words in my head and I wasn't scared.

I just thought I could make it work. I didn't exactly know how, but I just thought it would work out.

The first few days and weeks I felt like I was caught in a whirlwind. And that whole first year I don't think my heart rate dropped below 100.

I hired Kevin Stallings from Purdue as an assistant coach, and then Jerry Green said, "You know, I met a guy on an airplane and I think you would like to talk to him."

It was Steve Robinson, who was an assistant coach at Cornell. We arranged a meeting and talked for two hours. I went home and told Wanda, "I think I'm going to hire that guy."

She said, "Do you have any other information about him?"

"Nope, it's just a gut feeling."

Then Mark Turgeon, who was a graduate assistant under Larry Brown, wanted to talk to me about staying and joining my staff. He said, "I heard you talk about your love for North Carolina at the press conference, and you told that story about Galen Fiss and his love for the University of Kansas. That's the way I feel about Kansas."

I hired Mark on the spot because he had some local knowledge and also because I just loved the way he looked me in the eye and said, "The way you feel about North Carolina is exactly the way I feel about this place."

In September, two top recruits, Thomas Hill and Harold Miner, told me they were coming to Kansas, and we felt good about getting another prospect, Adonis Jordan. Then all hell broke loose.

On Halloween night, I was taking my kids trick-or-treating. We were walking around in the neighborhood where Bob Frederick lived and we saw his wife, Margey, and their kids. She said, "I'm glad I ran into you. Bob is trying to find you."

I called Bob at his office and he told me that the NCAA had released its findings from a recent investigation it had done on the Kansas program. I went straight to Bob's office and he told me the NCAA had put the program on probation for three years for recruiting violations involving the previous coaching staff. The outlook was bleak: we couldn't participate in the NCAA Tournament that year, we would lose three scholarships, and we weren't allowed to have any prospects on campus for a visit for a full year. I was crushed because the NCAA had led Bob to believe that nothing like that was going to occur. I had so much resentment toward the NCAA because nobody on my staff and none of my players had anything to do with the violations, so I thought they were punishing the wrong people.

Bob was just so apologetic. "Hey, we knew it could happen," I said. "We just didn't expect it to happen."

I called all of my assistants into the basketball office and apologized to them. I said, "This is a shock to me. I'm not sure where we go from here."

I told them I would understand if any of them wanted to leave for another job. Everybody was stunned. Then Jerry Green broke the silence in his own unique way. "Wow," he said. "This shit is getting serious." Everyone just busted out laughing. Everybody agreed that they were staying with me and that we'd keep pushing forward as best we could.

The day after the probation hit, Harold Miner called in tears to tell me he wasn't coming to Kansas because he thought the probation would hurt his clean-cut image.

Two days later, there was an article about me replacing Larry Brown in the *Dallas Morning News* that quoted a Kansas booster who a year earlier had been the president of the Jayhawk Club. He said, "Needless to say, we would have rather gotten a Gary Williams or a John Chaney or some of the other names we have heard about. All of us would like to have seen one with more of a proven track record. We didn't get one, and we will have to wait and see how it all turns out. I think it is causing some anxious moments among some of our people."

In that same article, a former Kansas athletic director compared my hiring to that of Gerry Faust, a high school coach hired to lead Notre Dame's football program in 1981, who was unceremoniously run out of town after five mediocre seasons. Joe Rushing, who was Thomas Hill's coach, called me after reading the article and said he'd told Thomas that he didn't know if I was going to have enough support to get the job done and that Thomas was considering other schools.

By that time Bob Frederick had told me that the night before I was hired, Margey had said, "Please tell me you are not going to hire that no-name assistant from North Carolina. The boosters will eat you alive." And later that same night, three of the university's largest financial contributors had gone to the chancellor's house to ask him not to let Bob hire me.

So I arranged a meeting with seven prominent boosters. We were going to meet for breakfast. Jerry Green said he wanted to go with me, but I wouldn't let him because I knew if he'd gone with me there would have been a fight. I went alone. "Guys," I said, "you're either with me or against me. I need you to be with me, but if you're not with me, don't hurt me. If you need me to prove myself I have no problem with that, but don't hurt me until you've given me a chance to get it done."

It was that kind of atmosphere. There was some doubt from the people who supported me and there was total frustration from the people who didn't. There wasn't anybody I could turn to except for my family and Bob Frederick and my staff, the people immediately around me.

The day after the newspaper article was published, Thomas Hill called to tell me he was going to Duke. We were still chasing Adonis Jordan, but four other prospects contacted us to cancel recruiting visits. It was the only time at Kansas that I really wondered, "My gosh, what did I get myself into?"

I SURVIVED MY first season at Kansas because of the players on my first team. They gave me a chance. They didn't care that I was a no-name without any head coaching experience. Those kids, Milt Newton, Kevin Pritchard, Mark Randall—all of them gave me a chance.

I had a lot of compassion for them and their disappointment over the probation. After winning the national title the year before, the remainder of that team wanted to go to the NCAA Tournament to prove that they could do some things, too. But they weren't going to get a chance.

From the first day of practice, my players tried to do what I asked them to do and believed that it was going to work. We had great kids with a ton of work ethic, but we didn't have many quality big guys or much depth. We opened up the season at the Great Alaska Shootout and we beat Alaska–Anchorage and California, and then we played Seton Hall in the final and we lost. That was the year Seton Hall ended up playing Michigan for the national championship. About two weeks later, we played Temple in Atlantic City on national television. Temple was ranked in the Top 5 and we played great and beat them. We got on a roll and pushed our record to 16–3. Then the bottom fell out.

Most people don't remember it, even a lot of Kansas fans don't, but

I do, because I lived through it. We lost eight games in a row. We only had 11 eligible players and then a few of those guys got hurt. And so all of a sudden we just had eight guys playing. We lost at Duke, and we lost at Oklahoma when they were No. 1 in the country, and then we lost at home to Kansas State. Then we played Oklahoma at home and we had some foul trouble in the first half. At halftime we got a junior varsity player, Brad Kampschroeder, to put on a uniform, just in case. Sure enough, we had three players foul out. I had our other five healthy guys out on the court and one of them picked up his fourth foul. I looked down the bench, and Brad Kampschroeder saw me looking at him. You have two responses from players, either that eager look of "Yeah, coach, I'm ready" or the one 180 degrees away from that. That poor kid sort of dove back into the bleachers where I couldn't see him. I just started laughing so hard. We lost to Oklahoma in overtime, and when we left the court, the crowd at Allen Fieldhouse gave us a standing ovation.

One Friday night during the losing streak, I took the team to a room downstairs in Allen Fieldhouse, and I made popcorn and put on the movie *Hoosiers*. We lost our next game. The next week I made popcorn again and put on *Rocky III*, and we still lost. A few days later, Jerry Green showed up at my house, walked into the kitchen, pulled open the silverware drawer, and started loading up all the knives into a bag he had with him. Wanda said, "What are you doing?"

He said, "It was not a good practice today. I'm getting all of the sharp objects away from the boy."

Wanda cracked up. I cracked up.

I was trying everything I could possibly think of. We had one kid, Milt Newton, who had been the second-leading scorer in the national championship game the year before, and he just couldn't make a shot. He was our best shooter, but he had lost all of his confidence, so I got the sports psychologist at Kansas to work with him. We played Oklahoma State, and Milt made four of his first five jump shots, and I thought, "All right, now Milt's going to be fine." Then he missed 16 in a row, finished 4-for-21 and we lost again. So we dropped from 16–3 to 16–11 before we finally broke the streak. We beat Colorado. We beat Nebraska. Then we were playing Oklahoma State at their place on Senior Day, and they hadn't lost at home all year. I did one of those dumb things that I've done several times as a coach. I told our kids, "We're going to win this game. We're going to go down there, and we're going to play well, and we're going to win the game."

So we had the ball out of bounds with 30 seconds to play, and we were down two. I called timeout and said, "Guys, this is what we're going to do, and everybody has got to believe that this is exactly what is going to happen. We're going to go for three, and we're going to knock in the three, and we're going to win this game right now. And then we're going to get the crap out of town as fast as we can."

Sure enough, Milt Newton knocked down a three with eight seconds to play, and we won—and then we literally sprinted off the court to celebrate.

Then there was some scuttlebutt about whether or not we should be allowed to play in the Big 8 Tournament because of the probation. The other coaches were concerned that if Kansas won the tournament, we could take an NCAA Tournament bid away from one of our conference teams, so they weren't exactly standing up for us. We played Kansas State in the first round. I thought we got a couple of bad calls from the officials at the end and we lost. At the press conference, I questioned some of those calls and then I said, "At least we won't have to listen to all the coaches saying we shouldn't be here." Those comments were not met with universal approval.

But the dumbest thing I did that first season was that I never signed my contract. I had asked Bob Frederick to make some adjustments to it because of the probation, and that process dragged on throughout the season. Looking back on it, if Kansas had wanted to fire me after we lost eight games in a row, I had no ground to stand on. I just had so much faith in Bob Frederick—and rightly so—but I wouldn't advise that for any young coach, that's for sure.

AFTER WE LOST Thomas Hill and Harold Miner, our first recruiting class looked pretty slim. I was still pursuing Adonis Jordan, but I didn't really know how good our chances were. I called Adonis and I said, "Sometimes you just have to have faith in somebody and that's what I'm asking you to do. Have faith in me."

When Adonis called back later that day and said he was coming, I walked to the back of our offices at Allen Fieldhouse. My assistants were there, and I motioned for all of them to come in. I wrote up on a blackboard: *Adonis is coming! Hooray! Hooray!* It was like a celebration for us, because after the probation we didn't know if we were going to get anybody.

The only other player we signed was a kid from Finland named Pekka Markkanen. Pekka's coach had sent me a videotape to watch, but it was shot at an unusual speed and we couldn't slow it down, so everybody just kept zipping up and down the court in fast-forward. I had to go by the word of a coach I didn't know, but I wasn't in a position to be too picky.

Before that second season started, I was walking through the gym while the guys were out on the court playing, and Kevin Pritchard yelled at me, "Coach, did you see what *Inside Sports* did? They picked us eighth in the league. There are only eight teams. They picked us last."

"Son, don't worry about it," I said. "We're going to be better than that."

"That ticks me off so much," he said. "I told all the guys that we're working twice as hard now."

One of the key players on that team was our junior center, Mark Randall. Larry Brown's coaching staff had almost run Mark off because he'd been hurt a lot, and even when he was healthy, he hadn't produced. They also had other choices. They just didn't have much confidence in him and he lost confidence in himself because nothing good had happened for him, but I knew how badly we needed him. We didn't have other choices. The year before I had told our coaches, "Mark's the only legitimate big guy we've got, so when we see him walking across campus, let's say, 'Gosh, Mark, you look good.' And if he walks out here on the court and doesn't trip, let's say, 'Gosh, you look better than Wilt Chamberlain.' We've got to give the kid some confidence." Randall averaged 16 points a game our first year, and the second year he was sensational.

We opened that season against Alabama–Birmingham in the Pre-season NIT at our place. Kevin Pritchard scored 22 points and we beat them by 26. At 6:30 the next morning I got a call from our assistant athletic director, who said, "At first, it looked like we were going to play the next round at DePaul, but they changed their minds. Now we're going to play at LSU."

I said, "What's going on?"

"Well, UNLV is No. 1 and LSU is No. 2, and they want to make sure they both get to the semifinals in New York City. They'd also like to see DePaul and St. John's get there, so they're sacrificing us."

So we flew down to play LSU and they had Shaquille O'Neal and Stanley Roberts, who was just as big as Shaq, and a great guard, Chris Jackson, who ended up changing his name to Mahmoud Abdul-Rauf when he played in the NBA. I added it up later and their starting lineup's first-year pro contracts combined to be $16 million. We had one pro who made $180,000. But I still thought we had a great chance to win. We got to the gym, and Dick Vitale showed up to watch us practice. Dick said, "Well, they're really giving you a tough road because they want LSU and UNLV in New York."

I said, "Dick, we're going to spoil the party."

"What are you talking about?"

"We're going to beat 'em." Then I called my team over to where Dick and I were talking. I said, "I just told Mr. Vitale here that we're going to spoil the party, we're going to win this frickin' game. They want LSU in Madison Square Garden, and we're not going to let that happen."

I let the team go back to finishing shootaround, and Dick said, "Now I know you're just a second-year coach. Do you really feel good about saying that?"

"Yeah. Dick, we're going to beat 'em."

So then we walked off the court, and Jerry Green said to me, "You're damn crazy."

We went back to the hotel and that night at snack I said to the team, "Guys, I want you to go to bed and think about who you're going to hug first at the end of this game, because we're going to win this frickin' game. We're going to move, we're going to pass, we're going to make Shaquille O'Neal and Stanley Roberts spin around so much they'll wear a hole in the floor." The players left and Jerry Green said, "You're damn crazy."

The next night we were spreading the floor and moving and cutting and slashing around so quickly that their big guys couldn't keep up with us; we played great and won the game. Everybody was running around hugging afterward. It was one of those really satisfying moments. The next day while we were at the hotel packing up the bus for the airport, this guy came over to me and said, "Coach, that was some kind of job last night."

"Well, thank you," I said. "Our guys really played well."

"The way you moved the ball, and the way your big guys posted up, I wish I could get my son to play like that."

"Well, thanks again. We were really good. How old is your son?"

"I'm Shaq's daddy."

BEATING No. 2 LSU earned us a trip to New York City to face No. 1 University of Nevada–Las Vegas. I went to Tavern on the Green for a press conference and they introduced me as *Ron* Williams. I stood up and said, "Folks, that doesn't bother me, because we are going to play our butts off and by the end of this tournament, you're going to know my first name."

UNLV had stars like Larry Johnson and Stacey Augmon and Greg Anthony and Anderson Hunt, all of whom would go on to play in the NBA. But I thought we could neutralize their pressure defense with backdoor cuts. We played almost a Princeton-style offense and they never figured us out. At one point in the second half we were up by 20 points and we ended up winning by 15. Their coach, Jerry Tarkanian, said afterward that he'd never had one of his teams handled like that.

In the next game we played St. John's in the tournament final and nobody on our team could guard their star player, "Boo" Harvey. I remembered Coach Smith once telling me about New York Knicks coach Red Holzman's theory that sometimes creating an obvious mismatch disrupts the flow of the other team. St. John's had another good player named Malik Sealy, and so there was a timeout and I said, "Terry Brown, you guard Malik." Terry was a shooter who couldn't guard his lunch.

Terry looked at me and he said, "Malik?"

"Yeah, you guard Malik."

Sure enough, St. John's came down the court and Malik started yelling at everybody that he had a mismatch and he was posting Terry Brown up, and their coach, Louie Carnesecca, started screaming to throw the ball in to Malik. Malik got the ball and shot a turnaround jump shot over Terry and missed. We got the rebound and came down and scored. On their next possession, Malik was posting Terry up again, and they threw it in there and some way, somehow, Terry got around him and deflected the ball, and we stole it and ran down and scored again. They came down a third time, and again they were trying to set up Malik in the post. They threw it in to him, and he turned around and dribbled it off Terry's foot, and we picked it up and raced down and scored again. Louie called a timeout, and they stopped posting up Malik, but by that time, Boo Harvey was either out of sync or mad and he missed his next two or three shots, and we won the game.

We went from unranked to No. 4 in the country. We won our first 19 games and wound up spending 14 weeks that season ranked at No. 1 or No. 2.

We beat Robert Morris in the first round of the NCAA Tournament and then we played UCLA. We had the last shot to win the game, but we missed it. I'll never forget that when we pulled into the parking lot at the arena before the UCLA game, Kevin Pritchard's dad was waiting for the bus. He told Kevin, "Son, you've got to play your rear end off today because there are 14 NBA scouts here." He wasn't as interested in our team winning as he was in how his son was being looked at by the pros. Kevin had never missed a big-time one-and-one in his career, and he missed one at the end of that game that would've given us a three-point lead. He'd never committed more than three turnovers in a game, but he had seven turnovers that game. I think that his dad and the stress just got to him.

We finished the year 30–5. We averaged more points than any other team I have ever coached and finished second in the conference regular season standings. Not bad for a team picked to finish last in our league.

WE STARTED THE 1990–91 season with two losses in the conference, but we bounced back to win our first regular season conference championship. Then we lost to Nebraska in the semifinals of the Big 8 Tournament. After that game I thought my team needed a pep talk. I said, "Guys, we still have the NCAAs, we can still accomplish a lot—"

Mark Randall interrupted me. "Coach, can I say something?"

I nodded and Mark stood up and said, "We're too good to do what we just did today. If everybody in this room would do what this man says and everybody in this room would pull together, we can make a run and we can win the whole thing." Mark wasn't emotional at all. He said it very matter-of-factly.

We beat New Orleans in the first round of the NCAA Tournament and beat Pittsburgh in the second round. Then we went to Charlotte to play Indiana and they were ranked No. 3 in the country. Two time-outs into the game, we were ahead 26–6, and the referees stopped the game because a bolt had come loose on the court and it was sticking up about a quarter inch. One of the referees, John Clougherty, called me and Bobby Knight out there, and John said, "I think we should wait a second until we get a maintenance guy to see if we can get this bolt hammered down."

Bobby Knight said, "If we're going to do that, can we start the damn game over?"

We dominated the game inside, including 15 offensive rebounds in the first half, and we won 83–65. Then we played Arkansas, which was ranked No. 2 in the country. Kevin Stallings prepared the scouting report for that game, and at our staff meeting, I said, "All right, give me a quick thought about Arkansas that I can share with the team."

Kevin said, "We have no chance. Their top seven guys are better at every position than we are. We have no chance."

"Kevin, don't say that. We can win the game."

"Coach, we have no chance."

"All right. I'm going to tell the team we're going to win the frickin' game."

"Coach, you know, that's worked in the past, but that ain't working this time."

"You just keep that to yourself."

And so we went into the team meeting that night, and I said. "Guys, we're in a great situation. We've already beaten the No. 3 team in the country, and now we're playing the No. 2 team, and we're going to win the game."

The players left and Kevin Stallings said, "You're crazy. We have no chance."

We played two days later, and with five minutes to go in the first half, the score was tied. Then Arkansas scored the next 13 points and we wound up trailing by 12 at the half. At halftime I was talking to the staff outside our locker room, and I told Kevin, "You don't say a word, because we're still going to win this frickin' game."

I told the players, "This is what's going to happen. It's our ball to start the half. Let's get a great shot and knock it in and then we need one stop. Then let's get another great shot and get another stop. I'm only asking for two stops. Then let's come down and let's make sure we get a good look again and let's knock that in, and by then the lead falls from 12 to six and they'll probably call a timeout and then we'll see them bickering at each other."

We came out, moved the ball around and Terry Brown got a layup. Then we went down and got a stop. We came back down and Terry hit another layup. We went down and got that second stop, and then we came down and Mark Randall got fouled and made one of two free throws. We got a third stop and Alonzo Jamison hit a three-pointer to cut the lead down to four. Their coach, Nolan Richardson, called a timeout. As they were walking off the court, two of their guys, Ron Huery and Oliver Miller, were yapping at each other, and I grabbed one of our players and said, "See?"

We outscored Arkansas by 24 in the second half. It was a great win and we were going to the Final Four. The neatest part of the game came afterward. My son, Scott, sneaked down on the court, came running up to me, and said, "Dad, you've got to let me go to the Final Four."

I said, "The whole family will go to the Final Four."

At the Final Four, we were playing North Carolina. Coach Smith and I spoke on the phone during the week a few times, and we decided that we didn't want to talk to the media about ourselves and our history together, but it was difficult because that's all anybody wanted to talk about.

At that point, in my mind I was still Coach Smith's assistant, but I was also the head coach at Kansas. I never called him by his first name; it was always "Coach Smith." There was still a sense of awe and I felt somewhat intimidated coaching against him. Meanwhile, Coach Smith saw me as an equal, a peer.

Preparing for the game was odd because Coach Smith and I had talked on the phone about once a week beginning the first day of practice that season about our teams' strengths and weaknesses, so we weren't going to surprise each other. Otherwise, I tried to treat North Carolina like any other opponent, except that I told our guys we couldn't call our plays verbally because we used the same terminology that they did.

Once the game started it felt exactly like every other game I've coached. North Carolina jumped out to a 24–15 lead, but our defense sparked a 17–1 run toward the end of the first half. We moved the ball well and we beat their pressure defenses. Mark Randall and Adonis Jordan each scored 16 points and Richard Scott had 14 off the bench. Our defense held one of UNC's primary scorers, Rick Fox, to just 5-of-22 shooting. We were in control the whole second half and we won 79–73, but our victory was overshadowed because Coach Smith was ejected at the end of the game. He had gotten a ridiculous technical foul for leaving the coach's box while there was a timeout for a substitution and then another in the final minute when the game was already decided. As he left the court, Coach Smith shook hands with me and all of my players. I felt bad for him because he didn't deserve that, but I also felt bad for our guys because Coach Smith's situation took the spotlight off of a great win for us.

I went back out to the court and watched Duke play UNLV in the other semifinal, and I was so mad at the Kansas fans because they were pulling for Duke to win. It was nothing against Duke; it was just that I felt we'd have a better chance to beat UNLV because we'd beaten them the year before, and I could tell my team, "Nobody thinks we can beat them again, but we know we can."

Duke upset UNLV and we struggled against the Blue Devils in the final. Alonzo Jamison, who had been the MVP of our regional and shot 60 percent from the floor for us the whole year, was 1-for-10 and Bobby Hurley made a terrible pass that Grant Hill turned into one of the greatest lob dunks in college history and we lost, 72–65.

My mother was at the game, and someone in the media came up to her afterward and asked, "How do you feel? Are you still proud of your son?"

She said, "I've always been proud of him, but this is one of the happiest moments of my life."

IN 1992 WE MADE a tremendous run through the regular season led by Adonis Jordan and a transfer from Northwestern named Rex Walters in our backcourt. We were a No. 1 seed in the NCAA Tournament, but we got upset in the second round by Don Haskins and Texas–El Paso. They were quicker than we were, so Haskins had decided to use a version of the "Four Corners" offense, which he hadn't used all season, to control the tempo of the game, and they beat us 66–60. I remember making some statements to the press after the game about how I was sad for our team, but I was happy for Coach Haskins, who was a coaching pioneer. He'd helped integrate the sport when he started five African-American players and beat Kentucky in the 1966 NCAA title game. I left the press conference, and this lady stopped me in the hallway and said, "Coach, hold on one second."

"Yes, ma'am."

"I just want you to know that I've never seen a young coach hold his poise and his composure and be able to handle the press like that at such a tough time. But I also want you to know I truly appreciate what you said about Coach Haskins."

Then she held out her hand and said, "That's my husband."

"Ma'am, I said that because I meant it. This is a hard time for us, but I'm really happy for you guys."

The next year we beat Jason Kidd's California team in the round of 16 and then we were playing Indiana in the round of eight to go to the Final Four again. What I remember most about that game is when they introduced the head coaches and I left our huddle to shake Bobby Knight's hand. Bobby wasn't there, so I walked all the way down to Indiana's bench. Bobby was huddled up with his team. One of their coaches told him I was there and Bobby turned around and said, "Oh, Roy, I'm sorry."

I said, "Coach, I have such respect for you that it doesn't bother me to walk all the way down to your bench."

He thanked me and patted me on the head and I turned around and walked back to my bench, and when I got there I turned around and Bobby had followed me all the way down to our bench. He said, "I just wanted you to know that I have enough respect for you to walk all the way down to your bench, too."

That was a cool deal. Then we played great and won the game to go to the Final Four again, in New Orleans.

In the semifinals we met up with North Carolina again. Donald Williams was sensational for them from the perimeter with 25 points and Eric Montross was more than we could handle inside with his 23 points. Rex Walters and Adonis Jordan each scored 19 points for us to keep it close, but UNC's defense caused us to take a lot of poor shots and they beat us 78–68. When the game ended I remember seeing Coach Smith clap his hands with satisfaction, and then he suddenly realized, "Oh my gosh, we beat Roy." I saw an instant 180-degree turn in his emotions from exhilaration to compassion. I saw pain in his face. I saw hurt. When we shook hands it was hard to speak because of the strong emotions we were both feeling.

I sent my team home, but Wanda and I decided to stay in New

Orleans to watch North Carolina play Michigan in the final. I became a fan. North Carolina was my favorite team other than the one I coached, and so I was in the stands waving a Carolina Blue pom-pom as the Tar Heels won the national championship.

After the game I told Wanda I wanted to go see Coach Smith. I knew the hotel where North Carolina was staying, so I walked over there and called one of their team managers, who told me which room Coach Smith was in. When he answered the phone, I said, "Coach, I was just coming to say congratulations."

He said, "Well, come on up."

I went up to Coach Smith's room and we watched the first half of the championship game on tape. I could tell he was proud of what his team had done, but we watched the tape like two coaches breaking down a game film. That was a thrill for me, but then I got out of there to let him enjoy the second half by himself.

BEFORE WE PLAYED California in the third round of the 1993 tournament, our coaching staff had watched tape of their team. I said, "Jason Kidd is special, but that other guard is pretty doggone good, too. I love his competitiveness. Who is that?"

Kevin Stallings said, "Well, that's the other freshman guard. That's Jerod Haase."

After we beat Cal the next day, I noticed that one of their players was in our locker room talking to Rex and Adonis, and I wondered what was going on. Then, right after the Final Four, we got a call from a guy who was a friend of Jerod Haase's. He wanted to know if we'd be interested in Jerod transferring to Kansas. We said we'd love to have him.

For the 1997 season we had one of the best teams I have ever seen. Our starting lineup included four guys who ended up being first-round draft choices in the NBA. We started Jerod and Jacque Vaughn in the backcourt, Paul Pierce at small forward, and Scot Pollard and Raef LaFrentz as our post players.

Before the start of the season, *Sports Illustrated* picked us No. 1. Everybody thought we were the big-time favorites to win the national championship. We won our first 22 games and nobody came close to us. Then we lost a game at Missouri when we had a one-point lead. Jacque knocked the ball away from one of their guys in the lane, and it bounced through his legs and into the hands of another Missouri player, who made the game-winning shot. We didn't lose another game in the regular season or the conference tournament and we spent the final 15 weeks of the season ranked No. 1 in the country.

But in the first game of that season against Santa Clara, Jerod had fallen on his shooting wrist, and it started bothering him more and more as the season went along. In the first two rounds of the NCAA Tournament, his wrist was so painful that he basically couldn't play. The doctors decided to give him a cortisone shot and he suffered an allergic reaction. At dinner the night before the third-round game, Jerod's wrist felt awful. We went to the shootaround the next day and he was in pain. At the end of the shootaround, I said, "Shoot a free throw for me."

His shot fell four feet short. I said, "Big fella, I don't know."

He looked back at me, and I'll never forget it. He said, "Coach, I would just like to try. My whole life I've been dreaming about this kind of team and this kind of moment."

"All right, we'll wait and see what it's like in warm-ups."

I was not feeling very good about it, to say the least, but as we went out to warm up, I said to Jerod, "All right, let me see you shoot a free throw."

This time he made it, but he doubled over in pain. Then he said again, "Coach, I would just like to try."

What could I say? I was almost crying. I had to let him play.

We were playing against a great Arizona team that had Mike Bibby, Jason Terry, Miles Simon, and Mike Dickerson. They had the most speed of any team I'd ever coached against. The first play of the game, Mike Bibby passed the ball over to the right wing, and Jerod knocked it away and went down for a layup. After he scored, he grabbed his wrist and grimaced in pain. He could barely dribble the ball. He couldn't shoot. He couldn't play, but I played him for 14 minutes anyway. When I finally took him out for good, everybody on our bench was so sad, because Jerod was a great teammate.

Without Jerod, we didn't play with the same confidence that we'd had all season and we couldn't match up against the quickness of the Arizona backcourt. We committed 20 turnovers and Bibby scored 21 points. We still had three shots in the final seconds to tie the game, but we lost 85–82. We finished that season 34–2.

We might have won that game if I had benched Jerod and prepared the team to play without him. But if someone had told me beforehand, "Roy, if you let Jerod Haase try to play, you're going to lose the game," I'd still do it the same way. I would still have played Jerod because he is the only kid I've ever coached who I thought cared as much about winning as I did. I was not going to deny that kid the chance to try.

That game was the most crushing loss I'd ever experienced as a head coach. It's hard to explain the sorrow that I felt for those kids. It was complete dejection. Until the day I die, I'll be trying to figure out how I couldn't get that bunch to the Final Four, and to this day I still apologize to them. If I coach for 50 more years, it will still be one of the biggest disappointments, if not *the* biggest disappointment, that I've ever had.

BEFORE THAT 1997 SEASON, I used a word that I probably shouldn't have used. I would say that I "desperately" wanted to win the national championship. We had the best team. We lost just two games, but we didn't win a national championship. We didn't even get to the Final Four. And it just crushed me. After that, I decided that I wasn't going to use the word *desperately* anymore.

I decided that my dream was to live long enough to someday coach my grandchildren in Little League baseball and basketball. That took the idea of winning a national championship and put it in the right perspective. It was still the most important thing in my professional career, but it wasn't everything. It wasn't going to dominate my life anymore.

In 1998 we had lost Jacque, Jerod, and Scot, but we still had Raef and Paul, so we knew we still were going to be pretty good. At the end of the season, we had won the conference again and then we won the conference tournament to climb to No. 2 in the country.

In the second round of the NCAA Tournament we faced Rhode Island, which had two very quick guards, Tyson Wheeler and Cuttino Mobley, and defense in the backcourt was not our strength. Mobley scored 27 points and Wheeler had 20 points, including five three-pointers, and they were the first opponent to shoot better than 50 percent against us in our last 26 games. They beat us 80–75.

Once again I was crushed. Wanda and the kids said all the right things to support me, but they knew that I had to get through it myself. I really felt like I'd failed my team again. Raef was a senior and Paul Pierce ended up going to the NBA after that season. That senior class had won more games in their four years than any other in Kansas history, but we hadn't even gone to a Final Four.

During that 1998 season, we were recruiting a really talented kid named JaRon Rush. He had committed to us, but there were a lot of weird things going on around him. There were articles in the news about how he was receiving gifts from a Kansas booster. Finally, I told our staff, "One more thing happens, and I'm not going to take him. I'm going to release him."

During the 100th-year celebration of Kansas basketball, we played a game against Missouri. We had a reunion and lots of our greatest players came back to visit. We played a great game and beat Missouri, and afterward JaRon was interviewed and he referred to me as "Roy" and questioned my substitution patterns.

I heard about that and I called my staff and said, "That's it, guys."

I called JaRon that night and I said, "Big fella, how you doing?"

He said, "Great."

"Well JaRon, I need to talk to you about your comments."

"I wanted to talk to you about that, too."

"No, JaRon, it's okay. We need to just stop this, because it's gotten personal now, and it's not going to work. So this is what you can do. I'm going to release you from your commitment, and you can go to UCLA or you can go to the NBA or you can go anywhere you want to go, but it's not going to be to Kansas, because I'm not going to coach you. But I enjoyed our time and good luck to you."

"But, Coach—"

"No, JaRon, let's just leave it like this. We can be friends now because anything else that is said is not going to be good."

And I hung up. I told Wanda it was the most satisfying two-minute conversation I'd ever had with a prospect.

While that was going on, we were also recruiting Korleone Young, but it was hard to get a straight answer out of him. Academically, we couldn't get Korleone to focus on what he needed to do to get into college, and then one day his Amateur Athletic Union (AAU) coach called and told me Korleone was going to the NBA. At the same time, we really thought we were going to get Quentin Richardson. Quentin and his dad both told me they thought Kansas was the best fit for him, but all of a sudden he announced he was going to DePaul. While I was spending all that time recruiting JaRon and Korleone and Quentin, I was also recruiting Tayshaun Prince, but I didn't have him rated quite as highly as the other guys, so I sort of neglected him. Tayshaun was a wonderful kid, a much more solid kid, and we probably could have gotten him, but I had put the emphasis on the other guys and we lost all three of them, and then we lost Tayshaun, too. I knew I had made some bad decisions on where to focus my energy, but the whole process just had gotten very seamy. In my mind it had become so distasteful that I wasn't sure I could continue doing it.

I went to Wanda and said, "I can't handle recruiting like this anymore. Maybe I have to go to the NBA."

TWELVE DIFFERENT NBA teams have contacted me over the years about their head coaching jobs. More than half of those came straight out and offered me the job. The others called and made me feel very strongly that they were recruiting me to come. When Michael Jordan took over the Washington Wizards he called and asked me if I'd be interested in becoming their coach. I said, "If you're going to play, I would consider it a lot more."

Three different people offered me the Boston Celtics job in 1997. I told M.L. Carr no. I told Larry Bird no. Then Red Auerbach called and I told him no. I told Red that my daughter was a senior in high school and I couldn't move her. Red said, "Well, how about if we just sign a contract and you'll be the coach next year?"

I told him I couldn't do that.

The Lakers offered me their coaching job three different times. I have always respected the Lakers because of Jerry West. In my opinion, nobody has done a better job running a franchise than he has, and when he offered me the job in 1992, that just blew me away. If I were ever going to do it, it would have to be with somebody as strong as Jerry in the front office and with an owner who would let his basketball people make the decisions. We talked salary with the Lakers the first time and I thought about it, but it didn't feel right. I told them no and they called back and asked me to reconsider. They lobbied Coach Smith, who said, "Roy's a college coach. Leave him alone!"

The Lakers continued to be attractive to me because Jerry West was eventually replaced by Mitch Kupchak, an old friend from UNC. Mitch offered me the job in 1999 and again in 2004, but my answer hadn't changed. The last time the offer came, Coach Smith wanted to get it out in the media that the Lakers had offered the job to me before they offered it to Duke's coach Mike Krzyzewski. I said, "Coach, that's not important." But it was important to him.

I'm not one of those people who think NBA coaches don't really coach. I think they coach a lot more in the pros than we do in college because of the 24-second clock, quicker possessions, 48-minute games. You know your opponents so much better in the NBA, so you've got to try different things. And I like the idea of no alumni meetings and no worrying about players' academics. You just coach. But I've always enjoyed the fact that I can mentor my college players off the floor and I don't think a pro coach could ever have that same impact.

The only time I ever had any real inclination to go to the NBA was during that tough time period in 1998 when recruiting got very difficult for me. I was vulnerable. If the Lakers job or the Celtics job had come along during that time, I might have taken it. But then my faith was suddenly restored.

WITHIN A FEW WEEKS of parting ways with JaRon Rush, I started recruiting Nick Collison from Iowa Falls High. Nick's best friend was a guy named Mike Lindeman, and Mike's sister, Joie, was Raef LaFrentz's girlfriend and a Kansas student. Sometimes when Joie came to the ballgames, she'd invite her little brother, Mike, to come down, too. Raef would give him tickets and Mike would bring Nick. One day my assistants told me that Nick was at the game, so I asked him to visit with me afterward. I said, "I'll be there to see you play before your season's over with."

Nick said, "Thank you, Coach."

I thought he was a mild-mannered, polite kid, and I really liked him. One day, later that season, I asked my assistants, Matt Doherty and Neil Dougherty, "How many more high school games does Nick have?"

Matt said, "Well, he's playing in the state final tomorrow night."

I said, "I have got to go see him play."

Neil said, "You know you can go see him play later on."

"I told the kid that I'd come and watch him play with his high school team," I said. "I'm going to watch him play Saturday. We'll practice early and I'll go watch the game, and then I'll come back for our game on Sunday."

I flew up to Iowa to see Nick play and he was sensational. He took charges, he blocked shots, he made passes, and he made lots of baskets. He was the most fundamentally sound post player I had ever recruited. He controlled the game like a point guard, calling out plays on both ends of the floor. His team won the state championship, and I headed out to the gym lobby, found a pay phone, and called Matt and Neil right away. "I just saw one of the greatest performances that I've ever seen, and you guys didn't think I needed to come now," I said.

I was dumbfounded that they'd said it would be all right to go see him later when I had told the kid I'd see him play a high school game.

On the last day of the spring recruiting period, I went to see Nick's dad, Dave, who was his high school coach, and I said, "Coach, what is the biggest negative you have about the University of Kansas?"

He said, "There's only one negative about Kansas: all those big-time players that you bring in. We just wonder if our son will get to play there."

"Well," I said, "do you know what day it is? This is the last day that college coaches can be out recruiting and I'm here at your school. I could be anywhere in America today, but I chose to be here. What that should tell you is that your son is one of those big-time players you're talking about."

Dave Collison looked at me. "I hadn't thought of it that way," he said.

That summer, Matt Doherty went to ABCD camp and he called to tell me, "Everybody's talking about this Drew Gooden kid."

I was at Nike camp watching Nick for two days, and then I changed over and went to the ABCD camp and watched Drew Gooden. Drew could run and jump and block shots, and he had an incredible knack for rebounding. The ball just seemed to find his hands. I said to myself, "That's what we want."

We started recruiting Drew. His parents were split up, but they were both very involved and wanted what was best for their son.

About a week later, Phil Jackson left the Chicago Bulls, and rumors were swirling that he was going to be replaced by Tim Floyd, the coach at Iowa State. I was in Las Vegas recruiting, and when I pulled into the parking lot, Tim Floyd pulled up beside me. He said, "I am going to take the Bulls job. Michael Jordan, as you know, is saying he's quitting. Is there any way you could convince him to let me talk to him. If you could just set it up, I'd really appreciate it."

"I'll do everything I can," I said, "but I don't think he's going to play."

I got Tim's number, and as I started walking away, he said, "Roy, let me tell you something else, too. When I go to the Bulls, Iowa State is going to lose a commitment from a kid from Sioux City who is a Kansas player if I've ever seen one."

"Is it the Hinrich kid?"

"Yeah, you would love him. Just watch him while you're out here."

I went into the gym and found Matt and we watched Kirk Hinrich play a game. As we were walking out, I said, "What do you think?"

Matt said, "Well, I was a little discouraged. He just got back from a tournament in Russia and I think he's tired."

I said, "I like him. He can dribble almost as fast as he can run. Yeah, he fumbled it around a little bit, but he has some unbelievable tools."

So we watched Kirk for the next three days and fell in love with him. All of a sudden I was recruiting Nick Collison, Drew Gooden, and Kirk Hinrich. With all three, the only people we had to deal with were their families who just loved their sons and wanted them to go to college and get a great education and have some great experiences. That was the kind of recruiting that I liked.

We ended up getting Drew first. He came to Lawrence on an official visit, and then a week later I went to his home in Oakland for a home visit. I pulled up in front of Drew's house, and neighbors started coming out of houses across the street and taking pictures, saying they were coming to the party. I was thinking I was there to make my pitch for Kansas. I got inside, and Drew's grandfather introduced me to the chef they'd hired to come cook the meal, and he said, "If we're going to have this kind of party, we wanted to really do it up right."

And I said, "Drew, come here. Have you forgotten to tell me something?"

Drew said, "Coach, I just decided I knew I wanted to come to Kansas, so why put it off? I canceled my other visits, and I just got caught up in everything, and everybody wanted to have a party, and . . . Coach, can I come to Kansas?"

I said, "All right, now that I know, let's go ahead and have a party."

As for Kirk, his dad was a high school coach and his mom was a teacher, so automatically I felt like I was ahead with them because those were people I knew I could relate to. Kirk loved our style of play. He had a sister at Kansas. And then we found out that he'd once played in a baseball tournament down in Oklahoma, and as the family was driving back to Iowa, they decided to stop in Lawrence to see Allen Fieldhouse—and so Kirk could have his picture taken in the gym. So we felt pretty confident. After his visit to us, Kirk called a couple of days later and said, "Coach, I'm coming."

Then I visited Nick at his home and I told him, "I won't offer the scholarship to anybody else until after you make your campus visit, but I'm probably going to need to know something pretty quick after that."

We thought it was going well, but Nick still visited Duke. When he got back, I said, "Is there anything I have to cover?"

Nick and his father were both on the phone, and his father said, "Well, Coach, the Duke people said that you're in line to be the next coach at North Carolina and that if Nick goes to school at Kansas, he won't finish his career with you."

And I said, "Let me tell you something. I'm going to be at Kansas longer than Nick is. I can promise you that I'll be at Kansas for his entire career." I remembered saying that and it was important to me, but I didn't think that it was that big of a deal at the time.

Nick and his family arrived for their campus visit on Friday and he had a good visit. On Sunday I said, "Nick, on Thursday I'm supposed to go to Juneau, Alaska, for Carlos Boozer's home visit. I don't want to go to Juneau, Alaska. Is there any information you can give me, because I've got this dilemma?"

We talked a little bit more, and I left the conference room where we were sitting to get some recruiting material from my office and then I came back, and Nick said, "Coach, I've got something to tell you. I'm coming to Kansas."

I just lost it and started screaming and cheering. I was overjoyed. It turns out that when I left the room, Nick's mother had looked at her son and said, "Why are you putting that man through this? You know you want to come to school here and you know we want you to come to school here, so why are you messing around like this? The guy is going to have to offer the scholarship to somebody else." So Nick listened to his mom.

Those three guys really changed everything. They reminded me that I could recruit good kids with good families. If it wasn't for those three guys, I don't know if I'd have stayed in college coaching.

They saved me.

WHEN NICK COLLISON, Kirk Hinrich, and Drew Gooden were freshmen at Kansas in 2000, we lost to Duke 69–64 in the second round of the NCAA Tournament. But what most people remember about that game is that at one point in the first half while I was screaming at one of my players, I wandered out of the coach's box, and Coach Krzyzewski yelled something about getting back in the box. He just got all over me, which ticked me off, so there was a timeout and I went marching down the sidelines toward their bench and I said, "Mike, I wasn't talking to the official. I'm talking to my player. I'm coaching my player."

He still didn't like it. He turned to the referee and said, "Do you think you can get Coach Williams to go back to his bench?"

I said, "I'll tell you what you can do . . ."

We got face-to-face there and said some more things you couldn't print in the newspaper. When I was walking back to my bench, the Kansas fans were going crazy. I found out later that there were a lot of UNC fans in the crowd, too, because the game was in Winston-Salem, North Carolina, and the Tar Heel fans loved the fact that I would go nose to nose with him.

The next year we finished 26–7 and made a great run, but we were a No. 4 seed and we lost to Illinois, a No. 1 seed, in the third round in San Antonio. Then in 2002, we brought in some good freshmen — Wayne Simien, Aaron Miles, and Keith Langford — and we had a big-time team. We went undefeated during the Big 12 regular season, the first time anybody had done that since the conference had expanded to 12 teams. We made the Final Four, and in the NCAA semifinal against Maryland, we started the game by taking several bad shots that all went in. During a timeout I told my team, "Guys, let's not live by that, because we could die by that. That's fool's gold. Let's get the shots we want." Then we took a few more bad shots and they didn't go in, and we started panicking and never really recovered. Looking back on it, I don't know if I did the right thing by questioning those shots, but I thought taking bad shots would eventually cost us the game, and it did.

Drew Gooden left after that season for the NBA, and we replaced him with a junior college transfer, Jeff Graves, and we knew we were going to be pretty doggone good again in 2003.

But at the beginning of the '03 season, Wayne Simien and Kirk Hinrich were both hurt, and we struggled out of the gate. We were ranked No. 2 in the country when we played North Carolina in the Preseason NIT, and we turned the ball over 11 times in the first half, fell behind by 21 points, and they beat us. Two days later, we played Florida and in the first half we missed all six of our three-point attempts and fell behind by 16 points. We woke up in the second half and cut Florida's lead to two, but we lost again. There was a story in the Baltimore paper later that week that began, "Which ranked team has been the biggest disappointment so far this season?" The answer was Kansas. We were 3–2. I didn't think it was any time to panic.

We started sharing the ball a little bit better, and we got on a run. We finished first in the Big 12 with a 14–2 record and we made it to Final Four again. In the NCAA semifinals we were playing Marquette with Dwyane Wade. Marquette had destroyed Kentucky in the round of eight, and Wade looked like Michael Jordan. I did not want our players to see how good he was because I was afraid it could shake their confidence, so we completely cut him out of the scouting tape. We didn't show them a single second of Dwyane Wade on tape, and when we went out there we were unbelievable. It was the greatest game I'd ever had a team play on a big stage. I try to never look at the score in the first half, so it wasn't until I walked off the floor at the half and looked up at the scoreboard that I saw we were up by 29. That impressed even me. I knew even Dwyane Wade couldn't make up that much ground. We shot 53 percent from the floor, made 15 dunks and eight three-point shots, and won by 33 points.

We played Syracuse in the NCAA final and I thought that we should win because I believed that we were the best team. I thought we should win because Nick and Kirk had come back for their senior years. I thought we should win because it was the right thing to have happen.

We went out and took some poor shots early in the game and Gerry McNamara made six three-pointers for them in the first half. We fell behind by 18 points before we started chipping away and chipping away. We shot a miserable 11-for-31 from the free-throw line in the game, but we still had the ball in the final minute down by just three. With two seconds left, we got the ball to Michael Lee. As he went up to shoot, Hakim Warrick came out of nowhere to block it, then Kirk missed a three at the buzzer, and the game was over.

When I shook hands with the Syracuse coach, Jim Boeheim, I knew he understood how I was feeling. I knew that he had been a jump shot away from the national title before and now he had one. I said, "Jimmy, I'm really happy for you."

He said, "Roy, I appreciate it. You're going to get yours one of these days, too."

That was a tough, tough night for me, but not only because we'd just lost the national championship game. I knew I was facing a big decision . . . again.

CHAPTER 8

Decision, Decision

IN APRIL 1997 Coach Smith, Coach Guthridge, Coach Fogler, and I met in Fort Myers, Florida, for a two-day golf vacation. During that trip, Coach Smith brought up the idea that he was thinking of retiring before the start of the next season. The subject of me possibly replacing him came up. "I can't tell you if I would take the job, because I don't know what I'd tell my players," I said. "Somebody tell me what I would tell my players."

Coach Smith retired in October. It was a sad day for college basketball and for me, because the man I saw as the role model for our entire sport was walking away. By that time, Coach Guthridge had decided to be his successor, but in my mind Coach Guthridge was only going to coach North Carolina for one season. He and I talked regularly during his first year, and he wavered about whether he wanted to coach UNC for a second season in 1999. He decided to come back, and then we spent another season talking periodically about whether he would coach a third. Whenever the subject of who would take his place came up, I told Coach Guthridge that I just didn't know what I would do if faced with that possibility. Those conversations drove me crazy because I was constantly enduring these heart-wrenching thoughts about having to make a choice between the two schools I dearly loved, Kansas and North Carolina. So when Coach Guthridge decided to remain at UNC for a third season in 2000, I called Coach Smith and told him that I was never going to even think about the North Carolina job again until it was actually open.

During our conversations in the spring of 2000, I got the impression that Coach Guthridge really didn't think he would coach the Tar Heels for another season. He sounded more likely to leave this time. One night during that summer, he called and told me he was pretty sure he was going to resign.

"Roy," he said, "I want you to take this job. You've got a good job, but whoever takes this job is going to get a *great* job."

I said, "Coach, I understand that."

The next day Wanda called me at my Kansas summer basketball camp. She told me to call Coach Guthridge. She had talked to him and she thought he might be wavering about the decision to quit. "You may be able to talk him out of this," she said. "You may be able to talk him into staying."

So I called Coach Guthridge. I really wanted him to continue coaching the Tar Heels so that I wouldn't have to face a decision about possibly coming back to UNC. "Coach," I said, "you don't have to do this. Just don't do it. Go ahead and coach another year."

The next day Coach Guthridge announced that he was retiring. I held a press conference in Lawrence later that day, and I explained that if the North Carolina job was offered to me, I would have to go back to Chapel Hill and talk to people before I could make any decision about coaching the Tar Heels.

"What do you have to find out?" one of the reporters asked. "You were there for 10 years."

"Yes, and I haven't been there for 12 years," I said. "I think I have the right to do that."

That night Dick Baddour, UNC's athletic director, called me at home and said, "Roy, we want you to come back and be the basketball coach at North Carolina."

"Dick," I said, "this is really going to be a hard decision. I'm going to need some time to get this clear in my mind. I won't drag this out, but give me a week to think about it."

It was a frenzy. I'd never seen anything like it before. I talked to Bob Frederick and Chancellor Robert Hemenway, who had replaced Chancellor Budig, and I asked them to give me some time to think.

Bob told me, "You write whatever contract you want and we'll sign it. You want a lifetime contract? We'll sign it."

I told him, "No, I'm satisfied with my contract."

He said, "Okay, other than that, you've got to make your decision. We're not going to put pressure on you."

The day before I left for Chapel Hill, I played 18 holes of golf with two good buddies, Randy Towner and Scot Buxton. When we were loading our clubs back in our cars in the parking lot, I said, "Boys, I think I've just played the last round of golf I'll ever play with you as the head coach at Kansas."

I did really feel that way, but I wanted something to tell me it was all right to leave. I know that sounds corny, but that's me.

I flew back to North Carolina with Wanda, and Scott drove up from Charlotte where he was working. Kimberly was a student at UNC. Coach Smith and his wife, Dick Baddour and his wife, and Wanda and I went out to dinner that night. They were recruiting me. Coach Smith said, "I want you to do what you want to do. I would love for you to be back here, but it's got to be what you want to do."

That night, I said to Wanda, "Let's go for a walk tomorrow morning before everybody else is up and see if the Davie Poplar will fall or something will give me a sign that it's all right to break my word to Nick Collison, because, honey, I told him I was going to be at Kansas for his whole career."

So the next morning we got up and walked and the Davie Poplar did not fall. Wanda said, "How are you going to feel if you don't go to North Carolina and they win the national championship?"

I said, "How would I feel if I left Kansas and they won the national championship?"

While I was in Chapel Hill, I could feel my mindset changing. I began to think, "You're happy at Kansas. It's your program. It has your fingerprints all over it. You've been there 12 years, your whole career, and you've always admired a coach that stays at one school his entire career." In the past, whenever Wanda and I had returned to Chapel Hill, we got chillbumps on our arms driving into town because the place meant so much to us. That didn't happen on this visit. The longer I was back in North Carolina, the more negative feelings I began to have about the move—which was strange to me. I'd thought that would be when the needle would swing significantly in UNC's favor.

I knew Scott wanted me to come back to North Carolina. He had just finished his career as a UNC walk-on, and his teammates would often ask him about me coming back to coach. I knew Kimberly would have loved to have me on the same campus with her. Wanda had made it perfectly clear that she would be glad to return to the state where both of her kids lived. When I'd first been offered the UNC job she said, "I could have my bags packed in about 30 minutes."

We left Chapel Hill and went down to our beach house in South Carolina. Some of our neighbors were flying UNC flags and others were flying Kansas flags. Everybody was giving me their opinion. I made out lists with everything on there outside of which place had the prettiest cheerleader uniforms, and they became so cumbersome that I tore them up and threw them away. Every five minutes I would flip-flop. I'm going. No, I'm not. I'm going. No, I'm not. North Carolina is home. Kansas feels like home. I'm happy at Kansas and I know my players. I don't know the players at North Carolina. Coach Smith wants me to come back. How can I tell him no? What the heck am I going to tell Nick Collison? There's nothing I can tell Nick Collison.

I couldn't eat, couldn't sleep, couldn't do anything. I flew back to Kansas City and there was a crowd waiting for me at the airport when I landed. Airport security had to escort me through the media to my car. I drove over to Allen Fieldhouse at about 2 o'clock in the morning, thinking there was not going to be anybody there, and there were probably 30 or 40 people walking like zombies around the fieldhouse. People had posted cards all the way around the arena with messages asking me to stay. Somebody had sewn a shirt to put over Dr. Allen's statue that said, "Roy, Please Stay." They had poems written on the sidewalk. I went and sat at the Chi Omega fountain in the middle of campus because that was a very peaceful spot to think. When I got back to my house I still couldn't sleep. The phone rang early the next morning, and it was one of my former high school players, David Wilson. I hadn't talked to David since I'd been at Kansas and I don't even know how he got my number.

"I saw you on the news last night when you got back to Kansas," he said, "and I want you to come back to UNC, but your players are going to love you regardless of what you do. You're always going to be our coach."

It was the toughest time that I'd ever had. It far surpassed, whatever pain, anger, and sorrow that I'd endured as a kid, because I didn't feel like I could make a decision that wouldn't hurt somebody that I really cared about. But when that young man called, it felt like a sign that the people who really cared about me would be all right if I decided to stay.

I went to my office at Allen Fieldhouse that morning and I called Bob and said, "I'm going to stay."

Bob let out a huge sigh of relief. "Coach, you have no idea how happy I am," he said. "This is a great day for Kansas basketball."

I asked him if we could put the news out in a press release, but he told me there were 60 media people in from out of town and we'd need to do a press conference.

I went back home and called Dick Baddour, and when I told him that I wasn't coming, he was silent for a few seconds. He asked me if there was anything he could do to change my mind. I said the decision was made. I said, "I've got to stay here."

Then I called Coach Smith. "I'm disappointed," he said, "but you've said it before. The people at North Carolina don't know what you have at Kansas and the people at Kansas don't know what we have here. You and I may be the only two people who know."

I walked out past the television camera crews in front of my house and I asked them not to follow me. I went across the street to the back of the driving range at the Alvamar Country Club. Several years before, they had made a practice tee there, and at some point even put up a sign that said, "For KU Golf Team and Coach Williams Only," and I went over there just to hit some balls to try to get my head clear.

When I got back to my house, Bob called and said, "Coach, we've had to change the press conference to the football stadium, because that media room over there is the only one big enough."

Ten minutes later, he called back and said, "Coach, we've got thousands of people already over at the stadium — we're going to put the press conference up on the video board."

I set a record that day. I drank eight 20-ounce Coca-Colas. I went into the press conference and I simply said, "I'm staying." The 16,000 people in the football stadium just went crazy. But I made one big mistake. I said, "The next time we're having a press conference like this, it'll either be because I'm retiring or dying."

That was the truth at the time. That was exactly the way I felt.

I was the king of the world at Kansas, but some people in North Carolina that I truly loved and I thought loved me just wiped me off the face of the earth. It hurt me so much more than anything I'd ever experienced.

That week, I told Scott and Kimmie that in life you want to have a group of people who are going to be with you regardless of what you do. I told them that some people are only going to be with you when you do what they want you to do, and there will be another group that is not going be with you at all, so you have to find a hard-core group that will always be with you.

Based on our talk when the process started, I thought Coach Guthridge would understand, but he didn't. Coach Smith handled it well and said he understood, but I knew I'd hurt him, too.

The bottom line was that I was really happy at Kansas, and that I just couldn't come to grips with what to tell Nick Collison. I had made him a promise.

. . .

COACH GUTHRIDGE REALLY struggled with my decision and he essentially didn't speak to me for three years. One time he was at a booster club event playing golf with a close friend of mine, Mickey Bell. Mickey mentioned my name and Coach Guthridge said, "Roy who?"

He wasn't the only one. Eddie Fogler only spoke to me two or three times over the next three years. Bill Miller, who had been a golfing and jogging buddy and one of my best friends in the world, spoke to me once and then didn't speak to me for almost two years until he was dying and I called him. Bill broke down when he got on the phone. Bill didn't want to go to his grave having those feelings, and he was mad at himself that he hadn't made the step, that I had to do it.

When I decided not to come back to North Carolina, they hired Matt Doherty, my former assistant at Kansas who was then the head coach at Notre Dame. I was happy with that decision. I thought Matt would be at North Carolina for the next 25 years and when I retired from Kansas, I'd move back to North Carolina and go play golf in the afternoon and then come watch Matt coach the Tar Heels, and that would be it. I thought Matt was going to be a perfect fit. I never thought the opportunity to coach at North Carolina would ever come again.

But, like I always had, I followed what North Carolina's team was doing. I watched their games on television whenever I could. During Matt's first season at North Carolina, we talked about once a week and I gave him advice whenever he asked for it. His team won 21 of its first 23 games, including 18 in a row, and climbed to No. 1 in the polls but then lost to Penn State in the second round of the NCAA Tournament. Before the next season, Matt called and told me he was concerned that his team might really struggle. UNC had lost a lot of its best talent. Brendan Haywood had graduated and gone on to the NBA, Joseph Forte had left early for the pros, and Julius Peppers and Ronald Curry had quit the team to concentrate on their football careers. UNC was not a good shooting team, they were not a good defensive team, and they were very inexperienced. At one point they started two freshmen in the backcourt for the first time in the history of the program. The team self-destructed and finished 8–20. That season I started getting anxious phone calls from friends of mine who were UNC alumni. They told me about the bad chemistry around the program. Matt and I talked even more often that season, and I tried to build his confidence. He had recruited Raymond Felton, Rashad McCants, and Sean May, three of the best players in that year's recruiting class, so I told him to hang his hat on that.

The spring after that season, Matt and I met up to play golf down in Pinehurst, and when I drove him back to Chapel Hill, I said, "Matt, you've got to reach out to the former players and the alumni, because they're going to be a source of strength for you."

He said, "Coach, I feel like I already have tremendous support from them."

"I don't think you do," I said.

"I go to my radio show every week and I get a standing ovation," he said.

"The people who go to those shows are the die-hard fans," I said, "but they aren't the masses."

At the beginning of the 2003 season, North Carolina beat my Kansas team in the Preseason NIT. But then Sean May broke his foot in December and that really torpedoed UNC's season. They finished 19–16 and missed the NCAA Tournament for the second straight year. Some of those same alums called me, saying it was getting ugly. They didn't think Matt was going to survive. I kept telling them that Matt was going to be fine, because I didn't know about the strained relationships between Matt and some of his players and their families. I just thought that he had a young team, and that when his freshmen got older they were going to be really good. I really believed that.

We won our regional in Anaheim to reach the 2003 Final Four and I rode the charter back to Kansas from California. I arrived home at 3 o'clock in the morning and I had 17 phone messages. One of them was Matt. He said, "First of all, congratulations on winning and going to the Final Four. I'm sorry you had to answer questions about the UNC job. I think I'm okay. I met with Dick Baddour again today, and I think everything is going to be fine."

I was elated for Matt and I was elated for me, because I didn't want to go through the decision again. I told Wanda, "I'm so happy that I don't have to think about the North Carolina job anymore, since that really is the only place I would ever consider leaving Kansas for. So why am I doing this to UCLA?"

UCLA had been in contact with me for about three weeks, and they were waiting until our season was over to talk to me about their coaching job. John Wooden had always been so good to me when my teams played at Pauley Pavilion and he wanted to speak to me about taking the job. Two other administrative people from UCLA had called and I told them I couldn't talk about any other jobs while I was still coaching my team, but they made me think that the position would be mine if I wanted it.

So I called UCLA and said, "I'm not going to take the job. I'm sorry I've made you wait this long."

I was ecstatic. Kansas was going back to the Final Four, I had told UCLA I wasn't interested, and Matt had told me he was going to be all right at North Carolina. All I had to think about was coaching my team. And then on Tuesday before we got down to New Orleans for the Final Four, the news broke that Matt was being fired. I called him the next day. It was a very uncomfortable position for me. Matt was very disappointed and didn't think what had happened to him was fair. I told him that I couldn't believe it. I was mad. I just couldn't understand it, either. But there was nothing I could say to Matt to make him feel better.

After I heard the news about the firing, I tried not to think about it. But it was hard not to. When I would watch game tape I could lose myself in the job at hand and I was all right, but then as soon as I took a break from preparing my team, if I was eating or walking or brushing my teeth, the decision I suspected could be coming again would creep back into my mind.

There was also another factor. Bob Frederick had retired as the Kansas athletic director in 2001 and was replaced by Al Bohl. Al and I were like oil and water. We just did not mix. I didn't think he ever had a grasp of what Kansas basketball really meant to people, and I never felt he was totally sincere with me. I never felt like he was in my corner. I think he felt threatened by me and saw our relationship as a power struggle.

I also didn't like the way Al treated people. In his first year, he fired the Kansas football coach in the middle of the season and sent an assistant athletic director to do it instead of doing it himself. Al and I started butting heads within six months of him getting the job, and it just never got any better.

The only time I was happy was when I was on the court. I just focused on my team and tried to ignore everything else.

When we lost to Syracuse in the 2003 NCAA championship game, it was a very emotional locker room. Drew Gooden was a rookie in the NBA, but he had flown in for the game, and he came in and hugged me and he was bawling like a little kid. He told me, "I wish I'd been here to help. Coach, I wanted you to win this so badly."

It was so hard knowing that Nick Collison and Kirk Hinrich had given me everything they had but had lost their last college game. At times like that as a coach you feel inadequate, because you don't know what to say to relieve some of that pain and you know it's not going to go away, anyway.

I did the postgame press conference, and I had just gotten back into the locker room with my team when our media relations director came in and said that Bonnie Bernstein from CBS wanted to interview me. I went out to see her and I asked her not to ask me about the North Carolina job. She didn't say anything. She asked me one question about the game, which I answered, and then she said, "Many people out there would like to know your level of interest in the North Carolina job, Coach."

I said, "Bonnie, I could give a flip about what those people want. As a journalist you have to ask that question and I understand that, but as a human being, all those people who want that answer right now are not very sensitive."

"If they offer you the job, though, would you be willing to take it?"

That's when I lost my temper. "I haven't thought about that for one second. I could give a shit about North Carolina right now. I've got 13 kids in that locker room that I love." I turned around and walked off.

I was steaming mad. I went up to my hotel room with my buddies and my family and I said, "Okay, you guys are not going to make the decision, but if you've got anything to say, say it right now, because I'm going to have to make the decision soon."

Nobody said anything. Everybody left and I told Wanda, "I don't know what to do, but I just know I'm so unhappy. And I've been unhappy for two years, except when I'm on the court."

She said, "Did Chancellor Hemenway find you after the game?"

"Yeah, he wants to meet with me at 9 o'clock tomorrow morning, but honey, I don't know what I'm going do. It's different this time."

On Wednesday Dick Baddour called to offer me the North Carolina job. I asked him to tell me why he had fired Matt. He said, "I brought in all of the players and talked to them individually, and it was not working. I had to do what was best for the program." He told me that many of the players had threatened to transfer if Matt stayed on as coach. Dick said he had no choice.

I said, "Dick, I don't agree with you, but there's nothing I can do about it now. Just please don't have anybody else call me. Just give me some space and some time and I'll make this decision. Give me a few days. I've been trying to win a national championship, and I would have cheated those kids if I had thought about this."

The previous day I had met with Chancellor Hemenway and he told me he was going to fire Al Bohl. He said it was because Al was not a good fit, that it was the best thing for the department. I thought part of it was because they wanted to keep me at Kansas and that in the chancellor's mind Al's departure would clear things up for me to stay.

He was partially right. A huge obstacle had been removed and initially I thought that I'd be all right at Kansas. But then I thought about how unhappy I'd been for two years and how the administration had allowed me to be that unhappy. I was back to flip-flopping again. On the even hours I was going to UNC and on the odd hours I was staying at Kansas. This time, Wanda didn't have any strong opinion about what to do. Kimmie had graduated from UNC and moved back to Kansas, and Scott was still working in North Carolina, so that wasn't a factor. Wanda did, however, make one statement that I'll never forget: "So many weird things had to happen for you to get another chance at this job. It's beginning to look a lot like destiny."

Two days later, I flew to Los Angeles to accept the John Wooden Legends of Coaching Award, and I got some of my Kansas buddies to fly out there with me to play some golf. Mitch Kupchak came to play with us because he was afraid there were too many Kansas guys in my group and they might sway my decision.

The first night, we all went to dinner at a restaurant in Los Angeles. The chef was a Kansas graduate. We all had a good meal, and then the chef brought out a cake with a message swirled in the icing that said, *Roy We Love You, Please Stay.*

I started to feel like there were Kansas people planted there, because folks I didn't know kept coming over to the table saying, "I hope you'll stay at Kansas." Mitch and Cody Plott, the two North Carolina guys at the table, felt like they were overmatched.

I received the Wooden Award, and one of the kids I had just signed to come to Kansas, Omar Wilkes, was also there to get his own award. He was the son of Jamaal Wilkes, who had played for Coach Wooden. So I was sitting there looking at Omar and I remembered back to the day I'd done his home visit, and I'd told him, "When you come on your visit to Kansas, ask the players about me."

Omar had said, "Coach, I don't have to ask the players about you. We talked to Coach Wooden and he told us that if he had a son, he would love for him to play for Roy Williams more than anybody else."

That moment had given me cold chills. Omar was just that kind of kid. I told Wanda, "How can I tell Omar I'm leaving Kansas? I just recruited him to come and I'm one of the biggest reasons why he's coming."

So at 11 o'clock that night we drove back to the airport to get on a plane to fly back to Kansas. Waiting for the plane, I was standing on the ramp with Dana Anderson, who was a close friend and huge Kansas booster. He told me about how he'd made a donation—which I later found out was $8 million—and that his hope was that if I stayed at Kansas for five more years that the school would change the name of Allen Fieldhouse to Allen-Williams Fieldhouse. "We want you to stay at Kansas," he said, "but I'm your friend and whatever you do, I'm going to be with you."

I said, "Dana, I really appreciate that."

I got on the plane and I said to myself, "I've got to make the decision before this plane hits the ground."

After we took off, we talked about the economy and politics and the Yankees for five minutes and then everybody else in the cabin went to sleep. I laid my head back, too, and closed my eyes, but I was far from sleeping. I went through the whole process again. I reminded myself again that I'd only been happy when I was on the court with my team and that every time I walked off the court I felt like I was fighting a battle.

And so before we landed in Lawrence, I made the decision. I waited to tell Wanda until we got back to our house. I said, "Honey, it's going to be North Carolina."

She said, "If that's what you want to do, I'm with you."

The next morning, I called Chancellor Hemenway and told him. He said, "I really hate that, but it sounds like you've completely made your decision."

Then I called Bob Frederick and he said, "I understand, but why don't you wait one more day?"

Bob was no longer the athletic director, but he knew that the department had written a deferred income clause into my contract and that April 15 was the deadline. It was April 14. He told me I'd make an extra $200,000 if I stayed one more day.

I said, "If they decide not to give me that money, then I'll know I have made the right decision."

Then I called Dick Baddour and Coach Smith and asked them to send a plane to get me.

The next two weeks were a replay of what had happened three years before. Only in reverse. The people at Kansas just wiped me off the face of the earth. I had told Chancellor Hemenway that I would be coming back to Lawrence for the Kansas season-ending basketball banquet, but then word got back to me that the school's administration was thinking about not letting me attend. A reporter questioned me about that, and I said, "I'm going to make them make that decision when I get there, because I'm going."

Two days later, I returned to Lawrence for the banquet. First, we had a team dinner at Allen Fieldhouse for the players and their parents, and then we went to the performing arts center for the banquet. We had a bus to take us 500 yards to the entrance so we could get in, because there were 1,500 fans there. We got off the bus, and over on the sidewalk I saw 30 of my former players, and that's when Wanda started crying. Kevin Pritchard walked up to me and said, "Coach, I'm here for you." Then the rest of the guys came up and hugged me and said they were going in there to support me and make sure that nobody would stop me from speaking.

When it came time for me to speak, I got up and started talking and someone from the balcony stood up and yelled, "You traitor!" Dave Collison stood up, turned around, and yelled back, "You ought to be ashamed of yourself."

The majority of the people in the room started standing, and then

The only photo I have of my mother, father, my sister, Frances, and me together.

Growing up, I loved to play the cowboy.

Frances washing the dishes and me not drying them.

The first big one I ever landed.

Baseball was my first love; I wanted
to be the next Mickey Mantle.

My sister looked out for me more
than I ever knew.

My mom and dad during
the good times.

Wanda Jones, my future wife, and I were just friends at Roberson High.

ROY WILLIAMS
Varsity Club I, II, III, IV; Paper IV
Basketball I, II, III, IV; Annual IV
Baseball I, II, III, IV
PTSA IV
Pres. Stu. Body IV
Escort Aries Ct. IV
Jr.–Sr. Com. III
Drama III, IV
Sq. Dance IV

I did not want to be on the square dance team, but my girlfriend, Pam, talked me into it.

WANDA JONES
Stu. Coun. IV (VP)
Beta Club III, IV
Drama IV
Paper III, IV
Annual IV
Jr.–Sr. III

MOST DEPENDABLE

Kris Mishoe
Roy Williams

I won the senior class vote for Most Dependable over Most Athletic, which I've come to appreciate over time.

Buddy Baldwin, the coach who made me want to be a coach.

This fine physical specimen became Roberson High's career scoring leader.

I remember this was a big basket I scored against Hendersonville High.

The 880-relay team for the Peacocks, part of our team that won an intramural championship.

Wanda and I started dating as freshmen at UNC when I slowed down enough for her to catch me.

My mother was so proud that I was the first in my family to go to college.

Wanda and Scott were the crowd when I coached the junior varsity team.

My first year coaching at Owen High when we finished 2–19.

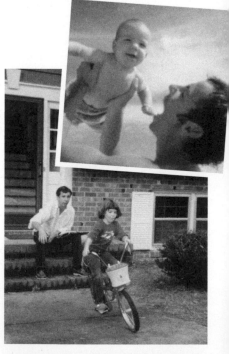

Every day of my 10 years as his assistant, Coach Smith prepared me to be a head coach.

I treasure the kind of family moments with my children, Scott (top) and Kimberly, that I did not have as a kid.

Me, Dean Smith, Bill Guthridge, and Matt Doherty at the 1993 Final Four. (All of us would coach the Tar Heels in the next decade.)

When my temper flares, I sometimes take it out on my sportcoat. I don't remember ever losing a game when I shed it.

I cried after Scott lived his dream and won a state title at Lawrence High in 1995.

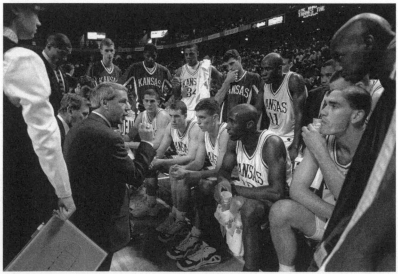

The 1997 Kansas team was one of the greatest I have ever seen and I'm still devastated that I couldn't get those guys to the Final Four. Four players on this team, Raef LaFrentz, Paul Pierce, Jacque Vaughn, and Scot Pollard, ended up being NBA first-round draft choices.

A promise to Nick Collison swayed my decision between Kansas and North Carolina in 2000.

Wanda and I returned to Chapel Hill in 2000 to see Kimmie on the UNC Dance Team.

A crowd of 16,000 Kansas fans showed up at the football stadium in 2000 to hear me announce, "I'm staying."

My 2003 press conference after I couldn't turn down North Carolina a second time.

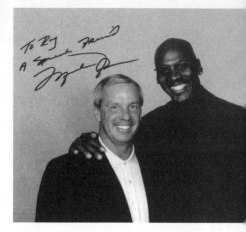

Michael Jordan and I have been close ever since I believed in him in 1980.

I pledge to my teammates and my coaches, that I will give 100% mentally and physically on every defensive possession these next 7 days. I CANNOT imagine letting my teammates down on this NOR CAN I imagine the hurt I will cause myself.

The pledge I asked my team to sign before the 2005 Final Four.

It was an incredible feeling of satisfaction to bring the players on this 2005 team, who had been through so much, to a national championship.

Twenty-two of my former players came for my Hall of Fame Induction in 2007.

Watching us play in the 2008 NCAA semifinals felt like a nightmare that will eat at me for the rest of my life.

Wanda, me, Kimberly, Scott, and his wife, Katie (l. to r.), on safari in South Africa in 2008. My family is who Roy Williams is.

My dad and Scott at the 2002 Final Four, the first of only two games my dad ever saw me coach.

My foxhole buddies and our wives during one of our recent golf escapes.

Senator Barack Obama played pickup with us in April 2008.

At our White House celebration in 2009, President Obama, who had picked us to win, said, "Thanks for salvaging my bracket."

After winning the 2009 national championship game, I told Tyler Hansbrough, "This is fitting, son."

One Shining Moment in 2009, the kind of moment I coach for.

The 2011 team had a lot of fun together. "I am having such a good time coaching you guys," I told them. "You have given me new life."

I experienced the three biggest shocks of my career in 2011, but that adversity really helped bond our players into a team.

Harrison Barnes hit this game-winner at Miami. He reminded me of Michael Jordan the way he became so confident taking a big shot and the way his teammates believed he was always going to make it.

After struggling through the humbling 2010 season, I wondered if we would ever get a chance to be the best again, so winning the 2011 ACC regular season championship was a surreal feeling.

As we finished off Duke to win the ACC regular season championship, everybody enjoyed the moment. "All year I've told you that our dreams and goals are realistic," I said to our players. "You guys believed and that's why we're champions."

1" />

2" />

Ever since I coached the junior varsity team, our chant coming out of every huddle is "Hard work!"

my players stood up, and there was a small ovation. Somehow we got through the night.

At the end of the evening, I went over to my buddy Scot Buxton's house. Twenty of my close friends were there, and we all ate ice cream as we shared memories of our Kansas times. Then Scot's son, Brett, asked if he could talk.

Brett said, "You're the only coach I've ever known at Kansas. I have looked up to you so much and I hate that you are leaving, but I know if you're doing it, it's because it's the best thing for your family. And I want you to know that you are one of my heroes."

It was closure with my best friends who knew what I had gone through three years before and knew what I'd gone through again this time.

I spent two days in Lawrence packing up. On our last night there, Wanda and I went to eat at El Mezcal, a Mexican restaurant. There was a lady and her daughter two tables over from us and they had sort of given me a dirty look when we sat down. They got up to leave and the mother turned around and stuck out her tongue at me. Then she walked out. That was pretty comical.

I had a clear conscience this time because whenever a Kansas recruit had asked me about how long I would be the Jayhawks coach, I had made sure that I didn't say the same thing I'd said to Nick Collison. Instead I had told them that 12 different NBA teams had called me about their jobs, so I wasn't going to the NBA, and I'd already turned down North Carolina, which was the only school that I would ever leave Kansas for. And so when I took the North Carolina job this time, I didn't feel like I had lied to anybody.

But in the following days people said some things that really hurt to hear. Wayne Simien, a sweet, wonderful kid who had missed the second half of the 2003 season with a separated shoulder, said, "I gave my right arm for that man." Chancellor Hemenway, who I'd worked with for seven years and had always introduced me as "the greatest basketball coach in America," began telling people that I'd become really hard to deal with over the last few years.

My friend Dana Anderson, who had stood on the airport ramp in Los Angeles and said, "Whatever you do I'm going to be with you," didn't speak to me for a year and a half. Then I heard that his mother passed away and I called him with my condolences. We both got very emotional and put aside our differences and to this day he is a great friend.

Kansas started showing a video before every home game that was all about the great history of the program, but they left out 15 years. My 15 years. It even reached the point that in 2008 when we were getting ready to play Kansas in the Final Four, there was a newspaper story about a barbershop in Lawrence that had put my picture up over the commode.

People would be surprised to know that I'm still a member of the Jayhawk Club. I'm still a season ticket holder at Kansas at the highest level because of the money that I contributed to the program during my time there. I've got six seats at midcourt on the second row. There are probably 20 people in that entire university and state that have given the Kansas program more money than I have.

As for the guy who called me a traitor at the banquet, I can live with that. That's just some fan expressing his opinion, but for the Kansas administration to think seriously about not letting me speak at the banquet? I'd given my heart and my body and my soul to Kansas for 15 years. It's not like I coached there for a couple of years and then as soon as somebody offered me a job for an extra dollar I took it.

It wasn't just the discontent. It was the anger and bitterness from people who I really thought cared about Roy Williams regardless, not just about what Roy Williams was doing for them as a basketball coach. That's what hurt me so badly.

Both times.

CHAPTER 9

Winning the Whole Blessed Thing

IF I HAD KNOWN how terrible I was going to feel telling my Kansas players I was leaving, I swear I would not have left. As a coach, it is the worst feeling I have ever had.

I really put a lot of thought into what I was going to say to them. I kept trying to think of something magical. Nothing came. Nothing. When the players walked into the locker room, they knew. They could see the look on my face and how emotional I was. I could see the expressions on their faces. I could sense the pain they were feeling.

I said, "Guys, this is the only time in my life I've ever felt like I feel right now, because I'm making a decision that I don't absolutely know is the right decision. But I've made the decision that I'm going to leave Kansas. I am not trading you for North Carolina's players because I would not trade you for anyone. I love you all. But the fact is, I haven't been happy for the last two years. I believe this is best for me and my family. I don't expect you to understand now, but hopefully at some point you'll know that I love you and that this is something I just had to do."

I walked out into the hallway and I felt awful because I had hurt them. I felt like I had chosen myself over 13 kids I really cared about. I felt dirty. I felt like I was skipping out on something. I wanted so badly to run back in there and say, "I can't do it. I'm staying here." But I had made the decision. I felt like it was the right decision, but that didn't change how bad I felt about myself right then. That moment was the lowest opinion I have ever had of Roy Williams.

I went to the airport and I'll never forget riding the plane back to Chapel Hill from Lawrence, with the pilot telling me that all the way across from middle America to North Carolina the air traffic controllers were saying, "Tell Coach, good luck. We're happy that he's coming home."

We landed at the Chapel Hill airport. Coach Smith was there. Coach Guthridge was there. Coach Guthridge said to me, "We're so happy that you're back."

That was a little uncomfortable for me; we hadn't really talked for three years and I knew he had been very mad at me. I understood deep down he was hurt because he'd wanted me to take over for him at North Carolina in 2000 and I hadn't done that, and that maybe he would have remained as the coach for another season if he'd known I would turn down the job. I gave him some leeway because I would always think of him as my coach.

We rode to the Smith Center and there were people along the sides of the road over the few miles from the airport to campus, holding up signs and screaming. Dick Baddour met us at the Smith Center and gave me a Carolina blue tie to put on. I told him I would not put it on. The tie I was wearing had blue and red on it, but it was not a Kansas Jayhawk tie like some people in the media thought. I was not going to change and just put on a UNC tie and act like the Kansas period of my life was over with. I was coming to North Carolina to coach the basketball team and I was going to give it everything I had, just like I had at Kansas, but I was not going to be phony.

At the press conference I spent about half my time thanking people at Kansas, and I heard later that some of the North Carolina people didn't really care for that. But it was something that I needed to do. I said that I was a Tar Heel born and I was a Tar Heel and Jayhawk bred, but when I die I'd be a Tar Heel dead.

The next day I met with the team individually and as a group and I told them I was going to help them win. I said, "I expect you to play unbelievably hard. I expect you to sacrifice and in the end you will be rewarded for those sacrifices. You will never work harder than I work, and you will never care more than I care, but I will ask you to come awfully close. This is the plan. You do what I tell you to do and we will make the NCAA Tournament this year. Then I'll get you a little help and next year we'll have a chance to win the whole blessed thing."

Some of the kids looked at me like I was crazy, some were skeptical, and some bought into it a little bit more.

My second day back at North Carolina, I wanted to watch the players work out for a few minutes, just to see what I had. I brought them in to do a little run-and-shoot workout. It lasted 28 minutes. That's all it was. Two guys threw up. I mean they were pathetic. Damion Grant got a rebound and was supposed to make an outlet pass, but the first time he tried it, he threw it 10 feet over the guy's head. The second time, he was standing 10 feet in front of the backboard. He was supposed to throw it off the board to rebound it and he missed the backboard.

I walked through the locker room and I overheard Byron Sanders talking to a teammate. "I know one thing," he said. "We're going to be in shape because he tried to kill us."

It was *28 minutes*. I was just dumbfounded that kids who wanted to be good college basketball players were that out of shape. I was thinking, "What in the world have I gotten myself into?"

DURING MY THIRD YEAR as an assistant coach at North Carolina we were all in the locker room before a game when the players started out to the court and I yelled, "Play hard, play smart!"

I began saying that every game. Coach Smith told me one time that the correct way to say it would be, "Play hard, play smartly," because smart is not an adverb. I told him, "Coach, that just doesn't sound as good to me."

I kept it going for the rest of my career as an assistant coach. Then I took that slogan to Kansas, and when I was talking to Coach Smith one night during my first year in Lawrence, I said, "I think I'm going to add one more thing. I'm going to start saying, 'Play hard, play smart, play together.'"

Coach Smith liked that, and they started saying it back at North Carolina, and before I knew it they were describing the "North Carolina way" as "Play hard, play smart, play together." It was funny because a few years later a Kansas alum sent a letter to all of the Kansas basketball lettermen, and he wrote something about how Kansas chanted, "Play hard, play smart, play together." Coach Smith is a Kansas letterman so he mailed me a copy of the letter and wrote on it, *Sounds like you guys are copying North Carolina!*

I called him and said, "Coach, you stole that from *me*!"

Before the 2004 season at UNC I had T-shirts made up for the players that said, "Play hard. Play smart. Play in March." I did it because nobody on our team had ever played in the NCAA Tournament.

The previous two seasons at UNC had been difficult ones. Things had gotten very personal with some of the players' families against the coach. Matt Doherty is a good coach and a good person, but it was not a good mix at that time. They'd gone 8–20 and 19–16, lost 36 games the last two years, which just doesn't happen at North Carolina. The players had been criticized by everybody. There was a lot of mistrust. A lot of bitterness. They'd been involved in a coach getting fired. It wasn't about the team anymore. Human nature says that you're going to try to protect yourself and a lot of the kids thought that their dreams and goals were slipping away. There were some highly recruited players who had gone through an awful time and they were asking themselves, "Am I ever going to be able to play in the NBA? Should I have left? Should I have transferred somewhere else?"

Then I came in preaching togetherness and they wanted to believe in it, but they were also worrying about themselves. Every player was wondering about his playing time and how much I was going to allow him to shoot. Lots of questions were whirling around in their minds, and it was hard to get everybody to sacrifice 100 percent for a common goal. There were things being said in the locker room that were disruptive. Players were jealous of other players, and people thought I was favoring one player over another. So it was a battle to get everybody on the same page. I thought they could play hard. I thought they could play smart. But I wasn't sure they could play together.

They weren't bad kids. They were good kids and they wanted to do the right thing, but in my opinion they had been through so much turmoil over the last few years that I'm not sure they wanted to trust me. They weren't sure they could. I needed them to give me a chance, and one of the key players to do that was Jackie Manuel.

I had looked at Jackie's stats when I arrived and saw he had taken more than 70 three-point shots during the 2003 season and hit only 26 percent of them. Also, Matt Doherty had told me about some difficult times he'd had with Jackie and his family. I called Jackie in and said, "This is the way it's going to be. I'm very difficult to handle if guys don't take good shots. I need you to take shots that you can make. I can't have you taking three-point shots and shooting 20 percent. I want you to be here. I've never been one to want to run anybody off, but if you don't think that's what you want to put up with, if you want to transfer, I'll help you."

Jackie said, "No, Coach, I want to stay."

Jackie was one of the keys because he changed his game. He sacrificed. He trusted me. He bought in to what I was saying quicker than anybody else, and he brought Jawad Williams and Sean May and Rashad McCants along after him. I began to tell the other players to do things like Jackie. I bragged on him and used him as an example all the time and the players used to tease him and call him my "son." But the faith that he had in me was crucial for us.

We won our first six games that season, and then in our ACC opener we played a close game against Wake Forest at home. With two seconds left in overtime, we were up by two points in a timeout. I told Melvin Scott and the rest of the players twice—it was the first thing I said when they came over to the huddle and the last thing I said when they left—"Do not foul an outside shot!"

We went back out on the court and three guys weren't lined up where I told them to be. Chris Paul took a jumper from the deep corner, and Melvin hit him harder than any of our football players hit a guy all year. I was surprised they didn't call it an intentional foul. Chris Paul made two free throws to send the game into double overtime, and then we lost in triple overtime.

Our problem was taking what I was saying and actually doing it. We fought that all year long.

In the middle of January we had a big win at home against No. 1 Connecticut. We were leading the game by 16 points early in the second half, but Connecticut rallied to take an 83–80 lead. Then Rashad McCants tied the game 83–83 on a three-point shot with just over a minute to play, and we got a stop and called a timeout. I diagrammed a play that we hadn't run the entire game to get Rashad open, and I said, "Guys, if you just believe we can win this game, we're going to have a lot of fun in that locker room." Rashad sprung wide open and hit another three-pointer with six seconds to play to get us the win. The crowd at the Smith Center stormed the court and we did have some fun jumping around in the locker room. I told the team it was the first time they made me feel like they all believed in what I was telling them to do.

Then we had a tough loss at home against Duke. We were up by five points with three minutes to play and we made three turnovers in a row to allow the game to go into overtime. In overtime, Rashad hit another huge three-point shot to tie the game with 13 seconds left, but then we let Chris Duhon drive to the basket for an easy layup in the final seconds to lose the game.

We lost five of our last seven ACC games on the road that season, because the players still didn't feel like they could totally depend on each other. Everybody was still looking for a shortcut, trying to win the game individually instead of doing their jobs and trusting their teammates.

In the ACC Tournament we were playing Georgia Tech in the first round and we had a one-point lead with 10 seconds left. After a timeout we didn't get lined up properly. We gambled for a steal from behind and that opened up the floor, and Jarrett Jack hit a 12-footer and we lost. It was just because we didn't do what I told them to do. We weren't disciplined enough. To reach around and try to steal the ball like you're on the playground against some guy that couldn't play dead in a cowboy movie was not going to get it done in the ACC.

Still, at that point we were 18–10 and we made the NCAA Tournament. In the first round we were matched up with Air Force, a very disciplined ball-control team, and I was thinking that was not the kind of team we wanted to play. Air Force totally controlled the tempo for most of the game, and we fell behind by six points with 13 minutes to play. But Sean May was just too big for them inside, and we put together an 11–0 run and pulled out the win. Then we played Texas in the second round. Sean was our only legitimate big man, and Texas was running in and out five 6'10" guys all game long. Afterward Sean said, "Coach, I just wanted the game to be over with. I was so worn out."

That was the mentality of the club. They were just finished. They didn't have enough discipline or toughness or experience. They just didn't know how to dig any deeper when the game got tough.

At the press conference after the game in Denver, there were some questions about whether any of our guys were going to declare early for the NBA draft. After the press conference, I ran into Doug Moe, the former Denver Nuggets coach, and he said, "Why would they ask you that? Somebody in the NBA would have to want your guys. Who would want any of those guys?"

DURING THE SECOND practice of the 2005 season, we left the court at the Smith Center and brought the players to our practice gym. When they got in there, they noticed that something was different. The players looked around wide-eyed wondering what was going on. I'd taken the rims off all of the backboards.

For 45 minutes we did nothing but defensive drills: denying the passing lanes, double-teaming the post, fighting through screens. We did that stuff over and over and over again, and it was very difficult. It was exhausting. None of the players ever touched a basketball. But they started to realize that we could get better as a team without shooting the ball. I'd made the decision to put Jackie Manuel in the starting lineup because he gave us a big-time defender in the starting five and I wanted to establish the attitude that we could win with defense.

In that same practice I reminded the kids that I'd told them in our second year together we could win the whole blessed thing. "We have big-time dreams," I said. "Every team in college basketball is thinking they have a chance to win the national championship, but that dream is realistic for us. We don't have to play over our heads. We just need to play as close to our potential as we possibly can and we can live our dreams."

I was passionate about that. I believed we were good enough and if they did what I told them to do, we had a chance to win a championship. I think believing it as strongly as I did gave them some confidence.

We had everybody back—Sean May, Rashad McCants, Raymond Felton, Jackie Manuel, Jawad Williams—and we'd added a talented freshman in Marvin Williams. Still, I was stunned when *Sports Illustrated* picked us No. 1 in the country. The local media hadn't even picked us to finish first in our league. We had a team led by a senior class that had gone 8–20 and then lost 27 games over the next two years and a junior class of Raymond and Sean and Rashad, three players who everybody thought were going to be great, but they had only one win in the NCAA Tournament. I knew we had a chance to be really special, but I was surprised that anybody else would think that way because our guys hadn't proven anything yet.

I had challenged every one of our players in our individual spring meetings. To Sean, I said, "You have to work harder than you've ever worked in your life. You've got to lose a little weight and you need to move around what you have left. You've got to have more stamina, more bounce, to be a top-flight college basketball player."

To Rashad: "You've got be able to put the ball on the floor and have a better assist-error ratio and be able to do a better job of guarding the basketball."

To Raymond: "You've got to shoot it a lot better."

To Jawad: "You've got to be more consistent and be able to handle some adversity if you get injured."

We lost Raymond for the first game of that season because he'd played in a summer league game that wasn't sanctioned. But I thought that was great because I believed everybody else would really step up and make up for Raymond's absence. That shows what I know. We laid a great big egg. It was as bad a game as I've ever had one of my teams play. Quentin Thomas was a freshman playing for Raymond, and he had three turnovers faster than I can eat half a box of popcorn, and Santa Clara beat us.

We got on the plane the next day to go to the Maui Invitational. I was steaming mad because I felt that instead of competing against Santa Clara, we just gave in. We thought we were going to sashay in there and be the big dog and Santa Clara was going to roll over. There's nothing I despise more than that.

So we got to the hotel in Hawaii and I told the guys, "We are not in Maui yet. We're going to go practice and I'll tell you when we're in Maui."

I had basically stayed up all night working on the practice plan. I knew one of two things was going to happen. Either we were going to show great effort and be glad to have it behind us, or we were not going to show great effort and I was going to fight somebody. They had made me mad, so I was going to make them mad. I was going to get even. I was going to run them until half the team puked. I was vicious and they responded.

Five minutes into the practice there was a defining moment. Rashad sprained his ankle and limped off the court and I thought, "My gosh, this is a bunch of crap." Rashad had a reputation, and deservedly so, that when times got tough in practice he wouldn't fight his way through it. But a minute later, Rashad had his ankle retaped and he came right back in and played his tail off.

For almost two hours in a high school gym that must have been over 100 degrees inside, every drill we did I demanded they do at full speed and be extremely competitive. Every little defensive drill that they hated, we did. Some of them we did two or three times. When we were finished, I wanted them to take a shower and eat and go to bed because they couldn't physically do anything else, and that's what happened. It was the hardest practice they'd ever had.

I didn't tell my players this, but in that practice I saw the competitive fire that I was looking for. I was screaming at them and they were busting their rear ends with no jabbering or complaining. Later, back at the hotel, I told Wanda, "We've got a chance to be pretty doggone good."

Before the first pregame meal at the tournament I told the players that I'd only lost the first game of the season twice in my career, but both of those times we'd played in the Final Four. We won the tournament opener against Brigham Young, and then in the second game against Tennessee, Raymond injured his wrist. He came back and played with it in a soft cast against Iowa in the final, and we won the Maui Invitational.

We got on a run and won 14 games in a row. One of those wins came at Indiana at the beginning of December, and I thought it was important to us because it was a very hostile atmosphere for Sean May, who was the top prospect in Indiana as a senior in high school and the son of a legendary Hoosier player. It was a very physical game for us at the end of a stretch when we played six games in 13 days. Indiana wasn't a great team, but they played a great game that night. Rashad made five three-pointers and scored 19 points, and Raymond had 18 and we were able to make plays at the end and win the game. The intensity and toughness that we showed was something that I loved.

That winning streak stopped in the middle of January. We lost a game at Wake Forest when we did not match their competitiveness. They pushed the ball up the floor harder than we did. They had us back on our heels. So I got after our guys a little bit. Some of the articles that were written after that game talked about how when things got bad, we got worse. They pointed out how we started complaining, we started going one-on-one, we stopped playing as a team. I challenged the players to make sure we didn't let that happen again.

The pivotal moment of the season happened right after our game at Duke in early February. We were down by one point and we had the ball at the end, but we never got off a final shot, and as our point guard, Raymond got the blame. The last play of the game had gotten too much attention, so I picked out 10 or 15 plays for the team to watch on tape. I showed everybody all of the mistakes that cost us the game and then I said, "Don't you all let them blame this loss on Raymond. It was my fault. It was your fault, Rashad. Sean, it was your fault. You guys who didn't play in the game, it was your fault because if you had worked harder in practice the day before when we said they were going to spread the floor, we might have handled that better."

I think that they all bought into that. They believed it. They became more of a team at that point. And from that moment on, Raymond was a different player. From that moment on, Raymond was willing to make big plays.

We beat Connecticut on the road in our next game and then won five straight in the ACC before we played Duke again in the last game of the regular season. We were down by nine points with a little more than three minutes left. It was Senior Day for us and you just can't lose on Senior Day. I got the team huddled around me, and Jawad had his head down. I flicked him on the forehead and I said, "Get your head up. We're going to win this game. If you all will do everything I tell you to do, I guarantee you we're going to win this game. It's got to be a total commitment. You have to do it right now better than you have ever done it before. And if you do that, if you'll give me total commitment on every possession, I promise you we're going to win this game."

I'm a little wacko, but I really did believe that we were going to win that game. So we went out and made a couple of plays and then Raymond was on the free-throw line and he missed and there was a loose ball and Marvin Williams picked it up and banked one in to give us the lead. That was the loudest I have ever heard any arena in my entire life. We won the game and we were the ACC champions. It was one of those incredibly emotional scenes. For the seniors, Jackie and Jawad and Melvin, who had been through the 8–20 season, it was a great accomplishment. I've never been so happy to watch three guys cut down nets.

In 2002 I HAD called Coach Smith from Kansas and told him that I thought we had a chance to win a national championship but that I was discouraged about how we were doing such a poor job boxing out on the boards. He said, "Make them sign a pledge that they're going to box out."

I said, "Coach, what do you mean?"

"Make them sign a pledge that they're going to box out on every possession."

And so everybody on our team signed a pledge and they seemed to respond well to the peer pressure that it created. We took care of business on the backboards all the way down the stretch that season.

In the first round of the 2005 ACC Tournament, our team played so poorly against Clemson that I threatened to take them back to Chapel Hill to practice that night. The next day we lost to Georgia Tech in the semifinals. Then in the NCAA Tournament we beat Oakland and then Iowa State, and then we outscored Villanova and Wisconsin, but we were awful defensively. I mean really awful. I thought we needed something to motivate our guys, and my assistant coach Joe Holladay said, "How about we make them sign the pledge again?"

I thought that was a good idea. We did it that Monday before the Final Four. An hour before practice that day I wrote this pledge up on the board:

I pledge to my teammates and my coaches, that I will give 100% mentally and physically on every defensive possession these next 7 days. I cannot imagine letting my teammates down on this nor can I imagine the hurt I will cause myself.

Underneath I drew 17 lines, and then I went out to the court.

When practice was over, I peeked into the players' locker room and all 17 guys had signed it.

I thought that was pretty neat.

AT HALFTIME OF the NCAA semifinal against Michigan State we were down by five points and I got after our guys. I said, "Why would you not box out? Why would you not take a charge? Fellas, this is the Final Four. Sean, I'll take a charge on you with Damion riding on your back. Let's wake up. How dare you do this to yourselves?"

We scored the first six points of the second half and then we picked up our defense. Michigan State made only 10 of 34 shots in the second half. We did box out. We did not back off and let somebody drive in and lay it up. We got turnovers that led to fast breaks that led to dunks. We got the lead and we'd get a stop and then another fast break and another and another. If that game had lasted long enough, we'd have won by a million.

Before the championship game, all I was reading about was how we were talented but we were not a team. That was an insult to me and to my staff and my players; it was like a slap in the face to what we'd worked on for 100 practices. And so I told the kids that. I said, "It should make you mad. I want it to make you mad. I want to shut them up."

Then I started telling them what some guy on TV said, what some other guy wrote in the paper, and then I saw that it was making them angry and I liked that. Finally, I told them, "Let's show them we're a frickin' team."

In the locker room before the final against Illinois, a team that had been ranked No. 1 for most of the season, I felt very confident. In each of the previous rounds, I'd written a number on the dry-erase board for the round we were trying to get to: *32, 16, 8, 4, 2.* I'd drawn boxes around the number and with each game the box got bigger. So that night I turned the board around and said, "This whole board is a box and if we win tonight, there's going to be a 1 in there. Phil Ford and Michael Jordan and Dean Smith are North Carolina basketball, but if we play our butts off tonight, you'll be North Carolina basketball forever. Tonight somebody is going to win the national championship. Why not let it be us?"

We came out attacking offensively and we got after them defensively and we surged ahead by 15 points. During timeouts, I kept telling them we were going to win it on the defensive end, and I thought we were playing one of our best defensive games of the year. On offense, Sean was kicking everybody's rear end, and at one timeout Jackie even said, "Guys, keep feeding the big dog. Let the big dog eat!"

Illinois made a run in the second half when Luther Head and Deron Williams made a bunch of threes, and they cut our lead to two with just under 13 minutes to go. Then Sean scored 10 of our next 13 points and we built our lead back up to 10 with nine minutes to go. We were up by six when there was a timeout with about seven minutes left. I was a little concerned about the look on our guys' faces. That moment reminded me of Coach Smith in the 1982 NCAA final against Georgetown and what I still think is the best huddle speech I have ever heard.

So I told the team, "We're okay. Why should anybody be worried? Guys, did you expect this to be easy? That is a really good team down there. They've won 37 games and they're not going to roll over and play dead, but this national championship is ours. We're exactly where we want to be. We're still in control. We're going to determine the outcome of this game."

I did see a little relief on their faces. Illinois fought back to tie the game 65–65, but then Raymond made a contested three-point shot and I thought back to the Duke game, when he didn't make a play at the end and got criticized so much for it. Now, he was not afraid to make a big play for us.

We took a 30-second timeout with a little more than two minutes remaining and the game tied 70–70. "Guys," I said. "I really don't have anything to say to you. We just have two more minutes to push and we're going to win the whole blessed thing. I wanted to give you a chance to catch your breath and just realize that every possession is crucial. We're fresh and we're into their bench already because Sean has kicked their tail. Think how fantastic this is going to feel. We're two minutes away from winning the national championship."

Then Rashad threw up a prayer, but sometimes prayers are answered because Marvin Williams tipped it in to give us the lead with just over a minute left. Then Raymond made three free throws and a huge steal, and Sean got the rebound of their last shot. I looked up at the scoreboard. We were ahead 75–70 and I saw the clock tick from two seconds down to one and then I looked back down and saw Sean still had the ball, and I looked at the clock and saw it tick from one to zero. The next thing I saw was Sean sprinting right at me. I'll never forget that big smelly, sweaty rascal hugging my neck, and seeing how excited he was. I told him, "Son, you have no idea what this means to me."

Sean said, "Coach, you believed in me. This is the happiest moment of my life."

I always told myself that if I ever won a national championship, I'd walk around the court with my fists up in the air like Rocky. But when it actually happened, I was in a fog. I had no idea what to do. I didn't know how to feel. I kept thinking, "Is this really happening?"

I hugged Marvin and I said, "Thank you so much for trusting in me and believing in me."

I saw Jackie and he said, "Coach, I love you."

I told him, "Young man, I will never forget this feeling for the rest of my life. Thank you for allowing me to coach you."

I wanted to say something to the three seniors, who were standing together with their arms around each other. I walked over to them and Melvin was saying a little prayer, and when he finished, I asked if I could join them. They put their arms around me in their huddle. I talked to them about how proud I was and said, "Treasure this moment. This has to be sweeter for you guys than anybody else."

Then I went to see my family in the stands. Wanda was crying and Scott was crying and Kimmie was crying and I was crying, and I hugged all of them. It was almost surreal. At that time a lot of it was relief, because my family had had to defend me for so long when people said I couldn't win the big one. I think it bothered them even more than it did me. They had been there for the lowest moments of my coaching career. I was glad to get that monkey off my back and I remember answering a question about it at the press conference by saying the same thing Coach Smith said in 1982, that I'm no better as a coach than I was three hours ago.

In the locker room I hugged Coach Smith and all I could think to say was, "Thank you."

Michael Jordan picked me up off the floor in a big bear hug and I said, "Thank you so much for being here."

"There is no way that I was missing watching you win your national championship," Michael said. "There may be more to come, but there was no way I was going to miss this one."

I turned to the team, and everybody got together and jumped around for a while. When we were done, I pointed at Michael and at

Coach Smith and said, "They are what made North Carolina basketball great, but now you all are a part of that forever."

When I got back to the team hotel, I was still in a daze. I went up to my room and there were 40 people up there. I thanked Bob Frederick for giving me my start as a head coach. I thanked Buddy Baldwin for instilling in me the dream to be a coach in the first place. There were a lot of tears shed, and it was just an incredible feeling of exhilaration and satisfaction that I'd been able to bring those kids, who had been through so much the last few years, to a national championship.

I told everybody in the room that I would've loved to be able to walk to the top of the escalator and be invisible and watch the reaction that our players were getting from the fans. I wished there was some way I could do that without people coming up to me. If only I could just watch my players, because that would tell me how nice it felt.

I didn't go to sleep at all that night. We flew back the next day and the reception in Chapel Hill was mind-boggling. We got back to our house and there were signs in our front yard, one of which read, "Roy and Wanda, thanks for 'heeling' our team."

That night I invited all of my coaches and their wives out to dinner to celebrate. I was physically and emotionally spent. I had nothing left. Neither did anybody else. About halfway through the meal, I saw Wanda yawning and Coach Robinson propping up his head in his hand and I said, "Let's get out of here and go on home to bed."

At 6 o'clock the next morning I met Coach Holladay in the parking lot at the Smith Center to go recruiting.

CHAPTER 10

Philosophy

WHEN I WAS TWO years old I went with my dad and some of my uncles to go fishing at a pond near where my aunt Doris lived. I was pestering them so much to let me fish that my dad found a little stick and tied a fishing line to one end of it with a hook and a bobber on it. I don't know if he even baited the hook, but he threw it out in the water for me. I was standing there holding the stick when all of a sudden the bobber sank, and I felt something tugging on the line. I had no idea what to do. I didn't have a reel. So I just turned around and took off running away from the pond as fast as I could with that stick, and I dragged the fish right out of the water up onto the bank. That fish was almost as big as me.

I'm still trying to land the big ones any way I can. Recruiting means everything. I know that Roy Williams is only as good as the players I can put out on the court. In the summer of 2000 I went to visit the legendary UCLA coach John Wooden and he said something that has always stuck with me: "Roy, you can coach talent. Some guys can't. Nobody can coach no talent, but you can coach talent." That has driven me ever since to make sure that I have talent to coach.

I recruit through a process of elimination. If I see a big guy who can't run, I don't recruit him, because I want our team to run. If I see a point guard who can shoot, but has no savvy, I won't recruit him, because I need a point guard who makes great decisions. Whenever I go out and recruit, I'm thinking, "This is the way I want to play. Can that kid do what I want him to do?"

I need guys that can pass, I need guys that can shoot, I need guys that play at a high speed and I need guys that are self-motivated, but I have to allow for some give and take, because not everybody is going to be perfect.

When I go into a gym to recruit, I climb up to the top of the bleachers, put my back against the wall, and I'm there to work. If I'm there to watch one individual, I'll watch every move he makes. If I'm watching a group of players at an All-Star camp, I wait for somebody to jump out at me and I'll write his number down on my pad every time he does something I like. In the summer of 1989, I was at a tournament in Louisville and they had four games going at the same time. My assistants had me watching a player on Court 2. Every time the play would stop on my court, I would glance over to Court 3, and No. 34 was just killing people. I kept writing down the number 34 over and over and over. He was so outrageous with his effort and rebounding and how he could run. At some point in the second half, I just turned away from my court and started watching No. 34. That player's name was Richard Scott and he ended up being a three-year starter for me at Kansas.

When I decide that a kid has the talent I'm looking for, then I try to find out about his character. I once had an elementary school principal in Wichita, Kansas, tell me, "Coach, I wish you'd say academics is the second priority."

"No ma'am," I said, "because if he's a great player and a 4.0 student but he's going to be a pain in the rear end, I want it to be somebody else's rear end."

I remember going to recruit Marvin Williams, and in one game he had 36 points. But that wasn't what sold me on him. Marvin fouled out of that game, and while the crowd was giving him a standing ovation, he walked over to the end of the bench and grabbed five cups of water and handed them to the five guys who were going back into the game. I said to myself, "I really want that kid."

If you're among the best in my talent and character tests, I'm going to show you how important you are to me. I pick one or two prospects every year to handle by myself. In the summer of 1992, I went to an AAU tournament and Eddie Fogler told me, "I just saw a guy that has Kansas written all over him." It was Raef LaFrentz. Raef was rated among the top 10 prospects in the country. I made nine or 10 trips to see Raef in Monona, Iowa. I would fly into a tiny airport in Prairie du Chien, Wisconsin, that had no rental cars. There was a car dealership about a mile and a half from the airport that would rent me a car. Sometimes I had to walk to get there. Then I would get a sandwich right across the street and I would drive about 20 miles across the Iowa border to Monona. I made that trip so many times that after a year or so when my plane landed, a guy at the car dealership brought my car to the airport and left it all warmed up and running for me on the tarmac with my club sandwich and a Coca-Cola sitting in the passenger seat. The people there were rooting for me to get Raef to come to Kansas.

I would call Raef every Sunday night at 9 o'clock. No other coach on my staff ever called him. He visited Kansas and then a few weeks later he visited Iowa, which was hard because I knew the home state pull was going to be a factor. The Sunday night after Raef's visit to Iowa, I called the LaFrentz house and Raef's mother told me, "Coach, Raef doesn't want to speak to you tonight. He wants to get his thoughts cleared." I thought it was all over with. I didn't sleep all night. I just sat in a chair and stared out into space. I called back a couple of days later, and that's when Raef's mother told me he had done the same thing with the Iowa coach after he visited Kansas. It was during one of our Sunday-night calls a few months later that Raef told me he'd decided to come to Kansas. I was ecstatic. He was the most highly rated recruit I had ever signed.

I tell every prospect I recruit that I'm going to try to outwork every other coach. Our players get one day off each week during the season, and on most of those off days I go recruiting. Once I was watching a recruit play and I had a stitch come loose in some dental work, but I stayed and watched the rest of that game while I spit blood into a cup. Another time I was at a prospect's game that didn't start until 12:15 a.m. I was the only college coach left in the gym and I was propping myself up against a railing to stay awake when the recruit's mother turned to me and said, "Coach, please go home." But I watched that whole game. I like to ask prospects, "Who is recruiting you the hardest?" If they don't say me, I'm mad and I'll go back to my staff and tell them we've got to do more.

I probably don't call recruits as often as other coaches because I hate the telephone. I can talk the paint off the wall face-to-face, but I don't really like talking on the phone. I tell prospects right up front that when I phone them, I won't talk their ear off for an hour like some other coaches. I want them to know that I care, but I believe everything is better in moderation. I don't send a bunch of e-mails to recruits. I send handwritten notes.

I don't recruit with a shotgun approach. I narrow down my focus as much as I can. If I want to sign two or three players, I will focus my attention on four or five candidates and they have to be kids that I'm going to enjoy being around every day. Since I became a head coach, I've had three recruits visit campus that my players thought wouldn't fit in, so I stopped recruiting all three.

Recruiting is like putting together a puzzle, and I mean that literally. When we recruited Paul Pierce at Kansas, we had four starters coming back, but we had no small forward. I asked my assistant Steve Robinson to make a little puzzle. He cut pieces out of a cardboard box; there were four corner pieces that represented our four starters and he left the centerpiece missing. We sent Paul the four corner pieces and then two days later, we sent the centerpiece in the shape of a star with Paul's picture on it and a message that read, *You are the missing piece to the puzzle.* That's what Paul turned out to be when we got him. Recruiting is about convincing kids that they are the missing piece that we need to be complete.

I'm a plodder. I'm methodical. I never stop recruiting. My life revolves around recruiting periods, recruiting trips, recruiting calls. The closest I ever came to a divorce was in my third year at Kansas when I took Wanda to Hawaii for the first vacation we'd had since going to Lawrence. Every afternoon of the trip I told her I was going jogging, but instead I put on my jogging shoes and went to a pay phone in the hotel lobby to make recruiting calls. When she found out what I'd been doing, she was not a happy camper. During warm-ups before we played the 1991 national championship game against Duke, I went around the corner from our locker room to a pay phone and made a recruiting call to Jason Kidd. All these reporters rushed up to me and

I said, "Guys, can't somebody talk to his father without you all hovering around like that?" I didn't say that that was who I was talking to, but it got them to leave me alone.

You have to call most prospects 10 times for every time they answer the phone. But Shane Battier had the most organized recruitment I've ever been involved in. He selected six schools and said he was going to have phone calls every Monday night. Each coach had 15 minutes. I made the phone call every Monday at 9:30.

One Monday night I was at Yankee Stadium watching the Yankees play the Texas Rangers. I was invited by my former chancellor at Kansas, Gene Budig, who was the president of the American League, and we were sitting in the first row beside the Yankee dugout with Marty Springstead, the league's supervisor of umpires. At 9:30 I told Chancellor Budig that I had to make a phone call.

He said, "A recruiting call?"

"Yes, how'd you know?"

"Because I know you."

Marty asked somebody to take me into the umpires' locker room. So I called Shane Battier from the umpires' locker room at Yankee Stadium, standing beside a guy who looked like he was 400 years old with mud on his hands rubbing up baseballs.

When I go to a recruit's home, I give it to him straight. I want recruits to feel like they're talking to a coach and not a salesman. I have a video with game highlights. I have articles with academic ratings. Then I tailor my talk to what I think is the most important factor for each prospect. At the end of the night I ask if there are any questions, and my hope is that he'll look me in the eye and say, "No, Coach, you answered everything."

Now I know recruits might say that just to get rid of me, because I'm not going to be the best for everybody, but I try to make our presentation sincere, passionate, and entertaining. I remember going to Adonis Jordan's home. Rick Barnes, the Providence coach, was scheduled to come in right after me. Rick arrived at the door 15 minutes early and rang the doorbell. Something funny had happened and we were all laughing and carrying on, and someone opened the door to Rick, and he said, "Sounds like you're having a party."

I said, "Coach, you're right, and it's going to last 15 more minutes."

That is my time to sell our program, to say this is how we see you fitting in and would you please come join us. Of course, you can't plan everything. I got to Jerod Haase's house, and his mom, Carol, said, "I've got some pizza for everybody. We have Canadian bacon and pineapple or vegetarian."

I do not eat pizza. I'd rather eat a napkin than a vegetarian pizza, so I chose the other one and they gave me two huge slices and I picked off every piece of pineapple and every piece of bacon and ate the crust and that's all I could stomach. It almost made me sick, but what choice did I have? I really wanted to sign Jerod Haase.

At North Carolina I use our rivalry with Duke as a recruiting tool. I'll say, "If you're a fan of Michigan or Michigan State, and those two teams play each other, the next morning you know who wins. If UCLA and Southern Cal play and you're a fan of one of those schools, the next day you know who wins. When Duke and North Carolina play, that night everybody in the country knows who wins. Why wouldn't you want to play in the biggest game there is in college basketball?"

For pro prospects, I also try to sell them on a dream. I'll say, "I know you want to be an NBA player and those NBA scouts want to see you perform on the biggest stage. Players that play in the Final Four always dominate the draft. You have big-time dreams and so does Roy Williams. What would be fun would be to see if we could reach those dreams together."

I never forget that everybody I recruit is somebody's child. In 1990 I went to visit Patrick Richey who was leaning toward going to Missouri. At the end of my presentation, I looked his mother in the eye and said, "If your son comes to Kansas, I will take care of him the same way I would want you to take care of my son if I sent him to live with you." I heard later that as soon as I left, Patrick's mother stood up and said, "Folks, we're going to Kansas!"

Of course, like every college coach, I've lost way more recruiting battles than I've won. When I was at Kansas recruiting Jimmy King, I spent a lot of time on him and thought he was the perfect fit for us. He visited Lawrence and absolutely loved it. Coming back, his mother picked him up at the airport and she saw a magazine with an article about America's best colleges. The magazine didn't list Kansas among the top 25 percent of colleges academically. She couldn't handle that. She wanted Jimmy to go to a great academic school. Jimmy called me up crying and told me he was going to Michigan. That just killed me. It was all about that one article.

So Jimmy went to Michigan and became part of the Fab Five and they made the Final Four his freshman and sophomore years. Then in his senior year we happened to be in Dayton, Ohio, in the same regional as Michigan, and we won our first-round game. When we got back to the hotel, standing there with all the Kansas fans were Jimmy King's mom and dad. Michigan had lost that day and they had come over to our hotel just to see me. His mom hugged me and said, "We are just here to help you celebrate. It was a tough day for us, but I just wanted to tell you that I made such a huge mistake. Watching you these last four years, Jimmy would have loved to have played for you."

That was all great, but we still didn't have Jimmy King.

So I enjoy recruiting when I get a chance to sit and talk with the kids and their families, and I love recruiting when I get in the gym, but there are other parts of recruiting that really stink. It can be demeaning. Kids have lied to me. I once had a recruit ask me to gather all of my assistant coaches and secretaries and everybody else we could find into my office, so he could commit to me in front of a huge group. We all cheered and hugged, and then six weeks later he called to tell me he was going to Michigan State.

The whole thing is an insane experience. Players are being recruited when they are still just kids. There are guys in ninth and 10th grade thinking about making commitments, and our admissions office will say, "How can we decide if a kid should come to college when he hasn't taken sophomore English?"

Nowadays, the NBA affects everything in recruiting. A lot of kids go to college with the idea of staying just one or two years, and that's not as fulfilling for me. I used to think it was a great thrill for a kid to be offered a scholarship to come to college. For some people, we're now just a bus stop.

Dwight Howard only visited one college, North Carolina. When he announced at his press conference he was going straight from high school to the NBA, he said that if he had gone to college he would have come and played for me. That was nice to hear, but he never played for me. I remember Dwight once showed me a paper that he'd written for an English class in the ninth grade titled "Dreams." He wrote that he wanted to be a starter in high school as a freshman, that he wanted to win four state championships, and that he wanted to be the first player taken in the NBA draft. His teacher gave him an A on it, and there was not one word in there about college. That was discouraging.

Sometimes I'll spend two years recruiting a kid, write him handwritten notes three times a week, call him whenever it's allowed, go to

see him play a lot, and then when he makes his decision to go somewhere else, he doesn't even call to tell me. I understand that every kid
isn't going to come play for me. It's just that when I come in second,
it upsets me. I invest a lot of myself personally, so it probably hurts me
more than some other coaches.

In the end, recruiting is like farming. Every day you pull the weeds,
water, try not to let it get too much sun and then you don't have any
idea until the crops come in whether you did worth a darn. You may
have a kid show up as a freshman and drop dead of fright before his
first game. I've had recruits arrive on campus, and then I say to myself, "Dang, he's not as good as I thought he was." Others come and I
think, "Dang, he's a lot better than I thought he was." You just never
know for sure what you've got until they're on your court.

IN THE SUMMER between my junior and senior years in high
school there were a bunch of guys who, two or three nights in a row,
had thrown eggs at each other, and the tension was building between
the two groups. One was my group of friends from the Biltmore com-
munity, and the other was from Valley Springs, but I had friends on
both sides. A lot of them wanted to fight, and I knew it could get
ugly. One night a few of us brought both groups together, and I said,
"Let's just have an egg war, and let's settle it. Let's have some fun and
get this over with."

We all agreed to meet on a Friday night at the Burger King in Biltmore and we made a game plan. We spent the next couple of hours
going around to grocery stores and we bought 111 dozen eggs. They
had 13 guys and we had 12. They had 63 dozen eggs and we only had
48 dozen. They had more money. We went out to the football field at
Christ School, and the war started at midnight. When you got tired
of being hit by eggs, you surrendered. We decided the battle would

continue until the last man standing. The winning team's prize was a watermelon.

Our team took one end of the field and theirs took the other, and at the start most everybody just charged each other. It looked like a scene out of *Braveheart*. I decided I was not doing that; I told one of my teammates to run with me and we would loop around and attack them from behind, and so we forced two or three of their guys to surrender right away.

That night I really thought I could be the next Johnny Unitas. I snuck up behind a guy with two eggs and he took off running. I threw one egg about 30 feet and I led him perfectly and hit him on the right side of his head. He stumbled a little bit and took off again. I threw the next egg a little farther and it hit him again in the same exact spot, and he went down to the ground and started yelling, "I give! I give!"

I was probably hit with more eggs than anybody that night, but I wouldn't surrender. Near the end of the war, our team had two guys alive and they had one. We surrounded their last guy in the corner of the end zone. We each had a half-dozen eggs and we were just pelting him until he screamed, "I give up!" Everybody had a great time that night.

That was the first time I ever brought a group together who didn't all think exactly the same way. I think about the egg war every season when a new freshman class comes in, another group of teenagers with their own competing agendas.

AN IDEA I live by comes from a John Wayne movie called *Rio Lobo*. John Wayne and Jack Elam are on one side of a creek shooting their guns at the bad guys on the other side. John Wayne looks down at Jack Elam and says, "Scatter gun's useless."

Jack Elam says, "Don't mind if I shoot, do you? It just makes me feel better."

I love that attitude: if you don't shoot, you have no chance of killing the bad guys on the other side of the river. If you don't shoot, you have no chance of making a basket. You have to be willing to try.

I balance that with an idea I take from the Clint Eastwood movie *Magnum Force*. At the end of the movie Clint Eastwood squares off with a dirty cop who had tried to kill him. He secretly activates a bomb in the cop's car, and as the cop drives off, his car blows up. Clint Eastwood says, "Man's got to know his limitations."

That's the other thing I think about when I'm coaching: everybody should understand what they can and cannot do.

Coach Smith never liked it when his coaching method was called "the system." He thought it suggested that what he taught was robotic. He preferred the word *philosophy,* so that's the word I use. My philosophy is that basketball is the simplest game in the world — *if* you can get five guys moving in the same direction for a common goal. Coaching is all about me getting my five guys to do what I want them to do better than you can get your five guys to do what you want them to do. If you have one guy looking out for himself, you're in big trouble. If you have more than one, you have no chance.

When I was on the UNC freshman team, my basketball idol was Steve Previs. He was the greatest teammate I've ever known. He lived by his favorite axiom, PMA, which stood for "positive mental attitude." No matter how badly I'd practiced or played in a game, Steve would always have something positive to say to me afterward to pump me up. He was like that with our whole team. He never cared one bit about his own statistics. There was not a selfish bone in his body. Every year I coach, I try to find a guy to be as good a teammate to my current players as Steve Previs was to me.

The strategy of a basketball game isn't that complicated. You get the ball. I get the ball. You get the ball. I get the ball. Those are the rules. The only way I get more shots than you is if I rebound the ball on offense and prevent you from rebounding the ball at your end. Then it boils down to the quality of the shot I get compared to the quality of the shot you get.

My offensive philosophy is that we're going to run. We're going to try to make the other team's players run faster and longer than they have ever run in their lives. In a typical game we want to have between 90 and 105 possessions, and we try to get that number up as high as we can, because if I'm better than you are, the more possessions we play, the more likely it is that I'm going to beat you. If I play golf against Tiger Woods for one hole I might beat him, but over 18 holes, I have no chance.

Coach Smith always said, "Let's be the actors and let them react." At some point every year I'll hold up a dollar bill in front of one of my players and tell him to put his thumb and index finger an inch apart on either side of the dollar. When I drop the dollar he won't catch it, which shows him how hard it is to react to my action.

In the halfcourt offense, we're going to share the ball. We're going to throw the ball inside and look for a good shot and if we don't like what we have inside, we throw it back out. I tell my players, "If you can shoot the ball well, shoot it. If you can't shoot it well, find something else to do that helps us." I had a player, Nick Bradford, come over to the bench one night and ask me, "Coach, don't you want me to shoot that shot? They're leaving me wide open."

I told him, "The coach of the other team is not dumb, son. He's leaving you open for a reason."

We always try to do what we want to do, not what the other team wants us to do. I've always been amused by football coaches who say,

"We took what they gave us." I don't want that. I want to take what I want. My thinking is, "This is the way we're going to play, so what will you do to stop it? We're going to run the ball and we're going to work on it every day in practice and take it to the highest level we possibly can, and then in the three days that you have to prepare to play us, there's no way you can practice defending it as well as we play it."

It's like the Green Bay Packers sweep with Jim Taylor and Paul Hornung or Southern Cal's Student Body Right. You may know exactly what's coming, but it's still pretty hard to stop.

People always talk about our fast-break offense, but actually I want our players to work hardest at the defensive end. I ask every player, "Do you remember the first time you were ever really guarded?" I believe we all do. For me, it was in the seventh grade at the YMCA. This guy was defending me so tightly that he wouldn't let me do what I wanted to do, and I thought, "God almighty, why are you doing this to me?" Bobby Knight said it best: "Don't guard someone like you like to be guarded."

We play man-to-man defense almost all the time because I can't coach zone. I despise it. There have been years when we didn't play zone more than 10 possessions the whole season. Still, you have to have it as an option. One of the few times I ever played zone for any length of time was when UCLA came to Lawrence in 1996, the year after they won the national title. They were drilling us. We were down 15 at the half and I went in the locker room and diagrammed the point zone. We had not worked on it one day that season. We played it in the second half and it was awful, but UCLA started taking outside shots and missing them, and we ended up winning by 15.

About 75 percent of what I do comes from Coach Smith, but we do differ on a few things. Coach Smith always taught players to switch on screens. I want my players to fight through them. He used to routinely run three different defenses on three straight possessions. I don't change that much. He played the Four Corners. I don't like to spread the floor much at the end of games. If I've got a six-point lead with four minutes to play, I want to beat you by 18.

The bottom line is that I want my players to understand that at some point in every game, somebody's going to give in, and I don't ever want it to be us. We want to be the last team standing.

I remember one day when Coach Robinson and I were walking from the locker room to the basketball office. We were side by side and as we approached the office door, he had his keys in his hand and I quickly reached into my pocket, grabbed my key, shoved it into the doorlock, and said, "Gotcha!"

Coach Robinson said, "I didn't realize it was a competition."

I said, "It's always a competition."

But winning is just as much about attitude. In my junior year of high school, our basketball team played at Enka High in the first game of the season. They were ranked No. 1 in Western North Carolina. They beat us, but it was a close game and it gave us some confidence. My teammate Walt Stroup was always confident. In the locker room after the game, Walt and I saw Enka's coach, Charlie Johnson.

"You guys have really improved," Coach Johnson said. "You're going to have a good year."

"You guys had better get ready," Walt said.

Coach Johnson said, "Excuse me?"

"You better get ready, because we're going to beat you next time."

I was thinking, "Walt, I'm going to hit you right in the mouth. This is the best team in Western North Carolina, and here you are making them mad."

Coach Johnson said, "We practice two hours every day trying to get ready."

Walt said, "You better start going three because we're going to get you next time."

I said, "Coach, thank you very much. Just overlook him."

The coach walked out and I said, "Walt, what are you thinking?"

"Roy, we're going to beat their butts next time. We're going to be good."

We played Enka again in late December. They were 6–0 and we were 3–3. Walt came over to my house for a pregame snack and I told him, "Now listen, don't you go in there and try to stir things up. Let's just play our tails off tonight and see if we can beat them."

Walt said, "We're going to beat those guys."

"I understand what you're saying. But don't be saying anything like that to them. Let's sneak up on them. Let's don't alert them to what's going to happen."

So we left to go to the gym and we walked in past the Enka locker room, and I was thinking that I had to make sure Walt didn't say anything to anybody. I went in our locker room and set my bag down, and I turned around and realized Walt was not there. I ran out and opened the door to Enka's locker room. Walt was in there and I heard him say, "I hope you boys enjoy your ride back to Enka, because your undefeated season is stopping tonight!"

I grabbed him and said, "What in the crap are you doing?"

"I just wanted to let them know we're going to beat them," he said.

"Are you crazy?"

At the end of the game, I was on the free-throw line and we were up by four points with 10 seconds to play, and Walt walked up to me and said, "I told you we were going to beat their butts."

To this day I tell that story to my players and talk to them about having confidence and really believing in something. Walt Stroup absolutely believed we were going to win that game, and that carried over to the rest of us.

EDDIE FOGLER ONCE called me "frighteningly organized." I do a practice plan every day and have it typed and placed in all of the players' lockers. I'll make out a weekly plan. I'll make out a monthly plan. I make out preseason plans. In my office files, I still have every practice plan I've ever written since I coached at Owen High.

All of my practices are organized to the minute:

5:22 Fast-break drills.
5:26 Defensive stations.
5:33 Box outs.

My practices do not run long.

During practices I want to show my team everything that they can possibly be exposed to in a game and what to do against it. I try not to do anything that doesn't correlate directly to our next opponent. I kid Jerod Haase all the time about how he and his former high school basketball coach used to run basketball camps and start out with a figure-eight drill. I told him, "Why would you practice the figure eight? That's the dumbest thing I've ever heard. You don't do that in a game, do you?"

In practice I am always evaluating and reevaluating my team. What are we strong at? What are we weak at? I try to improve our weaknesses and really play up our strengths. I ask myself, "What does our next opponent do really well that's a thorn for us? What could be the most significant factor in us losing?" Then I've got to find a way to hide that area and not allow it to cost us the game.

I am very demanding. When I was a young coach I would rant and rave like a lunatic. I would kick a lot of trash cans. Sometimes I would kick all of my players out of practice. At that time, I didn't have a record that led my players to think, "Hey, I ought to listen to what that guy says." The fact that I would put them on the endline and run them half to death put some fear in them. I wasn't really comfortable with that, but it worked and I was going to have to be comfortable with anything that worked. Over the years, my former players have told me that I've mellowed. I don't think I've mellowed; I just try to motivate more through sarcasm or appealing to their pride, which I think can be more effective than ranting and raving or running them.

Sometimes when I'm on the verge of blowing up, I think back to the best lesson I ever learned about controlling my temper. One day when I was home from college, I was driving on the highway around Asheville. It was a hot afternoon and I was in a car with no air-conditioning. There was a car in front of me in the passing lane just poking along. Finally, I changed lanes and saw there was a woman driving and a guy sleeping in the passenger seat. I yelled, "Lady, either drive faster or pull that old piece of s— ." The guy woke up and I saw that it was my uncle Gordon. I was yelling at my aunt Bertha. I hid my face, floored the car, and got the heck out of there.

But some parts of my personality I cannot change. The first time I can ever remember being superstitious was during my senior year in high school on the baseball team. Before our first game, I realized I had forgotten my socks, so I borrowed socks from a teammate and we lost the game. The second game I had my socks and we won, but

I forgot to wash them. We won our next game, so I didn't wash the socks. And then we won and we won and we won. We won 13 games in a row, and I became convinced that the unwashed socks were part of the reason. We reached the state playoffs against Holbrook High, whose pitcher, Wilbur Howard, would eventually play for the Houston Astros. He pitched a complete game to beat us. On the ride home I threw the lucky socks out the bus window.

Superstition is part of my college coaching career. During the 1982 Final Four in New Orleans, one of the vendors on Bourbon Street told me I should spit in the Mississippi River for luck. I did it every day we were there and we won the national championship. Now every time I've had a team playing a big game along the Mississippi, I spit in the river. Before every home game at Kansas I would go for a jog, stop at Phog Allen's gravesite, pat the headstone and say, "Doc, we need all the help we can get tonight." If it was a really big game I'd do that same thing at Dr. Naismith's grave as well. I never get a haircut on the day of a game and if I wear a tie for the first time and we lose, I'll never wear it again.

Common sense tells me that the result of a basketball game does not depend on whether or not I got a haircut that day, but it settles my mind to think that I have done something to help us win. As a coach, I feel really limited about how much I can affect the game. I just want to say I've done my part.

The other thing I must do before every game is take a nap. Right after our pregame meal, I sleep for 30 to 45 minutes. It's mandatory. It allows me to relax and have a clearer mind once the game starts. We can be playing Duke at Cameron Indoor Stadium on national television and I might not have slept at all the night before, but when I go home for a nap that afternoon I am out as soon as my head hits the pillow.

I try to arrive at the gym for home games an hour and half before the game starts. I check on the complimentary ticket list, and I meet with any prospects who are in town for the game. I go down to the locker room 35 minutes before the tip-off, visit with my assistant coaches, and watch the ticker to see other scores around the country. When all of the players are dressed and seated, a manager knocks on the door and I go in. I've seen NBA teams write 40 things up on the board before a game. I'll write down no more than three because that's all I think my players can absorb. I might write, *Five guys run both ways as fast as you can* or *Be strong with the ball, nothing casual* or *The team that wins the battle of the boards wins the game.* Once at Kansas, we had beaten Kansas State eight or nine times in a row in their building and I'd seen a lot of stories about them saying that the streak would end that night, so I wrote, *Watch them leave early.* It was the only thing I wrote. It was cocky, but it worked. At the end of the game, one of my players, Ricky Calloway, was on the free-throw line and he yelled over to me on the bench, "Coach, they're leeeeeeeaving!"

Another phrase I often write up on the board is *Lose yourself in the game.* Sometimes kids can choke on a big stage. If you lose yourself in playing the game, you don't worry about the result.

After that meeting, the players go out to the court for warm-ups and I meet them back in the locker room seven minutes before the game starts. I'll cover my three points of emphasis again and then we come together, kneel down on the floor, put our hands together, and I say the Lord's Prayer. I always add three words at the end. I say, "For thine is the kingdom, the power, and the glory, for ever and ever. *Together please, Lord.* Amen."

Then I tell them, "Play hard, play smart, play together," and I send them out for a final warm-up.

I usually get out to the court with two minutes left on the clock.

Usually. In December 1992 we were playing Michigan in the final of the Rainbow Classic in Hawaii. I sent the team out for the last time, then I went to use the bathroom, and the manager locked me in the locker room. Since that time I've made darn sure that a manager always knows I'm still in there.

In the final huddle before a game starts, we go over instructions for the opening tip, and then we put our hands in and chant something my teams have been saying since I was North Carolina's junior varsity coach: "Hard work!" It's something I've believed in since I was kid shoveling snow off the basketball court so I could practice or selling calendars or going right back out on the recruiting trail after winning a national title. The phrase is a reminder that nobody is going to outwork us. I think it pulls our guys together and gives them strength. It is what the players chant when they huddle for any timeout or any deadball. It's a constant reminder. *Hard work!*

I try not to look at the score in the first half, because I don't want that to influence my thinking about how we're playing. Sometimes if a team is taking bad shots and they're making them, a coach could be fooled into thinking his team is playing better than it really is and that just leads to problems later on. I try to look at the big picture and focus most on our rebounding and our defense.

I have always hoarded timeouts. I've said that when I die, I'm going to have more timeouts left than any other coach. I remember one time we were getting destroyed by Tyrese Rice in a game at Boston College and I never called a timeout. What was I going to say? Guard Tyrese? I think our guys knew we needed to guard him better. I will never call a timeout just so people will think I am coaching, because I really don't give a darn. I think I know a hell of a lot more about basketball than someone who's going to send a letter to the chancellor complaining that I just sat there and did nothing.

I try to pick my battles about when to argue with an official. After all of my years as a referee in intramurals, I know how hard the job is, so I'll only protest when I'm sure I'm right. When I do argue, I try to use sarcasm to mask my anger. I remember once when Ed Hightower was officiating a Kansas game and a Missouri guy threw an elbow that coldcocked one of my players. I saw it clear as day, and I jumped up and said, "Ed, didn't you see that?"

Ed said, "I saw it. There was nothing there."

I said, "Well, excuse me. I didn't realize you were God and you could see everything. Excuse me, God."

When Ed came back down the court the next time, I said to him, "God, in your spare time will you look at that play on tape. If you could do that for me, God, I'd really appreciate it."

That's when he almost called a technical foul on me.

A few days later, I got a handwritten note from Ed Hightower saying that he'd checked the tape and he'd missed it.

Sometimes I get so frustrated with a call or how bad my team is playing that I take it out on my sportcoat. I rip it off and throw it behind the bench. It's funny, but I don't think I've ever lost a game when I took my coat off.

In the second half, I start checking the score once the clock gets down to the eight-minute mark because by that time we have two opponents: the clock and the other team. That's when I'm usually pretty happy that I have lots of timeouts left to manage the end of the game.

When the game is over, I tell my players they have to beat me to the locker room. I don't ever want the whole team waiting around for one guy talking to his girlfriend. I usually give them some quick thoughts on the game and no matter how well we played, I can never be totally satisfied. Even after our best games, I'll say, "Everybody remember the easy one you missed, everybody remember the time you lost your man on defense, everybody remember the time you didn't box out." If we lose, I usually apologize to them and tell them it's my fault and I have to do better.

Then we put our hands in and I say a prayer. I always end that prayer by saying, "We do realize we're more fortunate than others. Amen."

I let myself enjoy a win for about 30 seconds before I start thinking about the next game. A loss sticks with me forever. Losing is deadening. For me, the lows are so much lower than the highs are high.

At the end of each season, I hear some of my critics in the media say, "Oh boy, Roy's going to cry again." I have done that a lot at the end of a year because I'm sad not to get to coach those kids again. I'm probably too emotional. I went through a stretch at Kansas where I actually tried to talk myself into not crying, but it was not me. I just can't help it.

When it comes to winning and losing, so many times I've had to remind people that it's not just my team playing out there, that the other team has something to do with the outcome. The tradition and history at North Carolina or Kansas makes fans think we should win all the time, but other programs have some tradition and history as well. And the teams that don't have it want to beat us even more because we have it. Sometimes when you lose, you just have to step back and say the other team deserved it more.

One of the best lessons I ever learned about sportsmanship occurred after my Kansas team won a game against Oklahoma. After the game, the Sooners coach, Billy Tubbs, gave me a little hand slap instead of shaking my hand. Two days later, Billy phoned me at my office and he said, "Roy, I just needed to call. The way I shook hands with you, that wasn't right. My wife, Pat, says you've said good things about me since you've been in the league and nobody else says good things about me, and now she's mad at me about it. Roy, I just want you to—"

I interrupted Billy and I said, "Coach, I don't have a problem with it. After a game, everybody's emotional."

"No, no. Roy, just understand this. Don't ever forget that I'm just an ass."

It was a neat deal, because every coach needs to get humbled once in a while.

I am humbled every time I drive back to Asheville on Interstate 40 and I see the exit sign for Drexel. Every time I see that sign it reminds me that in my first year at Owen High School we won only two games. We beat Drexel twice.

Every time I pass that sign, I think about how I'd like to find out what that Drexel coach is doing these days because I've been pretty lucky since then.

WHEN I TOOK the job at Kansas I did not want my players to wear Converse shoes, because North Carolina players wore Converse and I wanted to do something different. I called Nike. They did not return my call. I called them three times and they never returned a single call.

My friend Mickey Bell was working for Converse, and he said, "We want you to wear our shoes. We're going to make you an offer and I'll have it to you in a couple of days."

The offer wasn't a lot of money, but it was to Converse, and I didn't have any choice. So I signed the Converse contract. After my fourth season that contract expired and by that time we'd been to the national championship game, we'd won the conference and the conference tournament, and Nike was trying to recruit me.

Nike flew me to their campus in Beaverton, Oregon. A limousine picked me up at the airport, and when we got to the entrance of their headquarters there was a big banner that read, "Nike Family Welcomes Kansas Coach Roy Williams." They showed me a video of an Olympic long jumper winning a gold medal and then a highlight of me on the sidelines coaching in the national championship game, then a swimmer winning a gold medal, and then me on the sidelines again. I was blown away. Then they took me to the employee store and started loading me up with shirts and shoes, but I told them I didn't want the gear because I felt like I was taking advantage of them. Later, they sent me the stuff anyway. Nike CEO Phil Knight took me to a seafood restaurant, and it was about the best meal I'd ever had. Nike offered me a contract for more than twice as much money as Converse.

I flew back to Lawrence and called Mickey and we set up a meeting. I told Wanda, "Well, this is going to be hard, but I'm going to tell Mickey that I'm going with Nike."

She said, "Why?"

"They're a better company. They're a bigger company. They're more solid. The players like the shoes better. I've just got to do that."

That evening, Wanda, Mickey, and I sat down to dinner and Mickey said, "Well, you know I'm with you whatever you decide. It's not going to change our friendship. I'd love you to be with us, but I know you've got to look out for your family."

I said "Mickey, I've decided what I'm going to do."

"What?"

"I'm going to go back with Converse."

Wanda said, "*What?*"

Then I said to Mickey, "I just told Wanda two hours ago that I was going to go with Nike, and the only thing I've been able to think about since then is how I preach to our players to show loyalty to people who have helped you by doing what you can to help them. I've got to walk the way I talk."

AND I REALLY DO try to live by that rule. One day I was in my office in the Smith Center talking to one of my players and my assistant, Jennifer Holbrook, came in and said, "Former President Bush is on the phone for you."

I didn't know if it was one of my knucklehead buddies playing a trick on me or not, but I said, "Tell him I'll have to call him back."

When I finished with the player, I walked out to Jennifer's desk and I said, "Was it really President Bush?"

She said, "It really was."

Coach Smith taught me that your players are always your top priority. If I have a player in my office and the phone rings, I will not answer the phone. I have a Plexiglas paperweight that reads, "Statistics are important, but relationships last a lifetime."

When it comes to mentoring my players, I look at myself like a teammate. I am playing as hard as I can every day to get them to believe in what I believe in: that there's a right way to conduct yourself, there's a right way to answer people, there's a right way to dress when you go into a restaurant or get on a plane, and there's a right way to play basketball.

One of the ways I do this is through our "Thought for the Day." It's a concept I learned from Coach Smith. I have a file of over 1,000 inspirational phrases that I've collected from airline in-flight magazines, NBA scouts, PGA golfers, and lots of fans who have sent them to me in the mail: *See the rocks in your path not as obstacles, but as opportunities to climb higher* or *If you want to leave footprints in the sands of time—you better wear work shoes.* On the first day of preseason practice, the Thought for the Day is always the same: *It's amazing how much can be accomplished when nobody cares who gets the credit.*

Sometimes I'll spend 20 minutes before a practice picking the thought that I believe best pertains to the mindset of my team at that moment. Then during the first huddle of practice every day we spend a few minutes talking about it. We'll read the thought and then I'll ask the players, "How does that relate to basketball?" And then I'll ask them, "Okay now, how does that relate to life?"

Speaking of life off the court, most years I have an FBI agent come talk to my team about the dangers of gambling. I have a female faculty member talk to them about the meaning of the word *no.* Bill Chamberlain, my former teammate on the UNC freshman team, talks to them about making good decisions.

I try to constantly remind our players that at some point the ball is going to stop bouncing and they've got to have something to fall back on. Early each season I'll huddle the team and let the upperclassmen mentor the freshmen. I'll ask a senior, "Tell the freshmen what is the easiest way to get me upset. Is it a failure to do something on the court or is it a failure to do something academically?" That player will say that the worst days of running in practice are the days that I get a bad report on grades.

I also want my players to realize how fortunate we all are. Every year at Christmastime we go shopping for gifts for underprivileged kids. It's always an emotional day for me, and when our guys realize they're shopping for a child's only Christmas present, it gives them a different outlook. There's no question that it has a special significance to me because of how I grew up, but mostly it's about reminding our players that there are things more important than whether their jump shot is falling. Coach Smith once said that our program is the front porch of the university because we're the part that's most visible. I want our guys to have people see them in a very positive light.

I try to never blow smoke with my players. I tell them what they need to hear, not what they want to hear. I tell them the truth. When I was in high school, Buddy Baldwin told me, "If you tell the truth, you won't have to remember what you said."

Early in his Kansas career, Drew Gooden was convinced he should play on the perimeter and be allowed to shoot more three-point shots. One day I said, "Drew, I know you can shoot the three, I just don't think you can *make* the three." He was hurt that I didn't think he could play away from the basket, but two years into his NBA career Drew called me and thanked me for setting him on the right path to the pros.

I would not be good as a psychiatrist, because if anybody were to tell me that a man killed 12 people with a chainsaw because his dad knocked him around as a kid, I think that's a bunch of B.S. I believe that you get to make the decisions in your own life. It's not your dad. It's not your mom. You are responsible so you'd better make the right decisions. I try to coach my players like that.

That applies even to being on time. Everybody who knows me knows that I work on a strict schedule. I remember when Adonis Jordan was late for the bus on a road trip to Oklahoma State. Our bus was pulling out of the arena driveway when Adonis drove up. He grabbed his gear out of his car, but I met him at the bus door and said, "You're not going with us." I left him behind. He had to catch a ride with the radio crew. Four hours in a car with two old fogeys was a pretty severe punishment. Then I made him do the same thing on the way home. Adonis was never late again.

I remember when Rex Walters transferred to Kansas and I was

very hard on him in practice. The simplest way to get me mad is with selfishness, lack of concentration, or lack of hustle. Rex showed up with all three. Rex may have been the only player I ever threw out of practice twice. One of those times I told him, "Get out of here before you contaminate me and everybody else."

One day Rex called his father and said, "Dad, I want to come home. I don't think I can handle this man." His dad talked him out of it. The next season Rex was the best player in the conference, and as a senior, he led us to the Final Four and then got drafted by the New Jersey Nets in the first round. Rex grew more as a competitor than any other player I've coached.

I will never forget the words of Jack Johnson, one of my summer league baseball coaches: "You coach a guy and 30 years later you can still see in him something you gave him. You better be darn sure it's something positive."

One of my high school players, Stan Turner, once came to see me in his senior year. "Coach," he said, "I don't know what I'm going to do with my life."

Stan was really personable, the most well-liked student in his class, so I asked him, "Have you ever thought about going to Asheville-Buncombe Technical Institute in their hotel management program? I think you'd be good at that."

Stan came by the next day and said, "I think I would like to do that." Sure enough, he went there, and later on he became the general manager of a beautiful hotel in West Palm Beach.

One of my favorite stories is about Eric Davis, a player on the last North Carolina junior varsity team I coached. I had lost touch with Eric until he came to see me during my first season back at North Carolina in 2003. He told me, "Coach, you are the reason I am where I am today. After I played JV basketball I quit studying and I flunked out. I moved back home and one night my mom was watching Kansas play on television and she said, 'That man had faith in you that you could be somebody and here you are back at home on the street corners. That man had faith in you. Why don't you have some faith in yourself?' I called the university and begged them to let me back in school. Two years later, I begged the dental school to let me in. The reason I did that is because my mother said you had faith in me."

Today Eric Davis is a dentist. He gave me a picture of the two of us with this inscription: *The true measure of a man's greatness is not in the number of his accomplishments, but in the number of people's lives he inspired while achieving those accomplishments.*

I do have one huge regret about how I handled one of my players. Sean Tunstall was in four team pictures at Kansas, but he only played one season. During my first season as the Kansas coach, Sean was ruled ineligible as a freshman because the NCAA wouldn't verify a college board score. His sophomore year he could practice, but he couldn't play. But he played a significant role on our team during his junior year. In the NCAA Tournament semifinal against North Carolina, Sean made the basket that clinched the game for us.

The next year he was eligible, but I suspended him for the first semester because I didn't like what he'd done academically. I was just so frustrated with him. I did something I have always fought against as a coach, which is disciplining someone by taking away the one thing that he is successful at. But I took basketball away from Sean. His grades got worse. He left school, got involved with drugs, and landed in jail. Shortly after Sean got out of jail, he was shot and killed in a drug deal gone bad.

Sean's story is the reason that if I think there's any hope, I'll stick with a kid a lot longer than most coaches might, because I'm mad about the way I handled that. Sean was a good kid. At the time I thought I was doing the right thing for him, but now I think, "What if I'd let Sean play and just run him after every practice? Would that have saved his life?"

I'll never stop wishing I could do that one over again.

IN MY THIRD YEAR as an assistant coach at North Carolina, we were playing in the Great Alaska Shootout in Anchorage over Thanksgiving break. I got on the bus for the ride to the airport, and one of the hardest things I have ever had to do was to not get right back off. It killed me that my wife and my two little kids were going to be having Thanksgiving dinner together and I was not going to be there.

That feeling is the reason that every single year since I've been a head coach, Wanda has cooked a Thanksgiving dinner for me and my team. It usually doesn't happen on Thanksgiving Day because most years we are on the road. We do it whenever we can squeeze it into the schedule. One year we had Thanksgiving dinner on New Year's Day.

We like to describe the North Carolina program as a "family," and Wanda and I like to treat it that way. When recruits come on their visits, Wanda will fix breakfast at our house. I remember one Kansas recruit, Greg Ostertag, ate eight waffles with whipped cream and strawberries on top, after feeding on bacon and eggs first.

On the first day of classes each year, our players do a 12-minute run just to see what kind of shape they're in, and we follow that up with dessert at our house. If we're not playing in the final of our conference tournament, Wanda makes brownies and banana pudding and the players come over to watch the NCAA selection show.

My Kansas team celebrated my 200th career win at a Baskin-

Robbins. At the Smith Center after my 500th win, we had a huge cake that barely fit onto the top of a pool table. I shared that with my assistants, my players, the arena maintenance crew, and anybody else I could find.

It is all about enjoying the ride, a change in attitude that I adopted after the devastating loss in the 1997 NCAA Tournament. The legendary Marquette coach Al McGuire once said, "You've got to smell the roses along the way." I have tried to coach myself to do that more. I think I do a much better job of it than I used to.

Sometimes I'll lighten up a hard practice by letting my players run relay races where two guys put their arms around each other's waists and dribble a basketball from one guy's right hand to the other's left hand up and down the court, and they laugh through it like second-graders. Sometimes I'll take the team bowling. One time, after we'd done a clinic for kids, I let my team sing their way out of a practice we'd scheduled afterward. We'll make blooper reels that we run the day after games that show guys falling on their faces or walking off the court toward the wrong locker room. At Kansas in 1998 we began a tradition of bumping around in a mosh pit after big wins, and we still do that today. In 2009 I even agreed to do a television ad for Guitar Hero. First, I had to ask my players what Guitar Hero was. I had never seen the movie *Risky Business*, but when the ad's director pulled out a pair of briefs for me to wear, I told him that was not happening. We compromised on boxers and the other coaches in the ad—Bobby Knight, Mike Krzyzewski, and Rick Pitino—thanked me for that later. It was a hilarious experience.

During my final years at Kansas I'd fly home late at night from a recruiting trip, and on the drive home from the airport, it would often be 15 degrees outside. I would pull the sunroof back, roll down all the windows, crank up the heater, and turn on some soul music as loud as I could. I'd be singing and shimmying around in my seat to the Temptations as I rolled on down the highway.

I had learned to enjoy the ride.

CHAPTER 11

Stealing Brownies

THE NIGHT BEFORE I was going to meet Tyler Hansbrough and his parents for the first time, I left St. Louis around 11 p.m. to drive down to Tyler's hometown. On that trip, I got pulled over for speeding. I had no argument. The policeman took my driver's license back to his car and then walked back to my car, handed me the ticket, and said, "You should not have beaten my Missouri Tigers as many times as you did."

What he said hit me the wrong way. "I'm at North Carolina now," I said, "and if we get this kid I'm going to see down in Poplar Bluff, we're going to beat your butt again."

He was not amused. I started the car, pulled out, and drove no more than 500 yards when I saw the blue flashing lights in my rearview mirror again. I was thinking to myself, "That shows how dumb you are to say something smart-alecky to a cop. Aren't you always telling people, 'Do not pull the tail of the tiger when your head is in his mouth'?"

I knew I wasn't speeding this time, but I pulled over again, and now I was scared to death about what was going to happen. The policeman walked up to my window and said, "I forgot to give you back your rental car agreement."

At that moment, I knew recruiting Tyler Hansbrough was not going to be easy.

The first time I'd ever seen Tyler play was at the Nike All-America camp in Indianapolis the summer before his junior year. I was watching everybody that day, but I kept noticing this 6'9" kid who was running the floor and banging into everybody. I was thinking, "He's not that skilled and he doesn't look pretty, but he plays the way I want a big man to play."

I watched him the rest of that camp. Then I watched him in Orlando at an AAU tournament. I went to see him play three or four times during his high school season and then I made the decision that he was a guy I just had to have.

Once during his junior year, I flew out to watch him during a typical day. He and his teammates lifted weights at 7 a.m., they had a shootaround at 7:30, and then school started at 8. Then they played pickup games at 8 p.m. So I got there early and I watched Tyler lift weights and I watched Tyler at the shootaround, and then his high school's athletic director said, "Coach, what do you want to do the rest of the day?"

I said, "I'm just going to hang around and watch Tyler play pickup tonight."

"You want to go play golf?"

"Sure, I'm in."

So five of the coaches from Tyler's school and I left in the middle of that day to go to the golf course. We played 18 and afterward I said, "Am I going to get all you guys fired?"

One of them said, "No, we talked to the school superintendent and he's mad because he couldn't play with us."

Then we all went and got something to eat, and I went back to watch Tyler play pickup games that night. After the games, I walked up to Tyler's coach, John David Pattillo, and I said, "I can only say hello to Tyler, but can you remind him that when Coach Krzyzewski came here he just watched the pickup games, but I've watched him lift weights, watched him shoot, and then stayed all day and watched the pickup. That's the way I'm going to do it. I'm going to try to outwork everybody."

I thought that was something that might appeal to Tyler because he tries to outwork everybody, too.

In January of his junior year, Tyler came to Chapel Hill for what turned out to be the worst recruiting visit I have ever hosted. I think it was only the second time Tyler had ever been on a plane in his life. He was scared to death of airplanes, and we had a snow and ice storm. He was as shy as he could possibly be and all he was thinking about during his whole visit was how afraid he was on that plane and how he had to get on another plane to go back, and he didn't know when the ice storm would be over. It was very hard to break through his shell. He barely spoke for two days.

At the end of his visit, I drove him to the airport but his flight was canceled. And then the next flight was canceled. Then the airport closed. Tyler was beside himself. He was going to have to stay another night. I took him back to our house and he called his mom and his dad. Wanda fixed him dinner and we ate together in front of a ballgame on television, and I was trying to get him to relax. He said, "Coach, you're treating me like a king."

I said, "I'm just so sorry the travel is bad. At least I want you to feel like we're going to take care of you."

We had to scrape ice off of my car windshield just to get him back to his hotel room so he could sleep. The next morning I took him back to the airport and put him on the plane, and he was really freaked out. I drove back to my office and I told my assistants, "Guys, we tried, but it's not going to happen. There's no way we're getting that kid."

I spoke with Tyler's dad, Gene, the next week and I apologized for the way Tyler's visit had gone. Gene said, "Don't feel badly about it. Maybe we will come back another time and I can see the school with him because I like the way you've recruited him. I love your program. Maybe we need to take another look when you have better weather."

Then one night my friend Mickey Bell called me from St. Louis. "I don't know if you're going to get this Hansbrough kid," he said, "but he had some great things to say about you in the newspaper."

Tyler had said how he loved the personal notes I wrote to him that included some of our Thoughts for the Day. I had been sending him three handwritten notes a week, but after that I started writing even more often.

After Mickey called me, I called the Hansbroughs, and Gene told me, "Coach, I love your notes. We put them up on the refrigerator. It's the only mail that Tyler opens."

Tyler and Gene paid their own way to come for another visit to Chapel Hill during the first week of June. It was great weather. Tyler was a little more comfortable. He played pickup with our guys. Gene told me, "I've really studied the way you play and the way you coach, and I just want you to be his coach. I think this is the best fit for him."

Tyler's recruitment was as intense as any I have ever been involved in. During July I went to see every game he played during the recruiting period. Tyler had visited North Carolina, Kansas, Missouri, and

Kentucky. He had some Missouri boosters sponsoring his AAU team, and I knew he didn't want to hurt their feelings. His dad had gone to Missouri where he was the Big 8 high jump champion. His mother had been Miss Missouri. His dad had told me that he wished I was still the coach at Kansas because the distance was the biggest issue working against us.

In August I went to the 2004 Olympic Games in Greece as an assistant coach for the U.S. basketball team. The day Tyler made his college announcement, I called in from Athens at 5 o'clock in the morning. Coach Holladay told me that Tyler had said he was coming to UNC.

I knew Tyler's decision to come to North Carolina was important to us, but at the time I had no idea just how important it was going to end up being.

WHEN TYLER HANSBROUGH committed to North Carolina, he thought he would be backing up Sean May and Marvin Williams. Then we won the national championship in 2005 and I figured that Marvin would leave for the NBA after his freshman season. Two days after the national championship, I had just returned from a recruiting trip to see Ty Lawson when I got home and Wanda said that Sean May had called. I called Sean right back. "Coach," he said, "I know I told you I was coming back, but my dad and I have talked, and how can my stock get any higher than it is right now?"

I said, "Son, I understand."

I hung up the phone and I felt like somebody had just ripped out my stomach. I knew we were going to lose Marvin and Rashad McCants and Raymond Felton, but I really thought we'd have Sean back. Suddenly we had lost everybody. It put such a damper on things that we couldn't really enjoy the national championship.

At that point there was a controlled panic. We had lost our top seven scorers from the year before. That spring and summer we tried to recruit some more players who could help us that season, but we never did find anybody.

We had signed Tyler, Marcus Ginyard, Danny Green, Bobby Frasor, and Mike Copeland. It was a strong recruiting class, but now we realized we were going to be depending heavily on freshmen. Our starters ended up being Bobby and Marcus and Tyler, along with junior Reyshawn Terry and senior David Noel. David, who was originally recruited as a football player, had averaged 3.9 points per game the year before and he was our leading returning scorer. We knew we would have to build our offense around Tyler, a freshman, getting 20 shots a game. It was one of the few teams I have ever coached that didn't have a target on its back. *Sports Illustrated* didn't even pick us to make the NCAA Tournament.

Before the start of the season, I met with David. "You're going to have to be the greatest leader of all time," I said. "How you play and what you say are going to set the example for what I want everybody else to do." David embraced that challenge and it became David's team. He just let me coach it.

David hit the game-winning shot in our season opener against Gardner-Webb and began the season as the leader I had hoped he could be. But then early in the conference season, we lost consecutive games against Miami and Virginia, and I could tell David was feeling a lot of pressure. He was so stressed out that he was crying in the locker room after the Virginia game. I tried to console him a little bit that night and then I asked him to come visit with me in the office the next day. He came in and he broke down again.

I told him, "David, I know what your problem is. Raymond's in the NBA, Sean's in the NBA, Rashad's in the NBA, Marvin's in the

NBA, and you're not. You're still here. You want to do something like that for your family, too."

David said, "Coach, I just want to buy my mom a house."

"I wanted the same thing and, you know what, I did it," I said. "When I was 34 years old. It took me a while. You're going to be able to do that, too."

That day at practice our players were so tight we couldn't pass, dribble, or catch. Finally, I stopped practice and told them, "Guys, we are good. We don't need to be pressuring ourselves. We're going to be fine."

After that practice, I had a conversation with Reyshawn Terry and Wes Miller, a junior walk-on who had transferred from James Madison. I said, "Guys, this is when the young guys are going to really rely on your help. I need you to step up right now."

In our next game, at Florida State, I put Wes in the starting lineup and he hit six three-pointers to lead our team with 18 points. David sparked us on a second-half comeback and Reyshawn hit two free throws with 23 seconds left to win the game by a point. We would go on to win 10 of our last 12 games in the conference.

In the game at home against Georgia Tech, we fell behind by 13 points at the half. I was furious. My team had less intensity in that game than in any game I've ever coached. We were playing like prima donnas waiting for Georgia Tech to fold. It was a total team breakdown.

During halftime I overturned the Gatorade tray and then I grabbed a trash can and threw it against the wall and garbage flew out all over some of the players. I went absolutely bananas. That was the first time that those freshmen had ever seen that side of me. Maybe it scared them because Tyler was great in the second half. We just kept throwing it to him in the post because they couldn't stop him. He finished with 40 points, an ACC record for a freshman, and we won.

The next day was an off day, and one of our managers came by the office in a full sweat.

"You been getting a workout?" I asked.

He said, "No, I've been rebounding for Tyler. He's just down there shooting like crazy."

"Is he finished?" I said.

"No, he's got another manager."

I went to see Tyler and I said, "Big fella, don't you think you can take a day off?"

He said, "Coach, I missed five free throws last night. I've got to work on that."

I knew I was putting a big burden on Tyler's shoulders with that team. But Tyler had carried that kind of weight with every team he had ever played on and he'd always responded well, and I didn't have any other choice.

In the final game of the regular season, Tyler scored 27 points, including a three-point shot that turned out to be the dagger, and we beat No. 1 Duke on Senior Night in Cameron Indoor Stadium. Nobody thought we could handle J.J. Redick, who had set the ACC scoring record, but he missed 15 of his last 16 shots in his last home game, and we won 83–76. It was a great accomplishment and our guys acted that way in the locker room afterward, jumping around and screaming like little kids.

We wound up with a No. 3 seed in the NCAA Tournament and we met George Mason in the second round. They had a lot of experienced guys and I had a lot of guys who had never been in the NCAA Tournament before. We were out of sync. We couldn't make a shot.

All of a sudden our guys realized that if we didn't win the game our season was over, and the freshmen didn't know how to handle that. They got nervous and we got beat.

I wasn't upset with them. I had more fun coaching that team than any other team in my career, and in some ways I think that may have been my best coaching job. We won 23 games starting a football recruit, a walk-on, a guy who was only second-team All-State in high school, and two freshmen at the point guard and in the post. I think that team came as close to playing to its full potential as any team I have ever coached.

THE 2007 SEASON essentially started with what I call "the headband game." We were getting dressed to play Gonzaga in the semifinals of the Preseason NIT, and a few of our guys put on headbands. It irritated me because they had just decided to do that on their own. I didn't say anything about it because I didn't see quite as clearly before the game why it bothered me as I did during the game and afterward. Gonzaga beat us, and then I told our players, "By God, this is my team and this is the University of North Carolina and we don't wear that crap. Take those damn headbands off and I don't want to see them for the rest of your frickin' college careers." To me, the headbands made them look like individuals and we got beat that night by a better team.

With a significant boost from our freshman class of Ty Lawson, Wayne Ellington, Brandan Wright, and Deon Thompson, we won our next 12 games in a row and climbed to No. 1 in the country. Then we got fat and happy and lost a few games to Virginia Tech, N.C. State, and Maryland. In the last practice before a road trip to Georgia Tech, I didn't like the attitude of my freshman point guard, Ty Lawson. Ty wasn't hustling in the drills. He was just walking around. It was such a low level of effort that I didn't have a choice. I had to do something. Finally, I told him, "Ty, get off the court. As a matter of fact, just go to the locker room. And if you want to leave, just go ahead and leave, because I don't need you to go with me to Georgia Tech."

At the end of practice, I told the other guys, "Fellas, if Ty's on the bus that's fine. If he's not on the bus, that is all right with me."

I really didn't care. Some of my assistants cared and some of the players cared, and they talked Ty into coming to see me after practice.

I said, "Ty, you've got to make a decision. Do you want to be part of this team? Because I'm not going to allow you to just go through the motions."

Ty showed up for the bus to the airport, and when we got to the arena in Atlanta I told him he would not start and he would not be the first substitute at point guard. I played him just 10 minutes and we lost. I think Ty and everybody else on our team got the message that I was willing to move on and coach our team without any single player, no matter how critical he might be.

In the final minute of our Senior Day game at the Smith Center against Duke, Gerald Henderson tried to knock the ball loose from Tyler, but Tyler's nose got in the way. There was blood all over Tyler's face, and we found out later that his nose was broken. I do not believe that Gerald went in there with the intention of hitting Tyler. I think that he was very frustrated, and a lot of times in the heat of the competition, players do something they don't intend to do. Gerald got ejected from the game, and I was dumbfounded by broadcaster Billy Packer's response that Gerald shouldn't have been thrown out. I was upset that some people, including Mike Krzyzewski, said that Gerald was the victim. Tyler was the guy who had his nose broken. That really bothered me, even though I knew Mike was trying to take care of his player.

And I didn't like it in the press conference when it was suggested that we were ahead by so much at that point in the game that I should have already taken Tyler out. Duke's starters were still in the game. The crazy thing is that I had a substitute for Tyler waiting at the scorer's table before the free throw that led to all the commotion. If we hadn't missed the stupid free throw, none of that would have ever happened.

I remember Tyler came back out on the court while we were having our senior speeches. His jersey was all bloody and he had cotton balls stuffed up both nostrils so he looked like this big goofy elephant with tusks sticking out. He said, "Coach, don't I look great?" I had to laugh.

In the following days I was worried about how well Tyler was going to be able to play because he hated the facemask he was forced to wear to protect his nose. We won the ACC Tournament without Tyler being much of a factor. Freshman Brandan Wright led us in scoring in two of the games and won the tournament MVP.

In the second round of the NCAA Tournament, we were playing Michigan State and a few minutes into that game Tyler ripped the mask off because it was driving him crazy. He threw on his cape instead and played like Superman the rest of the game. Tyler scored 33 points and we beat Michigan State.

I remember the night before we played Georgetown in the round of eight, I woke up and looked over at the digital clock in my hotel room and it was 4:44 a.m. "That's a sign," I thought. "We're going to the Final Four."

That had been our goal all year long. We had a 10-point lead on Georgetown with seven minutes left in the game. We brought the ball down the court and Danny Green took one of the worst shots I have ever seen anybody take in a college game, a deep, deep three with no passes. I turned to my assistants and said, "What is he thinking?"

Georgetown then scored, and the next time we came down Reyshawn Terry took another quick outside shot and missed it. Then Georgetown went down and made a three-pointer, and all of a sudden our lead was down to five. Then we got tight and started short-arming our shots. We had the ball for a final shot with the game tied, and though Ty wasn't as aggressive as I wanted him to be, we still got the ball to Wayne Ellington for a pretty good shot. Wayne had knocked down that shot many times, but it didn't go in this time, so we went to overtime. In the overtime we panicked from the beginning and I could never get the guys to calm down. We got beat 96 84.

I felt terrible for our seniors, Reyshawn and Wes Miller, because both of them had come so far in their careers and I desperately wanted to get them to a Final Four.

Our locker room was one of the saddest locker rooms I could ever imagine. Most of the guys were crying and the ones who weren't looked like they were in shock. The cruel part of the NCAA Tournament is the suddenness, the swiftness, the finality of your season, when you lose. Boom and it's over.

I FIRST WENT to the Naismith Basketball Hall of Fame in 1983 when Coach Smith was inducted, and I sat there and thought it was really neat. Then Larry Brown was inducted in 2002 and I went again as part of the traveling party from Kansas. I remember one of the ushers said to me, "Coach, I hope one of these years you'll be in here." That was the first time I ever thought about it.

A couple of days later, I was talking to Coach Smith about Larry Brown's ceremony and he said, "One of these days you'll be in there."

I remember one evening Wanda and I were talking about a letter that somebody had written me that mentioned how someday I'd be a Hall of Fame coach. "You know," I told her, "I don't think I'll ever get there, but it would be a dream of mine."

That's all I ever said about it.

A few days after we won the national championship in 2005, I got a phone call from a friend of mine, Bill Frieder, who used to coach at Michigan. "Congratulations on winning the national championship," Bill said. "There was never any doubt in my mind, but this solidifies it—you're going to be a Hall of Famer."

I still didn't think too much about it. Then, at the end of a North Carolina practice in December 2006, I called everybody in and I was ready to give them some final thoughts from that practice, and Wes Miller said, "Coach, before we do that, we would like to be the first to congratulate you on becoming a finalist for the Hall of Fame."

That was a neat moment.

I knew something about what being a Hall of Fame finalist meant because for two years while I was at Kansas I had been a voter on the Honors Committee. I knew there were 24 people around the country voting and you had to get 18 of their 24 votes to be inducted, and that was difficult to do. I knew Bobby Knight didn't get in the first year he was nominated, so I put the whole issue on the back burner. I really didn't think it would happen. Then one day during the 2007 NCAA Tournament, I received a notice from the Hall of Fame telling me when they would be calling to let me know if I'd been elected.

We lost that Georgetown game, and three days later, my assistant, Jennifer, came into my office to remind me that the Hall of Fame was going to call that day. I had forgotten all about it. I was still pissed off at the world because of how we had lost the Georgetown game. I told Jennifer that I wasn't expecting good news and to close the door behind her on her way out because I didn't want anybody else to hear the phone call. I hadn't mentioned it to my staff because I didn't think I would make it in.

That morning I took a couple of minutes to think about what I was going to say when the call came. I rehearsed it in my head a few times: "I'm fine. I hope to coach a lot longer and I'm just flattered to be nominated and I understand how hard it is to get in. So don't worry about me."

Then the phone rang. John Doleva, the president of the Hall of Fame, said, "Coach, I want to congratulate you. You've been elected to the Naismith Basketball Hall of Fame."

I paused for a few seconds and then said, "Uh . . . wow. John, I had my speech all ready for what I was going to say to you when you told me I didn't make it. Very seldom in my life am I speechless. But I am speechless right now."

As soon as I got off the phone I called Wanda. She was not nearly as surprised as I was. A few minutes later the curiosity was killing Jennifer, so she came in and asked me and I told her I'd gotten in and that the Hall of Fame had asked me not to tell anybody else until the announcement was made over the Final Four weekend. Wanda and I told the kids and that was it.

I remember feeling very flattered, but honestly, it didn't take away the pain of the Georgetown game. That loss did not suddenly evaporate. At breakfast the next morning, I said to Wanda, "It's great getting into the Hall of Fame, but I would trade it for one more basket against Georgetown."

Wanda said, "That's the dumbest thing I've ever heard. There are going to be other Georgetowns."

I said, "Not for Reyshawn Terry."

We flew to the Final Four in Atlanta and the announcement was scheduled to be on Sunday night. On Saturday night I had dinner with my current and former assistants, something I try to do every year to catch up with everybody. At the end of that dinner, we were all out on the sidewalk and I told the group, "Hey, I need you all to keep this quiet, but I wanted you to hear it from me. I've been elected to the Hall of Fame. I want you to know from the bottom of my heart that I wouldn't be getting this honor if it wasn't for all of you. Thank you."

Then I called Coach Smith and Buddy Baldwin and told them both the same thing: "You are responsible for me being there."

That was in April and the ceremony was in September. I asked Jerod Haase, who I'd hired to be part of my staff at UNC, to handle requests from anybody who might call saying they wanted to come.

Twenty-two of my former players showed up. During a cocktail party before the ceremony, Wayne Simien walked up to me with this big grin on his face and we hugged, then separated for a moment, then bear-hugged again. Within two seconds I was so emotional I could barely speak because Wayne was one of the players I'd left behind at Kansas, the player who'd said, "I gave my right arm for that man." I told Wayne, "Young man, you have no idea how much this means to me for you to be here. Thank you for coming."

Wayne said, "Coach, I really wanted to be here. You'll always be my coach. You're like a second father to me."

It was one of the most satisfying feelings I'd ever had, but it was mixed with a little bit of sadness because I knew I had hurt that kid.

My Hall of Fame speech was only the third speech I have ever prepared in my life. The other two were for Roberson High School graduations. The hardest part about delivering the speech was being able to get through it without breaking down, particularly when I talked about my family and my former players. I thanked every player and coach by name who had come there to support me and then I thanked Coach Smith and said I hoped he would see the night as a tribute to him.

Mickey Bell told me before the speech that he had a bet with Coach Smith that I would start crying. I said, "Mickey, I've always wanted to beat you at everything." So I didn't cry that night.

A few people asked me for autographs afterward and wanted me to include an "HOF" for Hall of Famer. I wouldn't do it. I still wasn't comfortable with the idea. I think part of me was still afraid that somebody was going to call me and tell me that they'd counted the votes wrong.

We had a little private party after the ceremony, and when it was over, Wanda and I went upstairs. "You know, this is still hard to believe," I said.

I have to admit that the ceremony did scare me a little bit. I sort of felt like my life was about done because that was the biggest honor I could possibly get. I had to keep reminding myself, "Gosh, it's not all over with. You get to keep coaching."

So AFTER THAT, I went right back to coaching, because that's where the real joy is. I love playing road games. I love that atmosphere. I encourage my players to treat games away from home as a wonderful challenge. I like to tell my team, "Let's go into their living room and steal their brownies."

It's all about having the confidence and attitude that I can beat your butt anytime, anywhere, anyplace, anyhow. Coach Smith once told me that on the road he thought his team should play a little slower tempo, play a little more zone, be a little more conservative. There are very few things that I have ever disagreed with him about, but this is one. I want to attack your rear end even more at your place. I'm

going to show you that I don't care how many people are in the stands
screaming against us—we're coming after you. We'll shut them up.
We'll listen to them get quiet. I don't know if there's any better sound
than at the end of a road game when you hear that silence.

Our 2008 team never lost a game on the road. We won games at
Ohio State and Kentucky. We won by a point at Georgia Tech and
Virginia. We trailed by seven with less than three minutes to play
at Clemson and won the game in overtime on a three-pointer by
Wayne Ellington with less than a second left. We beat Florida State
in Tallahassee in overtime even after losing Ty Lawson to a sprained
ankle early in the first half. We came back from 18 points down in
the second half to win at Boston College, and we scored the last 10
points of the game to beat Duke in Cameron Indoor Stadium on
their Senior Night.

That's a lot of brownies.

We did lose two games at home that season, but we made it to the
Final Four brimming with confidence. Ty and Wayne were a dynamic
combination in the backcourt all season and Tyler was on his way to
winning the National Player of the Year award. I remember walking out to the court during the warm-ups before our semifinal game
against Kansas, and I believed that we were going to play great.

We got the opening tip and on our first possession our guys did
one of the things that we told them in the pregame they could not do.
Wayne tried to dribble the ball casually through the seam between
two perimeter defenders, and Kansas stole the ball and went right
down the court to score. We had also said in the pregame that we've
got to push the ball up the floor on every possession to attack their
defense before they got set, but after Kansas scored, Ty walked the
ball slowly up the court. The other thing we said that we could not
do was have our big men bring the ball down low and take a care-

less dribble. On our second possession, Deon Thompson brought the ball down and Kansas stole it from him and went down and scored. Then we walked it up the court again. We got to the first television timeout and I said, "Guys, we fought so hard to get here. Let's not tiptoe through the tulips. We've got to play."

Apart from what was going on in the game, I felt sick. I was sweating. I just felt awful. I was yelling at them during timeouts, and then I'd stand back up and I'd get really dizzy and have to grab the chair to keep from falling down. At one point in the game I turned to Coach Robinson and told him to call a play, because I couldn't. I could barely frickin' stand up. Someone gave me a towel and I was throwing up into the towel during the first half, and the way we were playing was making me even sicker. The sweat was just rolling down my forehead as we were just getting killed. Darrell Arthur and Brandon Rush were scoring at will and Cole Aldrich was blocking a bunch of shots for them on the defensive end. Kansas made 12 of its first 16 shots and scored 18 points in a row. At one point we fell behind 40–12.

As we walked off the court at halftime, we'd cut their lead to 17. I was mad, but I still believed we were going to win the game. I remembered back to the 2003 NCAA final when my Kansas team had been down 18 in the first half against Syracuse and we came back to have a three-point shot to tie the game at the end. In the locker room I reminded the players about how we had been behind Boston College by 14 points at halftime that season and we'd come back to win. I told them I thought we could do it again.

We came back out and made a run. We took better shots, we took better care of the basketball, we attacked them more instead of reacting so much to what they were doing, and eventually we cut their lead down to five points with about eight minutes left. Then Danny Green shot a three-pointer from right in front of our bench that could have cut the lead to two, but it rattled around and popped back out. We never got closer than that. It felt like we were the Little Engine That Could, but we just couldn't seem to climb to the top of the mountain. It wasn't until there were two minutes left in the game that I finally thought to myself, "Gosh, we're not going to be able to get this done."

It was such a sinking feeling. It felt like somebody reached in and grabbed my heart and shook it in front of my face. It was one of the most miserable nights of my career.

After the game I was criticized for not calling more timeouts when we fell way behind in the first half, but there were six timeouts in that half, and after each one, when we would leave the huddle, our guys did exactly the opposite of what I'd just asked them to do. We were like punch-drunk boxers who couldn't clear the cobwebs. In fact, after one timeout when we went out and made the same mistake I'd just been yelling about, I remember turning to one of my assistants and saying, "Boy, what good does it do us to have a timeout if they're not going to listen to us?"

I didn't sleep that night. That next morning, the first day that there's no practice and no game, is a terrible day. I felt lost. I also still felt very sick. I never left the hotel room and I was in the bathroom all the time. I lost six pounds in two days.

I normally don't go to the NCAA championship game if my team is not playing in it, but Scott and Kimmie had flown in for the Final Four, so I took them to the game on Monday night. I was pulling for Kansas. Two of my former players, Michael Lee and Brett Ballard, were now Kansas assistant coaches, and I wanted to support them. When we arrived at the arena we started down the steps to our seats and I saw another of my former Kansas players, Ryan Robertson, and he hugged me and said, "Coach, I'm glad Kansas is in the final, but I was pulling for you Saturday night."

That meant a lot to me. I was talking to Ryan, and this guy with him—I don't know who it was—gave me a Jayhawks sticker. Then Ryan said, "Coach, pull us through tonight."

We found our seats and I took the backing off the sticker and put it on my shirt. I didn't think anything about it. Next thing I knew, my picture was up on the video board. At halftime I did an interview with CBS, and they asked me about the sticker. I told them I didn't think it was a big deal because I coached at Kansas for 15 years, so of course I was pulling for the Jayhawks.

I forgot about it, until the next day when there was such a fury over the sticker. I didn't understand it at all. I just thought it was so unfair the way I was ripped. At the game, I was sitting in the North Carolina section with Wayne Ellington's family and in the row behind me were eight alums from the University of North Carolina, but the next day all I heard about was how I was sitting in the Kansas section. One reporter wrote a story suggesting that part of the reason we lost to Kansas was because I had said that I never wanted to play against my former team. That was such a silly statement to make.

A few weeks later I was at a North Carolina booster club meeting in Greensboro and I was very aggressive, very abrasive about the whole issue. I said, "Before I take any questions, I want to tell you folks something. In 1993 I was coaching at Kansas and we lost to North Carolina in the NCAA semifinal and I stayed for the final to watch Coach Smith win his second NCAA title. I stood there in the stands waving a Carolina Blue pom-pom all night. This year I was coaching North Carolina and we lost to Kansas in the semifinals and I stayed to cheer for Kansas in the final and wore a Kansas sticker. Why are people so mad about the sticker? What is the difference?"

When I finished, they gave me a standing ovation.

That Kansas game will eat at me for the rest of my career. Playing so poorly was bad enough, but playing so poorly against the team I coached for 15 years made it even worse. I wanted to win that game more than any game I have ever coached. I wish I could have figured out something else for our team to do, but looking back at it, I don't know what I could have done. Watching us play felt like a nightmare. I still to this day have not watched a tape of that Kansas game, and I probably never will.

THE NEXT GAME we played included a new player. A 6'2" guard named Barack Obama.

At the end of April I was on the road recruiting and I got a call telling me that Senator Obama's people had asked if he could play pickup with our team the morning after a campaign speech in the Smith Center. I thought it would be a great experience for my players.

At 6:45 a.m. the Secret Service cars pulled into the tunnel below the Smith Center and Senator Obama got out already dressed in his sweats and ready for a game. I gave him a quick tour of the arena and our locker room. He laughed with my staff about how he'd picked us to win in his NCAA Tournament pool and we'd let him down. We talked for a few more minutes, and I told him that I knew his former coach at Punahou School in Hawaii, Chris McLaughlin, because I had practiced my Kansas teams at that school during the Rainbow Classic. He was amused that we had that common ground.

We walked into our practice gym and our guys all had a chance to shake his hand, and then I asked them to pick teams. Senator Obama had more savvy than he did game, which I think is the right ratio for a president to have. He understood how to play the game, but he also had a little street in him. He could run the pick and roll. He could make a bounce pass off the dribble.

At one point he drove the ball to the basket right at Tyler. Our guys didn't go too easy on him. I remember one of our walk-ons, Jack Wooten, blocked the senator's shot and fouled him. Senator Obama told Jack, "Don't worry. The Secret Service won't do anything to you."

Later in that game, I called Marcus Ginyard over and I said, "Son, you know, you have a presidential candidate on your team. You may want to pass him the ball." After that, I think Marcus passed him the ball every time he touched it.

After the game, Senator Obama took a picture with all of us, and our guys told him how much they enjoyed the chance to play with him. Right after the workout, Marcus put up a sign in our locker room reminding everybody to register to vote.

A week later, I received a handwritten note from Senator Obama.

Coach Williams,

I wanted to drop you a quick note to say how much I enjoyed my visit to the Dean Dome. You and your team could not have been more gracious hosts and having the chance to scrimmage with the team (even if I didn't belong on the same court with them) was one of the highlights of the year. I was especially impressed with the attitudes and conduct of the young men you coach. It is testament to their character, their parents and the type of program you are running. Congratulations on all of your success and please pass on my regards to your team (as well as Happy Mother's Day to your wife).

Sincerely, Barack Obama

I can count on one finger the number of thank-you notes I've gotten from people getting ready to be president of the United States.

He earned my vote because I liked the fact that he was enjoying the ride. I'm not somebody who thinks you have to be president every moment of your life. I liked that he was interested enough in college basketball to be a fan. I liked that he filled out his NCAA brackets and I thought it was pretty neat that he'd picked us to win.

I wondered if he would do it again.

CHAPTER 12

Stress Relief

IN OUR LOCKER ROOM after losing at Wake Forest on January 11, 2009, I did what I have always done. I drew from my past.

I turned to Coach Robinson and said, "Coach, do you remember the 1991 season at Kansas?"

Coach Robinson's eyes got real big because he didn't know what I was doing, but he said, "Yes."

"Do you remember how our Kansas team started out that '91 season in the conference?"

"Isn't that the year we started out 0–2?"

"Exactly right, Coach. That's very good. Do you remember how we finished in the conference that year?"

"We finished first."

"Do you remember how we ended that season?"

"We played for the national championship."

"That's right. So, guys, we've been through this before. I've been through this before. Coach Robinson has been through this before. We've been 0–2 before and played for the national title. The season is not over. This is just a little bit of a challenge. So just follow along. Just do what we tell you to do and things will be fine. Guys, this game was extremely disappointing and we've got to play better, but my gosh we stunk it up and we still had a chance to win the dadgum game. This is just as much my fault as it is yours. I apologize and I've got to get better. But we're going to be all right, you've got to trust that. You've got to believe that. Do you believe that?

"What were our goals? Was our goal to beat Wake Forest? No. Our goal is to win the regular season championship and then our goal is to win the national championship. We haven't lost those opportunities. We can still reach our dreams."

I got a sense from each player that they were thinking, "Okay, huh, I guess we are all right."

Then I told them, "Let's keep this conversation in our locker room. Let's keep this to ourselves. But if you do what we ask you to do, I promise you we'll have a chance to be there at the end."

Pacing around the coaches' locker room a few minutes earlier, I had remembered how I felt when my 1991 Kansas team lost to Oklahoma State to fall to 0–2 in the Big 8. I remembered how at our coaches' meeting after that game I'd thrown a clipboard up against the wall in my hotel room in Stillwater, Oklahoma, and told my staff, "You guys get the hell out of here, I'll figure it out myself." But I also remembered how I'd decided that with the players I was going to be extremely positive and how well they'd reacted to that.

So that's what I did with my North Carolina team. I was going to do everything I could to make sure that they didn't fall off the cliff. Showing confidence in them was more important to that team than any team I have ever coached because of the high expectations they were facing. I didn't want panic to be an option. I had to keep saying we were going to be fine.

A coach can sometimes manipulate what his players think. I think we all try to convince our teams of something that isn't exactly right when we need to. But that night I believed everything I said and I wanted to help frame their opinion. Walking out of the arena that night, I said a little prayer to myself, "Lord, please let these kids realize that their dreams and goals are realistic. Amen."

On the bus ride home I watched the game tape. It reinforced for me that we had played very poorly and made a lot of silly mistakes. It gave me hope because I thought our mistakes were easy to correct. I was ticked off, as I always am, about losing, ticked off that we didn't show Wake Forest that we could stand up to them at their best. But I also felt pretty doggone good because I really didn't feel that anybody else would make us play as badly as Wake did that night.

I knew we were a good team. Tyler and Ty and Wayne were our three stars and Danny Green had already hit some huge baskets for us that season after stepping in for the injured Marcus Ginyard.

Before practice the next day, I asked myself, "As a player, what would I be thinking?" I can sense when my team is expecting to get hammered by me and sometimes I will fulfill their expectations, but I think that resorting to screaming and yelling at them shows a lack of confidence, not only in them but in myself. How can I expect players to be as good as I want them to be if I'm not doing the best that I can? I treated that practice as "get better," not "get even." I sensed they were going to have a great practice and they did. They were very attentive to doing things the right way and they saw better results when they took better shots. We showed them two hours of tape from the Wake Forest game. I kept asking them, "Isn't it easy to change that? All right, then let's change it."

As a coach, you always fear that if you tell your players what you expect to happen and the results are the opposite of what you said they'd be, you've lost credibility. I knew that if we laid an egg in our next game, I could lose some of their trust.

Fortunately, we won our next game at Virginia, but Wayne continued to struggle with his jump shot as he had all season. I knew I needed to figure out some way to help him get his confidence back. Before our next game, we shot videotape of Wayne's jump shot from every angle to check on his form. We sat him in a chair in the free-throw lane and had him taking one-handed shots to work on getting full extension and follow-through without getting his opposite hand involved. I knew he was thinking too much, so I reminded him to try to lose himself in the game and then I remember saying, "Keep shooting. You just need to have one of those games when you hit three or four in a row and you'll be fine."

In our next game against Miami, Wayne missed both shots he tried in the first half and he didn't score a single point. Then all of a sudden in the second half, he hit eight shots in a row. Seven of those were three-pointers. After the win, Wayne had this huge grin on his face and he told me he'd found his shot.

Two games later at Florida State, Tyler had his worst game of the season. He didn't shoot well, he got in foul trouble, and his 55-game streak scoring in double figures was broken. The game was tied with three seconds to go. I called a play with Tyler inbounding the ball to the midcourt line. "What if that's not open?" Tyler asked.

"Then just give it to Ty and he'll make a play."

Tyler gave my original play about one-tenth of a second to materialize and then he threw it to Ty, and Ty dribbled down the court and floated one up and won the game at the buzzer. It had been a miserable night for Tyler, but he showed what a great teammate he was by being the first guy to bear-hug Ty after he won that game for us. Tyler couldn't care less that his streak had ended as long as we won.

In early February we took our annual bus ride to Cameron Indoor Stadium to play Duke. The talk in the media was all about how Tyler and our other seniors couldn't possibly win all four of their games at Cameron, but I've always thought that being the underdog is a great position to be in if you're really good. In the postgame locker room after our previous game, I had told the team, "You know, guys, we probably can't beat Duke four years in a row over there. All those experts, they must be right. It'd be really hard to do that. But you know what? There's only one team in America that could do that and that's the guys sitting right here in this room. Nobody else in America could go there and win this game, but we can. So from tonight until we play them, let's think about how good this is going to feel when we beat Duke for the fourth straight time in their own gym."

We helped Duke defend us in the first half by clogging up the lane. But at halftime I went to the dry-erase board and drew our five positions, showing everybody where to go to open up some lanes for Ty to drive his man. I knew they couldn't guard Ty if we didn't help them. Ty drove to the basket over and over and scored 21 points in the second half, and sure enough, we beat Duke again.

We had won 10 games in a row since the loss at Wake Forest when we played at Maryland. It should have been 11 straight. We led by nine points with less than two minutes left when we went totally brain dead. We turned the ball over. We took stupid shots. We had to make five dumb plays in a row to give them any chance to win, and we made all five. We lost by three.

In the locker room I waited for a couple of minutes to let them think about it and then I went in there and ripped them pretty hard because we'd screwed up. I said, "I am really pissed. You know, part of this is my fault. If we had practiced late-game situations more, perhaps we wouldn't take stupid shots. Perhaps we wouldn't have panicked. Perhaps we wouldn't have turned the ball over stupidly in the backcourt. I'll take responsibility for that. Guys, if we had taken four shot-clock violations on our last four possessions we would've won the frickin' game."

At practice the next day I made them watch the whole Maryland game tape. That was really hard for them to sit there with me winding the tape back and forth, telling them how stupid this play was, how stupid that play was, how little effort we put in on another play. They had ticked me off, and I wanted them to know it. We sat there for nearly three hours watching tape and then we practiced for an hour and it was vicious. I think they got the message.

Before our Senior Day game against Duke, I put a lot of pressure on our underclassmen. I told freshman Ed Davis, "Tyler Hansbrough is going to go out the right way as a senior. It is your responsibility." I told freshman Larry Drew, "Bobby Frasor's going to go out the right way and if he doesn't, I'm going to be mad at you." I went on down the line. I was scared stiff that we would be so tight that we couldn't play. Then two days before the game, Ty jammed his toe in practice. It was swollen, so our doctors gave him a cortisone shot to relieve the pain.

We didn't know whether Ty was going to play until right before the game, and then he really struggled in the first half. At the end of halftime, as we were walking back out to the court, I grabbed Ty and I said, "Hey, put that half behind you and play your tail off in this half." Ty finished the game with 13 points, eight rebounds, and nine assists, and he made a key three-point play down the stretch, and we won the game and the ACC regular season championship. Ty would be voted the conference Player of the Year.

After the game the cortisone shot began to wear off and Ty told me he was really hurting. He left the gym with his dad and his dad suggested he try some Epsom salt and hot water. That was about the worst idea you could have. Ty's toe swelled up the size of a lemon.

I wanted to win a national championship more than I wanted to breathe, but I was not going to let Ty Lawson have another cortisone shot. Managing his injury reminded me of the way I felt at the beginning of the season with Tyler's shin. I worried about Ty every day at practice and I decided to sit him out of the ACC Tournament. We played Florida State in the semifinals and we got beat. I tried to reassure everybody in the locker room after that loss by telling them I'd been to the Final Four six times in my career and five of those six times my team had lost in the conference tournament.

President Obama picked us to win the NCAA Tournament again and it was broadcast everywhere. That was fine with me, because I couldn't possibly have felt more pressure than I already did going into the tournament.

I decided we could afford to sit Ty in our NCAA opener against Radford, but we played him in the next game against LSU. At one point in the first half, though, Ty's foot got bumped and he felt something pop in his toe. He limped to our bench and said, "Coach, you've got to get me out."

I thought he was done for the game, but he went back in a few minutes later. I could tell he was struggling to trust what he could do on the court. It was the same scenario as on Senior Day, because as we were walking back out after halftime, I grabbed Ty and said, "Remember, against Duke you didn't do too much in the first half, but you were great in the second half. Put that first half behind you. Son, we need you to be great this half."

We quickly fell behind by four points early in the second half, and at a timeout I walked into our huddle and barked at our seniors, "Is this how you want your careers to end? Then keep playing like this."

From that moment on, Ty had one of the best performances of any point guard I have ever coached. The very next possession, Ty made an unbelievable layup and there was a lot of chest bumping going on, and all of a sudden our team was feeling confident again. Ty attacked the rim every possession, and we were running and pushing the ball and LSU was having trouble getting back in time to keep Ty in front of them. Ty loaded everybody up on his back and won the game for us.

We normally don't like to make major changes in the middle of the NCAA Tournament, because in the past if we changed anything it really screwed things up. But against Gonzaga in the round of 16 game I thought we needed to make a change from how we had played ball screens all season. Their attack was to set a screen with one of their big guys, who would look for a pass cutting to the basket. We normally have our big guy step out and hedge, but that game, we decided to squeeze and go under, and our guys adapted to that idea very well. We shut down their favorite option and Ty scored 17 points in the first half. We won easily, 98–77.

Then we were playing Oklahoma and Blake Griffin, the guy who had the best season of anybody in the country. Again we made a major defensive adjustment. I decided to double-down on Griffin as soon as it was passed to him in the post. We had about 15 minutes during our one day of practice before the Oklahoma game to teach our guys when to double-team Griffin and then how to rotate to the open man. Our players did a great job of it. For much of the game, Griffin passed the ball out of the double-team and Oklahoma missed its first 15 shots from three-point range. We won 72–60. After the game I told our guys that I'd never seen a bad defensive team win a national title, and I thought we'd won our last two games with our defense. In the locker room that day the guys were so excited, but right before I walked out, I said, "Remember, we were here last year."

I said it again right before the NCAA semifinal against Villanova. I never mentioned the word *Kansas* because I thought that could bring back bad memories, but I repeated, "Remember, we were here last year." I also told them we should win the game because we were bigger and better than them. Reversing what had happened a year earlier, we jumped out to a 40–23 lead with Tyler outmuscling their smaller post players inside and then passing the ball out to open shooters when he got double-teamed. Tyler finished with 18 points and 11 rebounds, while Ty scored 22 points and Wayne had 20, and we won the game pretty easily.

After our game, I watched a tape of the other semifinal three different times, and I was surprised by how easily Michigan State beat Connecticut. I was happy, because I thought playing Michigan State would be great for us psychologically. I was thinking, "Hey, we beat the crap out of them earlier in the season, we can beat the crap out of them again."

In 2005 designer Alexander Julian had sent me a lucky suit to wear in the NCAA Tournament. I had worn it in the second game, the fourth game, and in the NCAA final, and we won the championship. He sent me another suit before the 2009 tournament, and I'd worn it in the second game and the fourth game. You bet I was wearing that suit for the championship game.

In our locker room before the game I said, "We're going to attack. We're not going to back down. We're going to attack and attack and attack. They're saying we can't beat them again because we beat them by 35. Hey, we can beat them worse. We can beat them by 45. We're better than they are. They say that Michigan State winning is going to fix the nation's economy—well then, I say, hell, let's stay poor a while longer. All of that stuff is B.S. This is a basketball game. That's all it is. We are better than they are. Now let's go play. Tonight somebody is going to win the national championship. Why not let it be us?"

The Temptations sang the national anthem. They are my favorite singing group, so I figured that was a good omen. Then Magic Johnson and Larry Bird were at center court for a ceremony. Magic, of course, played on a national championship team at Michigan State, and when he came off the floor he shook my hand and I said, "I know where your allegiance lies, but I appreciate you being here." Then I saw Larry and he whispered to me, "I really want you to kick their ass because I want to be able to talk junk to Magic."

In the first half of that game, I have never seen a team so driven by attitude. We played with such confidence. We played as aggressively as we could early and hit our shots and took their huge home crowd right out of the game. Wayne hit three three-point shots early and scored 17 points in the first half and we built the lead to 40–20 late in the half, but during timeouts I kept asking them not to focus on the score. The key factor in the game was Michigan State's turnovers and how we converted them quickly into points. Ty had seven steals at the half and our defense caused 14 turnovers. When I walked off the floor at halftime, I looked at the scoreboard and saw we were up by 21 points and I was mad because we'd played so great that I thought it should have been more. It wasn't a perfect half, but for a national championship game, it was pretty doggone close.

At halftime I said, "Guys, last year we were down 28 and did we not get it down to five and Danny had a shot go in and out that could have cut it to two? These guys could do the same thing. They can come back. Unless we don't let them."

I told our guys to keep attacking, but it did no good because in the second half our players couldn't stop watching the scoreboard. The whole half we were tentative, but we were playing so hard defensively that Michigan State could never cut our lead down to less than 13 points. We still had a comfortable margin with a minute to go, so I motioned to put in our last five guys on the bench.

All of a sudden Tyler was standing in front of me with the most amazing look on his face. It was pure, *pure* joy. At that moment, I realized how much winning that game meant to me. Tyler bear-hugged me and almost knocked me over and it was like Sean May in 2005 hugging me all over again. When he hugged me, it was the first time I actually realized we were going to win the national championship. Up until that moment, I hadn't had that thought. I was just coaching.

After the game I was in a daze. Again it reminded me of 2005. After we cut down the first net, I walked over to Tyler and we stood in front of the family section and I presented it to him. From the very beginning of the season, I had thought Tyler winning a national championship was the right thing to happen. I told him, "To me this is fitting, son. I want you to know that I will never, ever forget for the rest of my life being able to coach you."

The team then gathered for "One Shining Moment," the annual montage of highlights from the tournament that is shown up on the video board inside the arena. Watching that as the NCAA champion is the greatest time a coach can have. That's what you dream about. That's what every one of the recruiting trips, every one of the practices, every night you stay up late watching film, is all about. I remember watching the highlights and peeking over at Wayne, and he was crying, and I broke down and put my face in my hand. That's what I coach for.

Back in the locker room I stood at the dry-erase board and I said,

"We started with 64 teams and you divide by two how many are left?

They all shouted, "Thirty-two!"

"You divide that by two how many are left?"

"Sixteen!"

"Divide by two?"

"Eight!"

"Divide by two?"

"Four!"

"Divide by two?"

"Two!"

"Divide by two?"

"One!"

And I wrote a big 1 on the board. The players were all screaming. They really got into it. When the room fell quiet, I told them, "Fifty years from now, when they have another reunion in 2059, that night when you go out on the court, at 72 years old, you go out there and remember one thing, that no coach has ever felt more privileged, no coach has ever felt more proud of a team that handled things like you did. The adversity, the injuries, other people's expectations. I honestly feel like I'm the luckiest coach that has ever lived . . . I love you."

At the press conference after the game I said, "You can choose to believe it or not. I wanted this championship for Roy Williams, yes, and I'm extremely satisfied, but I so badly wanted this championship for Tyler Hansbrough. I know that's corny, but hello Pete, that's who I am. If you put $10 million in a pile right there and say, 'Roy, you can have that $10 million, but if you take it you'll forget that feeling you had when that big rascal came over and hugged you.' Well, you can have that $10 million. I wouldn't give $10 million for the feeling that I had at that moment."

I also shared what I'd said to our team after the Wake Forest game when we were 0–2 in the ACC. I truly believe that as a coach, that was the wisest thing I have ever done. That was a critical moment for getting our kids to believe that if they would just do what I asked them to do, we would be there at the end. I believed it. I think the kids believed it. In my view, that moment is the reason we were able to win the national championship. Who knows? My players may not even remember it.

TWO MONTHS AFTER the championship game, Coach Robinson and I were on a recruiting trip driving from Cincinnati to Cleveland and he asked me, "Do you think there's been the same excitement after the national title this year as there was in '05?"

I said, "Wanda and I have been talking about that very thing. We don't think so."

"Coach, I don't feel like it's been anything like it was in '05 and I talked to Coach Holladay and he feels the same way."

I said, "You know, back then the program was three years away from 8–20 and we were a little bit of the underdog because Illinois was the perfect team, and everybody thought we had all the talent but not the team. We surprised people a little bit. Maybe that was it. This year the expectations—"

Coach Robinson interrupted me and said, "Yeah, so just because we were expected to win it, people don't get excited by it? Everybody just says, 'Well, ho hum, they were the best team and they just did what they were supposed to do?'"

I started thinking about it more, and I realized that the level of euphoria from our alumni and fans just wasn't the same after the 2009 championship as it had been in 2005. I never want us to be spoiled. I don't want our fans to ever think we're supposed to win a national championship. That's a terrible feeling to have. In the 1980s I can remember Coach Smith saying, "What we need to do around here is go 8–20 one year to get people to appreciate what we do accomplish." It was extremely coincidental that he picked that record.

When we got back to our hotel after the 2009 championship, it wasn't the mob scene it had been in St. Louis in 2005. When I got home in '05, there were signs in my yard. That didn't happen in '09. When we got back to Chapel Hill the day after the '05 championship, everybody was so excited that people were still hugging each other. When we got back in '09, people weren't hugging each other anymore.

The best part for me is that to our 17 players it was the biggest thing that's ever been, and for our students it's a memory they'll treasure forever. That's who we should be coaching for anyway. To me, the 2009 title may be even sweeter than the one in '05 because of all the pressure I felt over the expectations before the season. Winning it all in '09 was a more satisfying accomplishment because of all the adversity we had. It was the hardest year I have ever had in coaching. Bobby Knight sent me a letter after the '09 season that said, "I want you to know what a great accomplishment that is to win the national championship when everybody says that's what you're supposed to do. You're the biggest target. You're the biggest game on everybody's schedule and if you think about it, the only way you can be successful is to win the national title."

I think we as coaches savored the 2009 championship more. Before the '09 national title game, Coach Robinson put a Ziploc sandwich bag in his pocket. When we won, he scooped some confetti off the floor to keep as a souvenir. I know I worked harder to enjoy it in '09. In '05 I started back recruiting on Wednesday after the championship. In '09 I gave myself until Thursday. We didn't go to the White

House in '05, but we did in '09 and I loved it when President Obama said, "Thanks for salvaging my bracket and vindicating me before the entire nation." I remember one morning I just sat back for a few minutes and looked over some of the stats from the championship game just to relive it a little bit.

In 2005 I didn't watch the championship game tape until the end of September. This year at the beach one night in June, I put in the tape. I watched the first half with my family and then I saved the rest. A few nights later, I was at my office late one night when everybody else was gone and I pulled up a chair and put the tape in and watched the second half. At first I was frustrated watching it, which seems weird, but I had the exact same feelings that I had during the game. I was coaching the game again. I was asking myself, "Why are we so tentative? Why aren't we more aggressive?" For some reason I couldn't tell myself, "Relax, you're going to win this game by 17." When it got to the end, I watched Tyler hug me and I got a little choked up and I had the same surprised feeling like, "By golly, we won the sucker."

CHAPTER 13

The 19th Hole

IN 1984 NORTH CAROLINA was playing in a tournament in
Tokyo and we played Arizona State in the last game on December 23. I asked Coach Smith if I could fly home and then
join the team again before our next game. He said I could and he
arranged for the program to pay for it because I couldn't afford the
trip. As soon as that game ended, Wanda had our bags packed and
we left out the back door of the arena and took a cab to the airport.
We flew from Tokyo to Seattle, and it was the most turbulent flight I
have been on in my entire life. That 747 bounced around like it was a
paper airplane. I saw somebody's drink bounce from two rows behind
me to two rows in front of me. Wanda squeezed my hand harder than
she ever has before or since. I was scared to death and we were both
about sick. We landed in Seattle, then flew from Seattle to Chicago,
then from Chicago to Charlotte, and finally to Asheville, so I could
spend Christmas Eve and Christmas Day with my children. On
December 26 I was on a 7 a.m. flight from Asheville to Atlanta,

then Atlanta to Los Angeles, and Los Angeles to Hawaii. I landed in Honolulu and I went straight to the gym with my luggage. I took off my dress shoes, put on my sneakers, and started working a team practice. People who were traveling with the team couldn't believe what I'd just done, but it's just what I wanted to do. It was worth it.

I have never been with my family as much as I wanted to be. Because of that, when my kids were growing up they never saw me taking a nap. Never. If they came in and I happened to be on the couch, I got up and I stayed up. Whatever they were doing, I wanted to do it with them.

Whenever I was home I would bathe them and I loved reading to them at night. I must have read *Goodnight Moon* 8,000 times. When they had their Little League games or their track meets, I tried to be there to watch them whenever I could. Because of what had happened when I was a kid, I wanted to make sure my children knew I was there for them.

Two years after I was hired at North Carolina in 1978, the NCAA changed the rules to say that the part-time assistant couldn't recruit. So for nearly six years I didn't recruit, and it almost killed me because those recruiting trips were where I thought I was making my biggest contribution. But looking back on it now, I realize it was a blessing, because it gave me a chance to be with Scott and Kimmie more when they were little kids.

Lots of nights I'd go home at 5 o'clock, and Wanda and I would get on our bicycles and put Scotty on the back of mine and Kimmie on the back of Wanda's and ride down to the neighborhood swimming pool. I wanted my kids to be able to swim better than I could. We had them taking lessons and they became good swimmers. The first time Scotty swam the whole length of the pool, I was thinking, "God, I hope he doesn't ask me to do that." I liked to get Kimmie to swim to me and then I'd back up a little bit more and back up a little bit more until she'd start giggling.

I remember the little things. Some good and some bad. We had a yellow jacket nest in the ground in our yard and one day those bees got all over both kids and they ran screaming to me. I was knocking bees off of them as fast as I could, but they both got stung a few times. Within five minutes, after I knew the kids were all right, I took a can of gas and poured several gallons down that hole. Then I lit a match and I blew that nest up so hard I could have killed a million bees, but I was going to make sure that none of them ever hurt my kids again.

Once Kimmie and I were at one of Scotty's baseball games. She was standing in front of me and I had my arms around her right at her chin. Scotty made a good play and I started clapping right in front of her face and I hit her. She had a loose tooth and I knocked her tooth right out, and for years she joked that I should be charged with child abuse.

I tried to be a good father in any way I could. One day Scotty asked me to teach him to field ground balls a little better, so we went out to practice. I was hitting balls to him and one of them took a bad hop and missed his glove and hit his finger. It turned it completely sideways and dislocated it. He came running to show it to me and he was really nervous, and I popped it back into place. I know doctors say you shouldn't do that, but that was my son.

Those kinds of memories mean so much because as kids get older, their father becomes less important. When I was an assistant at North Carolina, I'd get home and they'd both come running to me and Kimmie would jump up in my arms and hug me. Then one day I'm at Kansas and I came home and Kimmie was sitting on the couch with one of her friends watching television and she looked up at me and said, "Hey, dork."

A psychologist would say that I treasure those family moments because I didn't have them growing up. Maybe that played some part in it, but the real reason is that I loved spending time with my kids. I had gone from a troubled childhood to having the perfect family. That means everything. My family is what Roy Williams is.

Family dinners have always been very important to me. Whenever I was home we'd eat together. Sometimes it got in the way of the kids' social lives, but they allowed me to do that. It was our way of being together and it allowed me to catch up with their lives. Every morning I was home, I would fix breakfast—get out the cereal, make the toast, or fix Kimmie a plate of the little powdered doughnuts she loved and a glass of milk with chocolate syrup. It was a chance to have conversations with them. They were teenagers, so who knows whether it meant anything to them or not, but it was important to me.

One of my biggest regrets in life is that in Scott's senior year at Lawrence High in 1995, his basketball team won the state championship, and I missed 11 of his games, most of them because of our Kansas basketball practices. Looking back, I realize that all I had to do was change the practice time an hour in either direction. I regret that. I remember on the day of his state championship game, my Kansas team lost to Iowa State in the Big 8 Tournament. I left Kemper Arena in Kansas City and drove to Emporia and got there 15 minutes before the game started. I went from as low as I could be after losing to as happy as I could possibly be for Scott. I was a little jealous of him because I'd desperately wanted to play for a state championship when I was in high school. We have a picture from that day and my eyes are red because I'd cried watching my son live his dream. That moment made me forget getting my butt kicked in the Big 8 Tournament.

I enjoyed watching Kimmie's dance recitals just as much as watching Scott play basketball. I used to joke with Scott that he should have taken the dance classes to make his feet a lot quicker than they were. Kimmie has great feet.

When Scott went off to college at UNC, I drove with him from Lawrence to Chapel Hill. Wanda and Kimmie flew and met us and we got him moved in, and I'll never forget the feeling I had. We were standing outside his dorm and he was getting ready to go to orientation. We were leaving our son. He walked off in one direction, and Wanda, Kimmie, and I went off in the other. I handed Wanda the car keys and said, "Wanda, you drive and Kimmie you sit up front with her and don't either one of you turn around."

I sat in the backseat and cried, and when I'd finally composed myself I told Kimmie, "Maybe one of these days I'll be better."

She said, "There's no hope for you, Dad."

She was right. The exact same thing happened when we dropped her off in Chapel Hill three years later.

When Scott and Kimmie were in college and I was still at Kansas, I would come back at least once every year to see Scott play basketball and Kimmie dance with the UNC dance team. On Scott's Senior Day I had practice with my Kansas team Saturday morning in Lawrence and then the team flew on to Iowa State while I flew to Chapel Hill. Sunday morning I got a flight to Iowa State to coach the game that afternoon.

Kimmie danced as a sophomore and junior and I would go watch her and to this day when dancers go out on the court before the game, I watch them and I'm always thinking, "I wish Kimmie were here so I could ask her if they're any good."

There were plenty of times when I worried I wasn't there for my children enough. One summer, when Scott was 10 years old, he was getting ready to go to basketball camp at UNC, and he was acting sort of peculiar. I said, "Son, are you all right?"

"I'm just worried," he said.

"What are you worried about?"

"I am afraid I'm going to do something wrong. I'm afraid I'm going to embarrass you."

"Son, don't worry about that. You don't have to be a basketball player. Just go and have fun and if you decide that you're not having fun, I won't make you stay." I wanted Scott to understand that I loved him no matter what. Later in the conversation I touched on how much I was away from home. "Scott, you've got to understand that sometimes I'm gone and it's not because I want to be gone. It's the job. When I'm home I try to make the best of our time together. Do you understand the difference between quantity and quality? I'm not home in the quantity that other dads are, but when I'm home I want to make that good quality time."

"Sure, I understand," he said. "If you weren't gone, we wouldn't be getting all these good players and the teams that we're beating would probably be beating us."

There I was, trying to give my son some fatherly counsel and he was 10 steps ahead of me.

My children are my pride and joy. They have the kind of sincerity that makes people enjoy being around them. I owe all of that to Wanda. I remember telling her one time in our junior year of college that I wanted her to be the mother of my children, and there's no way that anybody else could have done the job that she's done. She has been the best teacher, the best mother, the best provider. She did such an unbelievable job of raising and guiding our children through the decisions that they've made when I wasn't there as much as I wanted to be. Wanda was often the mother and father both. Ninety percent of the things that our children learned when they were little, Wanda taught them.

I would always encourage our children to dream and Wanda was the more realistic one. She prepared our kids to handle everyday life. I remember a time when Scott told his mother he didn't need to study because he was going to play in the NBA and Wanda said, "You're not going to be a professional basketball player, son. Now go do your math homework."

I've been the luckiest guy because Wanda always took care of most everything. My duties are to coach the team and to take out the garbage when I'm home. Those are my only responsibilities. When I can do something as a father to help out with the kids, that's the icing. I never wanted to handle the finances. I have written two checks in 36 years of marriage, and both of them were at charity golf events when I didn't know how much the entry fee was. I don't keep track of how we're doing financially. I used to enjoy getting a paycheck, taking it home, and handing it to Wanda, but now, with direct deposit, I don't even do that.

When I was making $2,700 a year and Wanda stopped being a teacher because she was pregnant with Kimmie, I was never afraid of whether or not we were going to make it. I knew that she was watching it.

Wanda provides a perfect balance for me. She's so sensible. She's no coach, but a lot of times after games I like to ask her, "What did you think?" Over the years, I've learned from her take on games. When we were at Kansas that first year and lost eight games in a row, Wanda was not worried. She gave me the feeling that we were going to be all right, and I needed that support.

In 1999 when our team was struggling and I was at one of my lowest points as a coach, Coach Holladay came over to meet with me and we went down to our basement and talked for a couple of hours.

When he left, I came up into the kitchen and Wanda said, "You're not thinking about doing anything stupid like quitting are you?"

"No."

"Well, good," she said.

She knew that things were tough for me. I don't know whether or not she really wondered if I was thinking about quitting, but she wanted to make sure I realized what a bad decision that would be. She's never been one to pump me up or tell me how great I am. She only gives me that feeling when I need it — not when I want it but when I need it.

I've told Wanda that I want to die first because I don't know what I would do without her. For 40 years, she has been a great companion.

One of my favorite stories of us spending time together occurred during Tyler Hansbrough's senior year of high school in 2005. He had already committed to North Carolina, but I was flying out to see him play, and Wanda came with me. I reserved a private plane that was going to take us to Poplar Bluff. The pilot came out about 30 minutes before we were supposed to arrive and said that we couldn't land because an ice storm had closed the airport, so we were going to have to go to Cape Girardeau instead.

Ten minutes later, the pilot came out and said, "Coach they just closed Cape Girardeau. We're going into Jonesboro, Arkansas."

"All right, let's go," I said. "Can you call ahead and get me a rental car in Jonesboro?"

When we landed, I got my rental car and I called Tyler's dad, who said they were having sleet and freezing rain in Poplar Bluff. I asked him how long it would take me to get there.

He said, "Coach, that's an hour and a half. The players are going out to warm up right now."

"Maybe I can get there before the end of the game."

"Don't do that," he said. "That's silly. We'll be worried the entire time that you're going to slide off the side of the road."

"All right," I said. "Then I'll see you in a couple of weeks."

I was so frustrated. I asked the rental car agent where we could go to get something to eat. She gave me directions to a Sonic Drive-In. I drove there and bought two cheeseburgers and two chicken sandwiches for Wanda, me, and both pilots and drove back to the plane to go home.

I got back on the plane and we divvied up the food. On the flight home, I looked at Wanda and said, "Not many people have a husband who will put them on a private plane and fly them from Chapel Hill, North Carolina, to Jonesboro, Arkansas, to get a cheeseburger and then fly them back home. Honey, you have made the big-time."

She looked back at me. "Yes, this will go down as one of our most unusual dates."

EVER SINCE I WAS a Little League baseball player putting my uniform on 12 hours before the game, I have loved nothing more than being on a team. I have always enjoyed the idea of pulling together a group of guys for a common purpose and my dream back then was to be on a team for the rest of my life. These days my team is a group of friends I call my "foxhole buddies," and we will be together until the end of time.

They are Buddy Baldwin; Jerry Green; Scot Buxton, a neighbor during all my years in Lawrence; Randy Towner, the golf pro at Alvamar Country Club in Lawrence; Mike Davis, a former dean of the Law School at Kansas; Mickey Bell, a former UNC player who arranged my deals with Converse; Lee King, a UNC alum who I first met when my Owen golf team played at a course he owned;

Cody Plott, another North Carolina graduate who I played basketball against in high school and is now the president of Pebble Beach; Russ McCormick, a banker in Chapel Hill who helped me get my calendar business started; Billy Puckett, who was a year behind me at North Carolina and a fellow basketball camp counselor; Terry Allen, a former Kansas football coach; and Ted Seagroves, a friend who rides with me on recruiting trips and lives across the street. They are the guys that I jog with, the guys that I play golf with, the guys that I go on trips with, the guys that I would trust with my life.

I also have some buddies from my younger days in Asheville—Walt Stroup, Gene Allen, Curtis Ensley, and David Crandall—who I trust completely and who care about Roy Williams, not who Roy Williams is.

There is no reverence among us. I remember a game in 1994 when my Kansas team had the ball out of bounds down by a point with one second to play in the semifinals of the Big 8 Tournament. I called a play and we didn't score and we lost. After that game I saw Randy and Scot, and they said, "Gosh, we're so disappointed in you."

I said, "Guys, be careful. You're my best friends, but I might hit you with a hammer."

They said, "That was the perfect opportunity to run the barking dog play."

A month earlier, we had all seen a highlight on television where a high school team had a player run over to the corner and kneel down on all fours and start barking like a dog and everybody stopped to watch him while one of his teammates flipped the ball in to another teammate who scored the winning basket. Randy and Scot got me laughing just thinking about how I should have run the barking dog play, and it brought me back down to earth.

My buddies have a running joke about "the committee" that plans all of our outings together. It is a committee of one. Me. It will be January in the middle of our basketball season and I will call my buddies and tell them the committee has met. I don't even have to tell them the details about the latest trip I've planned. They're in. We get together each spring and fall to do a trip and it's seven or eight guys and their wives. Those trips are the highlight of my year.

The trips revolve not around basketball but around golf. Golf is my escape.

The first time I was ever on a golf course I was caddying for Buddy Baldwin, and he explained how hard golf was. When I first played the game as a senior in high school, I found out he was right. One of my uncles gave me a set of irons: a 3-, 5-, 7-, and 9-iron and a putter from a flea market, and I bought a used driver at a discount store. So I learned to play without a fairway wood or the other irons.

When I stopped playing competitive basketball after my freshman year in college, I knew I'd need something to replace it or I was going to go crazy. I played a round of golf at the UNC course and then I went back the next day, and again the next weekend. The golf course was a place where I could still compete. That summer I started playing a lot, and on into my sophomore year I played quite a bit. By the summer after my junior year, I'd decided I was going to try to be really good at it. My friend Gene Allen and I both bought a membership at Asheville Municipal Golf Course, or "Muni," as we called it. We played 26 days that June.

I continued to play during the summers through my five years coaching at Owen. But I have never played golf during the basketball season. I have always put the clubs away in October and I don't take them back out again until April, so it's a challenge to find my swing again each year.

One day on Muni I parred the first hole, eagled the second hole, birdied the third hole, eagled the fourth hole; I was five under after four holes. That was the first time I shot 69. The last summer before I came back to North Carolina as an assistant I got my handicap down to a 3. But in 10 years as Coach Smith's assistant my handicap never got back down to a 3, and then I became a head coach, and it's been going the wrong way ever since.

I had my first hole in one while I was at Kansas. I was thrilled. It was the 2nd hole at Alvamar, a 118-yard shot. I remember driving Wanda out there to see the hole and she said, "Gosh, that's so close it shouldn't even count."

Golf is even more fun for me now than when I was younger. Back then it was strictly the competition. Now it's the competition, but it's also the one place I can truly get away. When I'm playing, I don't think about who I need to call. I don't even take my phone to the golf course.

A golf trip is the one thing that really does relax me. Even when my game fails me, I still have a good time. I remember in the fall of 2008 I was playing with my buddies one afternoon and I walked to the 18th tee with a chance to make a birdie and shoot 80. I hit a great drive, but it flew a lot farther than I thought it would, and it wound up in a creek. Then I had a 40-yard pitch shot to a tucked pin over a bank with grass about a foot thick. My shot landed in that thick grass, and I hit it and I hit it and I hit it and I hit it and I hit it, and I could not get it out of the grass. I was laughing, but I was not going to quit. I walked back and dropped another ball, and I hit it in the creek again. Then I hit another shot into the bank of thick grass and took a few more swings. I finally got the ball up on the green and two-putted. My score on that hole was a 22. I said, "Guys, I'm not quitting on a 22." So we played a 19th hole and I parred it.

Nothing better illustrates my love of golf than when Wanda and

I were planning our wedding. I remember Wanda asked me, "What date do you want to get married?"

I said, "Whenever you want to."

"Where do you want to get married?" she said.

"Wherever you want to," I said.

"Who do you want to marry us?"

"Whoever you want to," I said.

My only request was that we get married at night because so many people get married in the middle of the day, and that just screws up a bunch of golf games. The day that I got married I played 36 holes.

I BELIEVE I AM a fine physical specimen, but there are times when my body fails me. I was on the 15th hole at Alvamar Country Club in 1995 when I hit a shot that I thought was perfect, and it landed in the lip of a bunker. I jumped up in the air and yelled, "Aaaaahhh!" And then the whole world started spinning every which way. I fell to the ground. I said to my partners, "Guys, I don't know what's going on. I'm really dizzy."

The second time it happened, I was on a trip with a bunch of other college coaches, and I was participating in a balloon toss, one of the activities they had planned for the event. My partner threw our balloon a little short and I stupidly dove for it and my chin hit the ground and all of a sudden, I couldn't tell which way was up. I felt like death warmed over.

The third time, I was playing golf again, and I hit a shot out of a bunker on the 6th hole and the wind blew sand in my face. I jerked my head around and I got so dizzy I threw up right in the bunker. I threw up on the 7th tee. I threw up on 8th tee. I threw up on the 9th tee. I decided not to play the back nine.

When I had another episode one day at a Kansas practice, school administrators became afraid that I was going to die on their watch, so they sent me to the Mayo Clinic where a doctor ran a series of tests on me. They made me sick as a dog. Finally, the doctor concluded that I had benign positional vertigo.

At the Mayo Clinic they also did full blood work and they checked my triglycerides, which are supposed to be 150 or below. My count was 455. They asked me to complete a questionnaire with a dietitian. The doctor came in to review it and he came to the question about soft drinks. I had written, *Coca-Cola Classic, 7–10 a day for 40 years.*

When the doctor saw that, he said, "Oooohhh."

I said, " 'Oooohhh' is not good if I'm the patient."

The doctor asked me if I could stop drinking Coca-Cola. So the next day I cut it out. Now I drink two or three Sprite Zeros a day and save my Cokes for when I eat a steak.

If it was up to Wanda, I would have quit coaching a long time ago. In her mind it's been very difficult for me mentally and physically. She would like for us to live some healthy time outside of the fishbowl. She's never actually asked me to quit, but after we won the national championship in 2005 she said, "We could quit right now. It would be a great time." If I had come back to Chapel Hill in 2009 and let everybody enjoy the national championship for a couple of weeks and then announced that I was retiring, that would have been a dream for her. Whenever I come home complaining about something at work, she says, "Well, I've got a cure. You could quit." She's been doing that for 10 years.

What Wanda sees is that when you're a college basketball coach people always want more. The administration always wants me to do more and the fans always want more. I could never do enough. In the first three months after the 2009 national championship, I had probably 100 people come up to me and say, "Great job, Coach, let's win it again next year."

I thought, "Can't we all enjoy this one for a little bit?"

Wanda and I both got a big kick out of a local newspaper poll that came out after the 2009 championship, which determined that 76 percent of North Carolina Tar Heels fans have a favorable opinion of me. When I read that I was thinking, "Gosh, in the previous five years we've won more games than anybody else in the country, we've been to three Final Fours and won two national championships. If it's 76 percent now, it isn't going to go anywhere but down. What the heck do I need to do to please those other 24 percent?"

Some of my friends still think I should try coaching in the NBA, but I've seen so many good people disappointed because of what happens to them coaching in that league. As an assistant coach at the 2004 Olympics I saw how some of the players' egos and immaturity destroyed that team, and I came back saying there was no way I could ever coach in the pros.

It would be easy to slow down, but I don't think I'm good enough to do that. I couldn't do it halfway. The fear of losing would not allow me to do that. Bob Frederick always used to say that he was surprised that after 10 years I still worked just as hard as I did the first day I got to Kansas. If you asked Coach Robinson right now, he would tell you that I'm a lot more mellow, particularly on the court, but that I work just as hard as the day he came to work with me 21 years ago. I'm never going to sit back and say, "Whew, I've made it." When it's time to work it would bother me like crazy if someone was out there recruiting and I wasn't. It would bother me a great deal if someone was out there watching tape and I wasn't. I'm probably a little wacko.

Hard work doesn't guarantee success, but without it you have no chance. I always want people to know that nobody's going to outwork me. I may screw it up. I may make a bad substitution. I may call a bad play. But there's no way that any other coach can outwork me. And that's what motivates me every single day.

Winning still drives me. When we won the national championship in 2005, I thought, "My gosh, how good would it feel to win a second one?" And after the 2009 championship, I was thinking, "Gosh, how great would it feel to win a third?" Maybe that's greedy. There's no question that I love the competition part. I want to beat your rear end. But I also enjoy putting a team together. Every year presents a different challenge for me.

If I live long enough to quit, what I will miss the most is building relationships with players. Those bonds are always going to be there and they are personal. They are not based on wins and losses but on something you gave them, something you tried to do for them, something you tried to establish in those kids that would affect their lives.

In the summer of 2009, I ran into Rex Walters, who is now the coach at San Francisco, and he said, "Coach, I just want you to know that every success I've had is directly related to my time spent with you." That is one of the greatest feelings you can have as a coach. My former players know that I care, that no matter how long they've been out of school, I'm always going to be there for them. I don't believe I'm going to get any little gold stars on my college diploma for every time I help one of my players, but it makes me feel great. As long as there are kids out there saying that I will always be their coach, I will be happy.

Coach Smith once told me, "Don't quit as early as I did." He re-tired at 66. I think he later wished he hadn't quit so soon, because he still loved the coaching part of it, but it was the press conferences, the booster club meetings, and the other stuff that wore him out. I'm 59 years old and I'd like to coach another eight to 10 years.

Wanda really roots for me to be good at golf because she thinks that if I were to give it up, I would never quit coaching. My buddies don't think I'll ever be able to retire, but I will. I'd always said that when the right head coaching job opened for me it would be staring me right in the face, and it was. And when the day comes that it's time for me to quit, it'll be staring me right in the face, too, and I'll say, "Well, that's it." I'm not worried about what will happen after that.

When I was a kid growing up with all the problems in our house, I always knew I was going to be all right. When I was 11 years old getting on the bus alone to go to the YMCA, I knew I was going to be all right. When I came to North Carolina as a part-time assistant for $2,700, I knew I was going to be all right. When I lost eight straight games in my first season at Kansas, I knew I was going to be all right. When I retire, I know I am going to be all right.

What would be ideal is to quit and then someday have a computer tell me what day I'm going to die. Then I'd see if I can play 18 holes for my last 365 days in a row. If I've got enough money to pay off my bets walking off the 18th green on my last day on earth, that'd be really a good deal for me. I'm one of those guys who was born with no money, and when I die, I hope the last check we write is to the guy that sells us the casket. And I hope the check bounces.

CHAPTER 14

Look Homeward, Angel

THERE IS ONE other reason I came back to North Carolina in 2003 that hardly anybody knows. The failing health of my dad and my sister helped bring me back. They were part of why I needed to be home.

I LOST MY MOM in 1992, and I have always regretted not being there for her when she died. My mom quit working at age 65. I had started a little fund for her to put some money aside. She quit because she wanted to spend some more time with her grandchildren. Nine months later she was diagnosed with cancer, and seven months after that, she was dead.

She had handled the first round of chemo pretty well. I was making the trip back from Kansas to North Carolina about once a week to see her, and one day the doctor had called me and said, "We can't get enough chemo to her the regular way. We want to put a catheter in her chest."

I called my mom about the surgery and she said, "Let's go ahead and do it."

The recruiting period had started and I flew to Los Angeles. I had this peculiar feeling, so I called Mom that evening and I said, "How are you doing?"

She said, "I'm doing fine."

"I'm thinking about getting a flight home tonight to see you through the operation."

"Oh, Roy, they're not even calling it an operation. They're just calling it a procedure to put the catheter in. It just takes 20 minutes and they're going to videotape it to use in some of the medical schools to show them how they're supposed to do it. So I'll try to look my best."

"Mom, are you sure you don't want me to come back?"

"No, you stay there and do your job and come back when you can."

"You sure you're okay?"

"Well, no. Actually, I'm really mad. They wanted me here at the hospital at 2 o'clock this afternoon and they're not doing the procedure until 5 o'clock tomorrow afternoon. Why didn't they just let me come in tomorrow so I wouldn't miss bingo tonight?"

So we laughed and I thought she was all right and I hung up the phone.

I went to the games to recruit that night and then I caught a red-eye to Indianapolis and went to a basketball camp there the next day. Phil Ford, who was an assistant coach at North Carolina at that point, was with us, and Phil, Jerry Green, Steve Robinson, and I went back to the hotel so I could call and make sure my mother was all right. We got back around 9 p.m. and Jerry went into his room and I went into my room with Phil and we were in there talking for a minute before I called my mom. There was a knock on the door and Jerry came in and he said, "Have you called yet?"

I said, "No."

"There was a message in my room," Jerry said. "Wanda called and she said your mother had cardiac arrest on the operating table. She passed away."

I had two thoughts. One, I felt my world had ended. The angel of the world had died. The person that I tried to make proud every single day of my life was gone. But I had this other feeling. I'm not the most religious person in the world, but I do believe in the Lord. I do believe in a higher being. When I first heard my mother had cancer I said, "Lord, I only have one request. Please don't allow my mom to suffer."

So the second thought that I had when she died, and the one I was able to live on, was that my mom hadn't suffered. That was the only way I could handle it. I didn't want to remember my mom in pain. I wanted to remember her being mad about not playing bingo.

The only way I got through it was because of Wanda and Scott and Kimmie. If I didn't have those three people to look forward to, I would not have cared about living. If it hadn't been for them, I would have had no more reason to keep going. I thought about how my mom worshipped them. She liked Wanda better than she liked me, and my son and my daughter were her dreams for the future. When I was a child, my mother was my hero and now my children are my heroes. And Wanda has been the strength behind everything that I've ever done. So even though I'd lost my mom, in that moment, I could think of my family and feel like the luckiest man there ever was.

I flew to Asheville and went to my mom's house. I got out of the car and just sort of stood there. I didn't know if I wanted to walk in the house. My mom had never remarried, but she had a friend named Leonard King who would take her to play bingo or out to eat. The first person to come out of the house was Leonard. He said, "I wanted to give you something. Your mom gave me this and told me to hold it until she got back out of the hospital."

He handed me two hundred-dollar bills, money my mom had won at bingo. I remember thinking that for my mom to have a hundred-dollar bill was like the craziest thing in the world.

Then Leonard said, "She would want you to have it."

I took one of the bills and folded it up in my wallet and I gave the other one to my sister.

The next night we had the visitation at the funeral home and my dad walked in. I hadn't seen him in a long time. "I'm not coming to the funeral tomorrow," he said, "but I wanted to see you and Frances. I wanted to tell you something. I have never regretted one damn thing I've ever done in my whole life except one. And that's the way I treated your mom. I loved her and I still do. All the rest of what those people say about me, I couldn't care less. They can all kiss my ass. There's nothing I can do to change what I did, but I'm sorry about everything that happened."

I hugged him and told him I appreciated that.

MY SISTER, FRANCES, was a lot like my dad in that she didn't always make the greatest decisions. She was married and divorced three times. She was a dreamer. She lived her whole life believing that one day she was going to hit the jackpot. She sold vitamin pills in a pyramid scheme, she started a housecleaning service, she sold time-shares in Myrtle Beach. She always believed that she was going to come up with an idea that was going to make a gazillion dollars, but that never panned out. She knew that I had found what I loved to do, and she was sad that she hadn't found something she loved like that, but she was very proud of me.

She came out to Lawrence almost every year to see a Kansas game and spend a few days with us. Once we went to one of Scott's high school basketball games and after the game I told her to follow me out. But when I got outside my sister wasn't there. I walked back in and Frances was standing in the bleachers looking totally lost and it dawned on me that something was wrong. The next morning at the breakfast table she told me, "Roy, I'm afraid one of these days I'm going to forget my children's names." How can anything be worse than that? Frances had been diagnosed with dementia in her early fifties.

I knew it would only get worse for her and part of why I came back to North Carolina is because I didn't want to be the rich little brother in Kansas just sending money. I visited Frances regularly when I moved back, but her health continued to decline. I really believe that the last basketball game my sister saw that she knew what was going on was the 2005 NCAA championship game. She would fade in and out watching it on television with her son and daughter, but I like to believe she knew that we won that game.

The last nine months of her life, my sister didn't know who I was. At that time, I wanted to go see Frances and I didn't want to go see Frances. I felt so guilty that I didn't want to see her, but I hated seeing my sister like that. I saw her at Christmas in 2006 for the last time and she died three months later. If only she had been healthier, I think Frances and I would have grown closer than we ever had a chance to as kids. She would have really enjoyed being the big sister of the basketball coach at North Carolina.

THE LAST TIME I ever saw my dad was on a Wednesday in May 2004. I was going to St. Louis for a meeting, and I got a charter plane to fly me from Chapel Hill and stop over in Asheville so I could visit with him. Over the years, we'd seen each other on Christmas a few times. He came to watch me coach two games. He had never come to my house. By the time I came back to North Carolina, my dad had late-stage cancer. We saw each other about a dozen times during that first year I was back.

When I arrived at his house on that May afternoon, he said, "Well, good God, look what the dogs drug in."

Later, he said to me, "You know, I really didn't do a good job with you as a father."

I said, "I was all right."

"No, I could've taught you so many things."

"You did."

"What the hell did I ever teach you?"

"Daddy, I just looked at what you did and I tried to do the opposite."

"That's the only goddamn way I could ever have taught you anything."

Then I said, "Daddy, you did something else, too. When you came to Mom's visitation I appreciate you saying what you did."

He looked at me and said, "It's still the only goddamn thing I've ever regretted in my entire life."

As I was leaving, I said, "I'll be back on Sunday."

I will never forget that he said, "Well, maybe I'll be here, maybe I won't."

That next Sunday, as I drove to Asheville, I was heading toward my dad's house when I decided I needed to stop at a golf course right near the airport because I wanted to work on my putting. So I putted for about 30 minutes. Then I thought to myself, "It's time to go now."

I got back in the car and drove over to my dad's house, and my half brother, Danny, came out of the house. "He's passed," he said. "He's been gone for about 30 minutes."

I said, "I know." I knew because I didn't want to see my dad like that anymore. The last thing he had said to me was, "Well, maybe I'll be here, maybe I won't." That was right somehow. It was like my mom saying, "Why didn't they just let me come in tomorrow so I wouldn't miss bingo tonight?"

At my mom's funeral when I delivered the eulogy, I said, "Life was never easy for my mother, but she never belabored that point. She never made me feel like she was feeling sorry for herself, and that made me feel how strong she was. Very seldom did we ever tell each other, 'I love you.' But there was never a moment in my life that she didn't make me feel like I was the most important person in her world. I thought she was an angel, but she treated me like one."

My dad had heard about the eulogy. He asked one of my cousins, "Do you think Roy will talk at my funeral like he did at his mom's?"

That was my dad's way of asking me. Because he wouldn't actually ask me. He had too much pride. But he knew my cousin would tell me.

So I spoke at my dad's funeral, too. I said, "The song that came to my mind when my mom died was "Wind Beneath My Wings," because that's what she was. The song that reminds me of my dad every time I hear it is "Papa Was a Rolling Stone," because he was married five times and the only thing he ever left us was alone, where he laid his hat was his home, and he spent all his time chasing women and drinking. That was my dad.

"He didn't always do a great job living, but my dad was really good at dying. He had three grandsons and he had three shotguns and before he died, he gave each grandson a shotgun. He had two sons, my half brother Danny and me, and he tried to mend fences with both of us. Before my dad died, he cleared everything off his chest and all of us in this room should hope to be able to do that. I know Daddy would want everybody to say I love you more than he and I ever did, and so I would hope that all of you would take the time to tell people that you love them. My dad would like that. My dad made some mistakes while he was alive, but he tried to make amends before he died, so I believe he died a contented man.

"Some of you may be upset about the bad things I'm saying about my dad at his funeral. You know what? It doesn't bother me, because my dad told me one time that he didn't give a damn what other people thought. Well, I'm Babe's son."

MY MOM DIED on July 7, 1992, and in my wallet to this day I've still got that folded-up hundred-dollar bill. Whenever I see it there it reminds me that if there's ever a really, really, really rainy day, I'll be all right, because my mom will still be leaving me that dime.

I REALLY DON'T SPEND much time thinking about where I've been in my life or how much different that is from where I am now. But I will say that as a person and as a coach, I have never experienced anything like the changes in the two years since this book was first published. Most people would probably think my perspective began to shift on January 4, 2010, when our loss to the College of Charleston began the downward spiral of the most exasperating and humbling season of my college coaching career. But it really began three days earlier.

I HAD FIRST HEARD the news in June of 2009. On Father's Day. Wanda and I were driving back home from the beach one night when we got a call from our son, Scott. We talked for a while on the speakerphone, and Scott wished me a happy Father's Day. At the end of the call he said, "Oh, by the way, Katie's expecting."

"Expecting?" Wanda said. "Expecting *what*?" We were stunned.

Then I said, "Are you telling me what I think you're telling me?"

"Yeah," Scott said.

"When?"

"January 1."

After we hung up, the thing I remember most is that Wanda and I didn't say anything to each other for several miles. My mind was racing.

Many years ago I read an article about Jimmy Valvano. One of his dreams in life was to do things with his grandchildren that he neglected to do with his own children, because he felt guilty about how much time he'd spent away from his kids while coaching. Jimmy passed away before he ever got that chance. For years, I've been thinking about that. During a lot of my children's lifetime, there were so many things I missed. So the moment I heard that I was going to have a grandchild, other than almost wrecking my car, it was a pretty neat deal.

It was something that I had been pestering Scott and Katie about, at first sort of casually, then more straightforwardly, and then more bluntly, until the day I finally said, "When are you guys going to get started so we can have some grandchildren?"

The anticipation was phenomenal. Every time I saw a little baby or passed a store selling baby clothes or toys, I thought about it. But what it all meant didn't really strike me until the day the baby arrived. I had just come home from our January 1 basketball practice when the phone rang, and within a half hour, Wanda and I were driving to the hospital in Charlotte. We took two cars because I had to be back in Chapel Hill for practice the next day. We got there two hours later, and probably 30 minutes after that, the baby was born. We were sitting in the waiting room with Katie's parents when Scott walked up with a big smile on his face. He didn't tell us boy or girl. I had told him early on that I didn't want to know, and they felt the same way. I wanted to be surprised. We followed him down to the delivery room. I was the last one in, holding the door for the other grandparents, and my heart was pounding. "Well," Katie said, "why don't you guys come over here and say hello to your grandson, Aiden Allen Williams."

That was the moment when time stood still. Allen is my middle name and Katie's father's first name, and when Katie said that, I had to turn around and walk back toward the door. I wanted to get away to someplace where people couldn't see me, but there was no place to hide. I had to compose myself for a couple of seconds before I could even go over there and take a look at the little rascal. I thought of my mother and I wished she could have been there to see him.

People have asked me what I would have done if the birth had happened on a game night. The answer is easy. I would have missed the game. I hadn't told anybody, but I'd already made up my mind that if it happened, Coach Robinson and the rest of the staff would coach the game and I would come back when I could. I knew there would be other basketball games, but there would never be another first grandchild. Luckily, it didn't come to that. That's how I know Aiden is my kind of kid. He was punctual.

I went over to the hospital the next morning to see my grandson again, and then I left to come back for practice. While I was driving back to Chapel Hill, the phone in the car kept ringing over and over with people calling to find out the baby's name and statistics. That ride was a blur. I was so far past elated that I don't know if there's a word in the dictionary to describe how I was feeling. During that whole trip I completely forgot about basketball.

THE 2010 BASKETBALL SEASON changed my perspective as well. It is mind-boggling to think that in the span of one year I went from the greatest season I've ever been involved with, as far as margin of victory all the way through the NCAA tournament, to the worst season I've ever been involved with.

I remember years ago, after I'd just taken my first head coaching job at Kansas, I attended a farewell party at Coach Smith's house on the night before we left for Lawrence. Coach Smith walked me out to his driveway. "The biggest worry I have about you is how hard you take the losses," he said, "because I assure you they are going to be much more difficult for you as a head coach."

Our next game after Aiden's birth was at the College of Charleston, and we had an 11-point lead with four minutes to play. Charleston scored the next eight points of the game and had the ball with time running out. I was on the sideline with my arm in a sling from the shoulder surgery I'd had in November, and I was jumping up and down but couldn't get anybody's attention. Instead of doing my usual jumping jacks, I could only wave one arm. We had a player who was supposed to foul and he didn't foul, so instead of sending their guy to the free-throw line for a one-and-one, the guy shoots a three and ties it up, and then we lose in overtime. We almost never lose a game like that. We win games like that.

Three games later, we played Georgia Tech at home, and I remember five things happened at the end of that game that could have gone either way, and if any one of the five had gone our way, we would have won. But we were 0-for-5. We had to make a great comeback just to have a chance to win that game, but that's what North Carolina does. And to lose it at the end, that is *not* what North Carolina does.

Now there was some doubt. We'd lost a home game. That was the game that got our guys thinking, "Oh my gosh, what is happening?" The difference between winning and losing is often so small, but the impact can be so huge. I really believe that if we had won that game, it would have changed our whole season.

As a coach you're always considering worst-case scenarios. After losing to Georgia Tech, Coach Robinson and I were sitting in the coaches' locker room one night after practice. "Steve," I said, "we've got to get this turned around because—"

"One loss leads to another one," he said, finishing my sentence. We lost eight of our next 10 games.

I've been asked a million times what went wrong that season, and that's easy to answer. You don't have to be a nuclear physicist to figure it out. I had said in the preseason that we were thin in backcourt experience. I was worried about our perimeter shooting because we had nobody that had ever done it in crunch time. And we had nobody on our team who'd ever been asked to be "the man." Nobody like a Sean May, Tyler Hansbrough, Raymond Felton, or Ty Lawson who I could point to and say, "All right, this is the play we're going to run, and they know we're going to run it, but you're going to score anyway."

Still, I thought our depth up front might be such a strength that it might overcome some of those weaknesses. In golf you can hit it a little sideways, but you can overcome that if you make all the putts. But then our big guys all of a sudden started getting hurt. There was no strength for us to build on. We had too many holes. The guys we were depending on to cover up those holes became holes. And then, when you lose a couple of games, the fans tend to panic and the players start saying, "Oh my gosh, what are we doing?" That lack of confidence grows like a snowball rolling downhill until the players begin to think, "How are we going to screw this one up?"

We were in a team meeting one night, and I asked Coach Holladay if he had anything to say.

"I'm just so confused about why this team won't do what you've asked them to do, when every other team that you've coached has tried to do that to the best of their ability and they've been successful," he said. "I'm dumbfounded about why these guys aren't giving you that kind of effort mentally and physically."

He was right. I could never get that team to do the simple things that I'd gotten every other team to do for the previous 21 years. I was saying the same things during our 90th practice that I was saying the first week, and I could not get them to do them. They kept making the same mistakes over and over.

I went back and looked at old practice plans to see if I'd left something out. I asked myself, "Am I running them too much? Am I not running them enough?" I even had the players write down things that they wanted everybody on the team to focus on, and I asked them to include me. A few players wanted me to shorten practices, and I threw those out because that was a cop out. Some of them wanted me to be more demanding. I was trying to be, but you can't ask guys to do multiplication tables when they haven't learned how to add yet.

Another day I had the team and the staff vote for which five guys were playing the hardest, and we posted it up on the board in the locker room. It was brutal. My thought process was, "What would I think if I was a player and Coach put those names up on the board and I wasn't one of them? That would kill me." That meeting was hard for me because I was astounded that guys weren't hurt as much as I wanted them to be, that it didn't bother them as much as it would me. And it hurt me because I hadn't been able to get them to feel as invested as I thought they should be. I even asked one of those guys, "Did that embarrass you?"

"A little," he said.

"Did you expect it?"

"Yeah."

"Then why not change?"

THE LOSS AT DUKE to end the regular season was a low point. I have never had to sit through anything like that. Duke had everything going in their favor. It was Senior Night, and none of their players had ever beaten us in Cameron. I was dumb enough to think that was great, because nobody thought we had a chance. I felt like we could really stick it to them. We could do something to hurt their psyche for a long time. And we were awful. They totally dominated us from the first whistle to the last. It was embarrassing. The level of the beating was something that I'd never experienced before as a college coach. We looked like we didn't have any idea how to play. It was the last regular season game, and I remember we had a shot clock violation right after a timeout. "Guys," I said, "how can that happen?"

I left Cameron and drove straight down to the beach and got there at 2 o'clock in the morning. The team had the day off, and I wanted to collect my thoughts before the ACC Tournament started. I couldn't sleep that night. The next morning I planned to sit on the porch to try to relax a little bit, but I couldn't. I went for a walk four times that day. I could not sit still. I wanted to do anything to avoid sitting there, because all I could think about was how badly I got my butt beat the night before. So I was walking down the street and a guy passed me on a bike, and he said, "You guys got killed last night!"

I said, "You think I don't know that?" For a moment, the "mountain" came out in me, and I wanted to go over there and see how tough he was.

There were also a few college kids standing there. "Hey, Coach," one of them said, "don't worry about that guy. Can we have a picture made with you?"

I laughed. "You sure you want your picture made with *me*?"

I was humbled, but I was not about to give up. I honest-to-goodness believed we would go to the ACC Tournament and win the thing. What a neat deal it would be, because everybody had counted us out and said we were not going to make the NCAA Tournament.

After we lost to Georgia Tech in the first round, I was walking off the court in Greensboro, and I was bewildered. I can remember stopping for a second on the way back to the locker room and thinking, "Gosh, we're not going to make the fricking tournament. How could this happen?"

One of the few things about the season I'm proud of is that after that loss, I asked every one of my assistant coaches, "Do you want to go to the NIT?" Every one of them said "No. No. No." The seniors had told me they had taken an informal vote, and some of the players on our team didn't want to go. I came home and asked Wanda about it, and she said, "No." I woke up the next morning and told myself, "If we get an NIT bid, we're going, because if somebody invites me to play, I'm going to go play. How could it get any worse than it is right now? Playing more can only help us, because we're at rock bottom."

So we made a nice little run to the finals of the NIT, and we built a little of our confidence back. In the locker room after the loss in the championship game, Coach Robinson pointed at me and said, "Coach Williams is really the only one who wanted to do this, because he thought we could still do something positive. We did."

The other thing I'm proud of is what Deon Thompson talked about at our postseason banquet. "Coach never gave up," he said. "He never let us give in. Every game he came to practice coaching us the same way he did last year when we won a national championship. He always believed we were going to get it turned around."

I guess that's what the captain of the *Titanic* thought: "We're going to stop sinking any minute now." But I did come to practice every day, and told the guys, "Hey, if we give in, we know what the result is going to be. If we don't give in, we could get rewarded." It wasn't that I had to give myself a pep talk. I honestly thought that we were going to turn it around. I have always believed that you never lose a game; the clock just runs out on you. I thought our team was going to be a good team, but the season ended before we really had a chance to show it.

Two days after our last game, the Final Four began. I had been to every Final Four since I became a head coach, 21 years in a row. In 2010 I didn't go. I was worn out and my team wasn't there, so I didn't give a darn. On the night of the championship game, I watched *Dancing with the Stars*. I wanted to watch Erin Andrews and to see if Pamela Anderson could dance. I clicked over to the NCAA final at one point, saw one play, and then turned it right back. Eventually, somebody told me that Duke won. Duke is a conference team and nobody can have more respect for what that program has accomplished than I do, but that doesn't mean I have to sit there and pull for them. I don't think Mike was pulling for us when we won it the year before. The bottom line is that I was like a spoiled little brat thinking that if you won't let me play, then I'm going to take my ball and go home.

The season was hard. I didn't handle the losses well. Losing feels like somebody reaches into your chest and jerks your heart out and shakes it right in front of you. That sounds very dramatic, but coaching is my livelihood. It's not my life, but it is my livelihood and it is my passion. It was tough to get smacked right between the eyes again and again.

My worst record as a head coach had been 19–12. In 2010 we had 17 losses. There's a long way between 12 and 17. And to not even qualify for the NCAA tournament? I felt worthless. I felt like a failure. I haven't felt that way very often in my professional life. Winning a national championship the previous April wasn't nearly as high as the lows were low after losing at home to Georgia Tech, Virginia, and Duke a few months later.

During the 2010 season, I'd go to sleep and wake up an hour later. Sometimes I'd go two nights in a row without sleeping at all. I'd be up watching tape, writing down notes. The doctor told me I needed to start taking some sleeping pills. When I'd stay up all night—night after night after night—Wanda would say, "Are you trying to kill yourself?"

It didn't feel real. I remember lying in bed when I couldn't sleep all those nights and thinking, "I wish I could go to sleep and wake up and realize that this has all been a nightmare." But it lasted so long, I knew that I hadn't slept long enough for all that bad stuff to happen.

I don't think I'm important enough that some higher power sent Aiden here to make sure Ol' Roy would be okay. I think his arrival was a coincidence. But it was a wonderful coincidence. I could have made it through that season without him, but it would have been so much harder. He was something else to live for. Something there to make sure I got my exercise, to make sure I took my heart medicine. He soothed my soul.

I remember how Aiden saved me after we got killed at Clemson. We couldn't fly home, because there was too much ice on the plane, so I sent the players back on the bus. Wanda and her parents were at the game, and they were going to Charlotte afterward to see the grandbaby, so I joined them. The next morning the little boy fell asleep on my chest while we were lying on the couch. That's the first time those two worlds met. I had been so distraught, just ruined. Seeing Aiden didn't make me forget the loss, but it showed me something else beyond basketball. I thought, "That was ridiculous last night. I'm really ticked off, but gosh almighty, this is about as nice as it can be." It didn't erase the hurt, but it made me feel really good at a time when nothing else in the world could have.

ON AUGUST 1, 2010, I turned 60 years old. All I really wanted to do that day was to have dinner with my family. Scott, Katie, Aiden, my daughter Kimberly, and Wanda and her mom and dad were all there. Dinner was about as countrified as you can get: fried chicken, biscuits and gravy, corn, green beans, and potatoes. I really wanted some family pictures made, because I only have one picture of me with my sister and my mom and dad. So Scott set up his camera with a timer, and he took some pictures of the four generations. It was one of the great days of my 60 years.

I can remember when I thought 60 was ancient. Kimberly likes to say, "Daddy, one of these days you are going to mature, but I don't know when." She's right. Earlier that summer, two people bet me $25 each that I wouldn't cut all my hair off. So I did it. Cutting off all of my hair just to say I beat people is not terribly mature. That $50 was not going to change my life, but I wanted to beat them. That kind of thing makes me feel that while I may be getting older, I'm definitely not mature yet.

I will admit that the 2010 season aged me as much as any season I have ever coached. It was also a season when I spent more time thinking about aging because of what I saw happening to Coach Smith.

During my first five years back at UNC, Coach Smith came to practice four times a week. I'd walk over to him at water break, and during those two minutes we'd talk. I loved that part of it. I thought I was so lucky to have another set of eyes that I trusted so much, whose only goal was the same as mine: to make the team better.

The past three seasons Coach Smith has rarely come to practice. I have missed having him there, but I've missed it more for him, because I know he is not doing what he really loves to do. During my first few years back at UNC, there would be a phone message from

Coach Smith after every game congratulating me on a great win or telling me to remind one of the players to sprint back harder on defense. The past couple of years he has never called me after a game. That's sad.

Coach Smith has more pride than anybody I've ever known in my life. He was so proud of his basketball knowledge and his mind and his memory and his relationships with the players. The memory loss that he's recently suffered is the worst thing that could possibly happen to him. It's cruel. He shouldn't have the last years of his life take him so far away from what he stood for. That's the hardest part. It would have been great to have him around in 2010 to ask, "Coach, every time we play man-to-man defense out of bounds, I think they're going to score a layup. What do you think about playing zone?" I didn't have that. We did end up making that change, but it seemed strange not to have his approval.

Coach Smith still has good days. He sent me a handwritten note during the 2010 season that said exactly what he would have said to me 15 years ago. The writing was so clear; the punctuation and grammar were perfect. A couple of days later, I thanked him for the note, and it took a few seconds for him to remember that he'd sent it to me. During a team party at my house after the 2010 season, I introduced Coach Smith to Aiden, and a few minutes later I was holding Aiden and Coach Smith came over and said, "Oh, that's the cutest baby . . . now whose baby is this?" I don't think he has much memory about what happened to our team during the 2010 season and that's okay with me. I don't want him to remember that.

Every time I see Coach Smith, I have such mixed emotions. In the summer of 2010, I played nine holes of golf with him and Coach Guthridge. It was the hardest nine holes I've ever had to play, because the Coach Smith I've known was always playing mind games with you, knowing how the bet stood and wanting to get 25 other bets down. He loved to compete, and that was the first time that Coach Smith and I ever played golf that there wasn't something bet. We were just playing golf, and that felt so unusual. Still, I was really happy I'd had a chance to spend some time with him.

My favorite moment from the 2010 season came at our 100-year celebration of North Carolina basketball when I walked Coach Smith out to the center circle at the Smith Center along with Coach Guthridge and Eddie Fogler. It was the most emotional time I have ever had that did not involve my family. I started crying, Al Wood was crying, Walter Davis was crying. Lots of the players were emotional. After the ceremony, I walked Coach Smith back into the tunnel and at that moment his mind was as clear as it has ever been. "Coach," I said, "you did great, and thank you very much."

Coach Smith looked back at me with tears in his eyes and he said, "No, thank you." And he hugged me. That is a moment I will never forget.

FLYING HOME FROM NEW YORK after the last game of the 2010 season, I was relieved. I am always relieved when the season is over. I was also still unbelievably mad, surprised, confused, and thinking, "How in the crap could this happen? This is not supposed to happen. Okay, what am I going to do to make sure this doesn't ever happen again?"

That season, I doubted myself as a coach more than the first 21 years put together. Buddy Baldwin said to me three or four times that season, "Coach, you cannot get that dumb that quickly. Even *you*." There's some truth to that, but it didn't make me feel any better. I was still the one going through it. I can't just say that the kids didn't do it, because it was *us*. That was the part that was killing me. It was not just the players' fault. Sure, I can't make the three-point shots, I can't shoot the free throws, I can't not turn the ball over, I can't invest on the court. I can't do any of that for them, but I had to find a way to get them to do it, and I couldn't. I blamed myself. I failed. That is hard to take.

Part of doubting yourself as a coach is that it makes you wonder, "Am I ever going to have a chance to be the best again?" There are no guarantees. I went to the Final Four as an assistant at North Carolina in 1982 and then I didn't get back until Kansas got there in 1991. I can still remember during a dinner at the 1991 Final Four when Coach Smith said to me, "Man, after '82 neither one of us thought it would take us this long to get back, did we?"

During the 2010 season I was always coaching for the moment, coaching for a practice, coaching for a game. But after the season, I did sit back and wonder if I could get us back to where we'd have an opportunity to win it all. That's the unknown. I wanted that the day after we won the championship in 2009, but following the 2010 season, that desire was so much deeper. I don't ever want to embarrass the program, and I felt like I'd embarrassed the program that season. I just hoped to bring our team back to where all of the players who had ever played at North Carolina could be really proud of us again.

I met with our athletic director, Dick Baddour, shortly after the 2010 season, and he told me he thought I needed to let go of what happened. I told him I couldn't. I know that he was right, but if you haven't walked in my shoes, you don't know the pain, you don't know the regret, you don't know the anguish. It eats at your soul.

THERE WERE PLENTY of times during the summer after the 2010 season that I felt like climbing up on top of the Smith Center and jumping off. The off-season was really difficult. It seemed like an eternity, the longest I have ever endured as a coach by far. I was ready to start practice the day we came back from the NIT in New York. I was dying for another chance to compete.

It helped that my friends in the coaching business, and even some of my enemies, really supported me. All of those guys have gone through seasons when it just didn't work. It makes you realize that you're not alone. Coaches understand.

Feeling like I had embarrassed the program was hard to deal with, but it drove me. I tried to look back at every single thing I did with the 2010 team to see if I could figure out what I did wrong. One of the things that went through my mind was how every year my assistant coaches tell me that I've mellowed compared to when I first became a head coach. So one Sunday night right after the season, I took the players over to the track and ran the crap out of them. In recent seasons we'd done all of our conditioning work in the gym, so going to the track added more of an element of stamina and mental toughness to it.

We did one of my conditioning drills from the fall of 1981 that I'd created for guys like Jordan, Perkins, and Worthy. I wanted to show the current guys what tough really means. They ran a timed half-mile, three 400-meter runs, and five 200-meter sprints. They were shocked. They didn't think they could do it. One of the players was throwing up at the end of the track. I liked that. I told them I was done being Mr. Nice Guy and that something had to change, because I wasn't going to go through another season like 2010, and if I couldn't get them to play the way I wanted them to play by coaching them, teaching them, or pleading with them, this would be another option. Coaching by fear doesn't bother me if it gets the results we're all looking for.

Then during my postseason player meetings, I talked with David and Travis Wear about what I wanted them to work on over the summer. Their dad called me a couple of weeks later. I thought he wanted to talk about what I'd told his sons to practice so he could get them started on it at home. Instead he said, "Roy, I'll just get right to the point. The boys are not coming back. I want their release immediately." I was stunned. I didn't know what to say. It was not a pleasant phone conversation. He said that his boys weren't happy, and I just didn't believe that. I asked if I could speak to the boys and he said it would serve no purpose. That was it.

The Wears were two kids that I really enjoyed coaching. I thought they were really going to be good players and that they could really help us get back to where we wanted to be. They were going to play at least 45 minutes a game for us combined in 2011. Then all of a sudden the rug was pulled out from underneath us. I was just dumbfounded. Reality set in pretty quickly, and I realized that it doesn't make any difference how I feel. We've got to move forward.

The remaining players took that news and used it to help them bond. During the second session of summer school, we had everybody on campus except for Leslie McDonald and Larry Drew. It was fantastic for our guys. It was John Henson, Tyler Zeller, Kendall Marshall, Harrison Barnes, Reggie Bullock, Dexter Strickland, Justin Watts, and Will Graves, and every day they were playing pickup against all of our NBA alums who come back to play in Chapel Hill each summer. The two teams never mixed. Our players told me it was vicious. The alums said they'd never played in summer games more competitive. There were nine current or former NBA players out there including Marvin Williams, Raymond Felton, and Sean May, and our eight guys were trying to kick their tails.

On the first day of classes in August, we always do a 12-minute run, and then we come over to our house and I talk about the season and what I expect out of them. I gave my talk, and then at the end I asked if anybody else had anything to say. Will Graves said, "Coach, I need you to say something that you haven't said yet tonight."

"What's that?" I said.

"About winning a national championship," Will said.

Every other year that Will had been playing, I'd said, "I'm looking at a team that's good enough to win the national championship." I believed that for the 2011 team. I hadn't said it to the team because we were so young. I was thinking short-term goals more than long-term goals. But I said it again that night.

One day during conditioning in September, I was standing at the finish line as my assistants were calling out times. John Henson had just finished running and two other guys had run similar times. John looked over to me in a panic, asking, "What was his time? What did he run?"

"John, relax," I said. "Sam Perkins hated this program, but you know what he told me one time? Sam said, 'Coach, sometimes you've got to shut the hell up and run.' John, that's what you've got to do. These are times you can make. These times are realistic for you. Are they easy? No, but life's not easy, so just shut the hell up and run."

John looked at me and he said, "Okay." Then John took off running and he was fantastic.

No one liked the conditioning program at all, but I was determined to add some toughness to the team if they didn't have enough by themselves. It was really hard, but I was really proud of how they handled it. It made them a lot tougher mentally. They knew there was no sympathy from me. "You can complain all you want," I told them, "but keep it to yourselves, because it has no meaning to me. Guys, everybody wants to be like Mike. Well, then *be* like Mike. Shut up and do it."

During that time period I was seeing Will Graves get into the best shape of his life. I began to think he was going to have a great year. Then all of a sudden, one week before the start of practice in October, I had to dismiss Will.

That was another big blow to us that I really had a difficult time handling. Losing Will is going to affect me for the rest of my life because I stuck by the kid when everybody else was telling me to forget him. I was shocked when I found out I was going to have to let him go. I couldn't believe that he had made the same mistakes again. I had suspended him in 2009 for the whole second semester, and at that time I said, "Will, if there are any more problems, there is no decision to be made. You have one foot in the grave and the other on a banana peel. So don't screw it up."

I had a difficult meeting with him and his mother. They asked for one more chance. I absolutely loved the kid, but I had already given him all the chances I could, and he understood that.

I knew it was going to be hard to replace what Will could do for us on the court. He was a senior. He was our most experienced player, our best perimeter shooter, our best defensive player on the perimeter. Before the next practice, I pulled the team together and told them, "We've got some more adversity to handle. Will's not going to be with us, but we've got to move forward." That was really a hard day because those kids were counting on Will and felt like he'd really turned a corner and was going to be one of our leaders.

WHEN WE LOST to Minnesota and Vanderbilt in the Puerto Rico tournament to fall to 2–2, I wasn't alarmed. Those teams both had plenty of talent and experience, and we were only ranked in the Top 10 because of our reputation and expectations. Then we lost at Illinois and against Texas in Greensboro, and I still wasn't ready to panic. I'd said during the preseason that my team was going to get better and better as the year progressed, and I really believed that.

The one worry I did have was how the players would handle those losses, because lots of people were jumping off the bandwagon and badmouthing us. I know they were all thinking, "Here we go again. It's going to be just like 2010." But I kept telling our players, "We have big-time dreams and big-time goals. They are realistic. We just have to do it."

When Harrison Barnes struggled early in the season, I talked to him about expectations. I told him that he shouldn't be concerned with that stuff. He is one of the most stoic and focused kids I've ever coached, and I thought that if anyone could handle it, it would be Harrison. But I still worried about him. I even had a conversation with his mom at some point later in the season when I told her, "I was beginning to wonder what happened to that guy I recruited."

She said, "Well, I was beginning to wonder who that guy was disguised as my son."

What I kept saying to the press is what I believed. If Harrison Barnes is my biggest worry, I'm okay because before everybody else started seeing his productivity and success in the games, I could see it during practice. He started doing things that made me stop and go, "Wow!" I could see it coming.

During the Virginia Tech game at home in early January, Harrison made two or three really bad plays in a row, and I took him out. I was sitting between Steve Robinson and C. B. McGrath. "Guys," I said, "I am not that bad of an evaluator of talent. That kid is a lot better player than he's showing. I'm going to let him sit here for a couple of minutes, and then I'm going to put him back in because he might make a big play for us."

I put Harrison back in, and in a four-minute period he made three baskets that were just huge in helping us win that game. To me, that was the game that really helped Harrison take off. I said to myself, "That's what I thought we were going to get."

The next game against Georgia Tech was the turning point of our season. I was so pissed. I was mad with the way we started. I knew we were very lucky to be down only one point at the half, and then we came out in the second half and stunk it up even worse. We lost by 20 points, and I was off-the-charts angry.

I remember Coach Smith telling me many times, "You're better off not saying too much to the players after a game. You think you have the right opinion, you think you have the facts, but you're always better off looking at the tape and making sure. You want to be confident that what you're saying is true." But after that game I couldn't help myself. In 23 years I have never jumped on a team like I did those guys that night. Not even close. I ripped into them because I thought we didn't concentrate, we didn't play hard, and the players started blaming each other. I said, "How can we not know who we're guarding? How can we not run back on defense or have two guys run to the same guy and leave a wide-open three-point shooter? How can we make one pass and shoot a bad shot?"

Then I got after them because we had guys wearing five or six different kinds of shoes. Even though I knew it made no difference, I said, "And another thing. Everybody is going to wear the same fricking shoe! We're going to look like a team when we're on the court, even if we don't play like one." It had nothing to do with the game, but it made me feel better. Finally I said, "We are not going to be like last year where it's okay to lose. This team is not going to be like that. You are going to change or I'm going to kill you."

I still had the belief that we were going to be really good. In 2010 it was more of a hope than a belief. In 2011 I strongly believed it. I was so pleased about the wins at Virginia and at home against Virginia Tech because we didn't play well and we had to really tough it out to win. We would not have won those games in 2010. So I had that as a crutch. I felt like we just laid an egg at Georgia Tech. The year before we'd laid a lot of them, and I'd be damned if I was going to let them lay any more eggs in 2011.

I first started thinking about making a lineup change about six games into the season, because we were really having trouble scoring and Kendall Marshall had been making some pretty good decisions on the offensive end. Then all of a sudden Kendall had a bad game at Illinois, so I couldn't put him in the starting lineup yet because he was struggling. I can't count more than five times as a head coach that I've made a major change to the starting lineup during the season, but after the Georgia Tech game I had a meeting with my staff the next day, and I told them I was thinking about making three changes to the starting five: Dexter Strickland, Tyler Zeller, and Larry Drew. Z didn't deserve it as much, but I really thought I needed to shake things up. Then Leslie McDonald got hurt and couldn't practice or play in the next game, so I couldn't sub out Dexter. Then I thought, "That's not fair to Z." So the bottom line is that I only changed Kendall for Larry.

Before practice started I said, "Guys, do you think I'm the kind of coach who's going to sit back and let that kind of stuff at Georgia Tech happen and not do anything about it? I started to change you, Z. I started to change you, too, Dexter. Today I decided not to, but that doesn't mean I won't change you guys tomorrow."

Then I pulled Larry aside and I said, "Larry, this is not permanent. It can be if you don't play well and Kendall plays great. It's not just your fault, but I've got to do something, and this is what I've chosen to do. Maybe this will take some of the pressure off you, because you've had more pressure on you than any player I've ever coached."

Larry wasn't defiant. He didn't throw his arms around my neck and hug me either. It was very matter of fact. Larry said he just wanted us to win. We had a great practice that day.

We won our next four games and we were really good. Our offense ran more smoothly. I realized that while starting Kendall wasn't intentionally permanent, it was going to be awfully hard to make a change back now that Kendall was playing so well and Larry was giving us such a great defensive presence off the bench. Those four games were the best of Larry's career, and he really seemed to be buying in to what we were doing. He had nine assists and one turnover in 19 minutes at Boston College. Then three days later, on February 4, I got a phone call from Larry Drew, Sr., who said, "I'm pulling him out of there right away."

"You've got to be kidding me," I said. "It's the middle of the season."

It was so unexpected that Larry's roommate Justin Watts didn't even know about it. That morning Ed Davis called Justin from Toronto and asked, "What's Larry doing?"

Justin said, "What are you talking about?"

Ed said, "He's outta there."

Justin said, "No, he's not. He's in the bedroom." Then Justin went into the bedroom and came back out and said, "Yeah, he is outta here."

Losing the Wears, Will Graves, and Larry Drew were the three biggest shocks of my 23 years as a head coach, and they all happened within nine months, but at least I was learning how to deal with that kind of change. Again I knew I had to attack the situation head on. Right before practice on the day Larry left, the team huddled up and I went around to every player and said, "If there's anything going

through your mind to say about this, go ahead and say it." Some of
the kids were really hurt, but all of them agreed that if Larry didn't
want to be with us, then that's fine and let's move on. They rallied
around Kendall. As a team we never discussed Larry again.

From that day forward our players became so much more focused
on being a team. Now everybody was just concerned about winning.
Everybody was just concerned about our team. Now everybody could
trust each other.

Before our next game against Florida State, Kendall came to see
me. He was struggling with what had happened. He was nervous. I
reminded him of a story David Noel had told me about a time when
Kendall was just a sophomore in high school visiting campus playing
pickup with our team during the preseason, and yet he was confident
enough to point at David to tell him where to go so he could get him
the ball. I told Kendall just to be himself and he'd be fine.

The Florida State game was played in transition, Kendall's kind of
game. He was the quarterback. The orchestrator. He had 16 assists in
the win, and our crowd really got behind him because they didn't like
what had happened either. Florida State's coach, Leonard Hamilton,
told me afterward that he wished I'd made that lineup change just
one game later.

Then we played at Duke. We were the more aggressive team early,
and we stunned them. We were up by 14 at halftime, and I told our
staff that we had to try to be just as aggressive and not allow our team
to look at the scoreboard. But Duke got three offensive rebound baskets in the first three minutes of the second half and took it to us. We
hung around and cut their lead to three points in the final minute,
but we lost.

Always on my walk from the court to our locker room after a game
I try to think about the best way to address what has just occurred.

That was a night when I decided to be very straightforward. "I am ticked off," I told the team. "I am not into any moral victories. I don't want anybody saying that we almost got them. That's a bunch of bull. Let's not try to gain anything by telling ourselves that we played the top-ranked team in the country on their home court and beat them for 25 minutes. I'm not into that crap and you better not be either."

It was during that stretch of the season that Reggie Bullock became very limited by a knee injury and we finally had to shut him down. We were so used to adversity at that point that we didn't feel sorry for ourselves. It hurt from a coaching standpoint, because Reggie had the potential to be our best outside shooter, and when we lost him we were down to just eight scholarship players. We started substituting around TV timeouts to give our starters a three-minute break but only miss a few seconds of game time. We were so much more concerned about foul trouble. Guys had to fight fatigue. We really had to call on the toughness we'd built in the preseason conditioning.

We won a close game at Clemson when Harrison made the ferocious dunk. We ground out an ugly win at home against Boston College when we scored only 48 points. We battled through some rough patches to win at N.C. State and at home against Maryland, and then Harrison hit the game-winning jumpshot in the final seconds at Florida State, just as he had earlier in the season at Miami.

Everybody acts like they want to take the big shot that's going to decide the game, but not everybody really does. But Harrison, like Michael Jordan, is so focused that he doesn't think about the result or what's at stake. He's just going through his routine and making a play. He's not thinking, "Oh my gosh, this is a game-winner." He's just thinking, "Gimme the ball. I know I can do it." With every one of those clutch shots, Harrison became more confident, and the other guys began believing he was always going to make it.

By the time we met Duke again in the final game of the regular season, it was for the ACC championship. Toward the end of the season the press kept asking me if I'd seen this coming. I said that I hadn't, but not because I didn't believe in our team.

I remember one time I met with Coach Wooden, and he told me that before each season he used to pull out his team's schedule and would write down what he thought UCLA's record would be at the end of the year, seal it, put it in his desk and then open it after the season. I've never done that. I never think beyond the next game. Did I think we could be really good? Yes. Did I expect we could win the conference championship? I never thought that far ahead.

Against Duke I felt like all of the pressure was on us, but I didn't want my team to feel that way. I tried to be very confident, telling them that the only reason Duke beat us in Durham was because we stopped playing.

It was our Senior Day, but we had no senior starters and I had my whole staff asking me, "What are you going to do about the senior walk-ons? Are you really going to start those guys?" I worried about it, too. I remembered watching my son start as a senior against Duke and how Chris Carrawell scored two baskets against him. But finally I told myself, "I've started my seniors every year. We've never lost a game in the first two minutes. Those guys have been fantastic for us. This could be the moment of their lives as basketball players."

Also, I thought if I decided that we couldn't start the walk-ons, that would cause the starters to feel more pressure. We started three walk-ons and we were fortunate that Duke missed some open shots in those minutes, but the emotion of playing those guys and how our crowd responded to them set the tone for the entire game.

Once the game started, I never felt like we were going to lose. We got up by 12 points at the half and Duke came out and scored the first seven points of the second half. It was just like the game at Cameron, only this time we didn't panic. Harrison quickly scored two big baskets to take the lead back up to 12. We calmly answered all of their runs.

It was a surreal feeling cutting down the nets that day. I went around to each of my assistant coaches and said, "This is really good because nobody expected us to be here except us. I guess everybody's back on the bandwagon now." Then I got the team together out on the court, and I said, "Remember, all year, I've told you that our dreams and goals are realistic. You guys believed and that's why we're champions."

After that game someone asked me if I thought the struggles of the 2010 season made me a better coach. I do believe it made me appreciate what we had previously accomplished a bit more, and it made me try to enjoy the wins with the 2011 team more regardless of how poorly we played. But did it make me a better coach? I don't think so. But I have always been driven by fear of failure. Now I had experienced it and I didn't want that to happen anymore.

A COUPLE OF WEEKS before the end of the regular season we were talking in a staff meeting about problems that were happening on and off the court at other schools. At that point in a season, some coaches do not like their team at all and some teams do not like their coach at all, and that's sad because it takes all of the enjoyment out of coaching. "Guys," I said to my staff, "do you realize how much fun this group has been to coach?" I knew how lucky I was, and I decided that I was going to share that with our players.

Before practice that afternoon, we all huddled and I said, "I am having such a good time coaching you guys. You have given me new life." It felt really good sharing that with them.

It wasn't a battle anymore. The previous season had been a battle every day. I had never thought about quitting. I had never thought that I couldn't coach anymore. But if we had endured another season in 2011 when I couldn't get the kids to do what I wanted them to do, I'm not sure what I would've done. The 2011 team renewed my enthusiasm, renewed my confidence, renewed my faith in my coaching and my love for being a coach. They renewed my belief that what we were trying to do was right.

I'm a strong believer in toughness and that if my team just hangs around and never gives up, we are always going to come back to win. That was never more evident than in the ACC Tournament. After we won the regular season championship, our guys heaved a sigh of relief and thought that we'd really accomplished something. Then all of a sudden we were in Greensboro playing Miami and getting our butts kicked. We fell behind by 19 points with just under 10 minutes to go in the second half. I kept telling our players that if we didn't give up, I believed we were going to win the game, and I reminded them how we'd come from way behind to win at their place earlier in the season. We just kept plugging away until we won it at the buzzer.

Obviously, we learned nothing from the Miami game. In the ACC semifinal against Clemson, we fell behind by 14 in the first half. But in the second half, Harrison started making a bunch of baskets, and our team got so excited about what he was doing that it carried them along. I had no idea Harrison was on his way to 40 points. I just knew he was scoring every time we needed a basket. It reminded me of Al Wood scoring 39 points against Virginia in the 1981 NCAA Tournament semifinal. During that game, I remember Coach Smith turning to me and asking, "Do you think Al needs a breather?" I said, "Coach, let's wait until he misses one." That's the way I felt about Harrison that day.

Losing to Duke the next afternoon in the ACC championship game did teach us a lesson. We fell behind early and this time our guys couldn't fight back and win. I told them, "If that happens again, our season's over. We go home." Our guys realized that in the NCAA Tournament they had to be ready to play from the very start.

Whenever we play against a big underdog in the first round of the NCAAs, I am reminded of what Coach Smith always told the press in that situation. "Remember," he'd say, "they give out scholarships, too." But then the day before the Long Island game, I noticed one of their players asking one of our guys for an autograph for his little brother. Normally that might have worried me, but before the game I really thought we were ready and I was pleased that we got off to a better start and won the game easily.

Then in the next round against Washington, they kept making shots that our defense wanted them to take. I kept telling myself that they were not going to keep making those shots for 40 minutes, and finally, they didn't. We rallied to go up by one point with seven seconds left, and I called for the out-of-bounds defense that Vanderbilt coach Kevin Stallings had taught our staff the previous summer. That defense had caused a turnover or a timeout in almost every game that season because it's so hard to inbound the ball over John Henson. Sure enough, John tipped the pass, we got the steal, and Dexter hit two foul shots to help us win by three.

Before our next game, against Marquette, I made a point with the team. "I'm tired of listening to how Marquette is going to beat us because of how hard they work," I said. "I'm tired of hearing how they're lunchpail guys. How they don't have McDonald's All-Americans, they eat at McDonald's. You're telling me that Marquette's going to beat us because they want it more than you do?" A lot of the experts picked Marquette to win. We were ahead by 25 points at the half and it was never close.

As our staff looked at tape before the Elite Eight game against Kentucky, we thought the two most improved teams in the country were probably North Carolina and Kentucky. I felt that we were really going to play well. I had been lucky enough to coach in nine Elite Eight games previously and win seven of them. I even made a statement one time at a clinic, which I will never make again, that the two easiest games to coach in college are the Elite Eight game and the national championship game because you don't have to supply much motivation. Because of what's at stake, the want-to should naturally be there.

But at the start of the game against Kentucky, we did not have that fire, that sense of urgency. The players told me later that they felt like they were overconfident because they had already beaten Kentucky in December. That exposed the inexperience of our team. I've always felt that if somebody beats me one time, I want to beat their butt even more the next time we play because I am not going to let somebody do that to me again. That was Kentucky's attitude.

We did make a great run in the second half to get the score tied with three minutes left. But Kentucky hit some big threes down the stretch, and we just couldn't make the big shot this time. It was so hard to lose like that, because you don't know how many opportunities you're going to get, and the way the tournament played out, I believe if we had beaten Kentucky, we would have been the best team at the Final Four.

I have been in some tough locker rooms: in 1997 when my Kansas team lost to Arizona and I was convinced we had the best team in the country; in 2003 when we lost to Syracuse and I believed Kirk Hinrich and Nick Collison deserved to win it all. But this one was the toughest. The suddenness of your season ending is always the biggest shock in college basketball, and those kids were so young that it hit them really, really hard. Not a single player on our roster had ever lost a game in the NCAA Tournament. None of the kids in that locker room had ever experienced that finality. They were just destroyed. Normally I expect all of my players to look at me when I'm talking, but when I looked around that locker room there was not one player making eye contact. Some of them had their heads down crying. Others had towels draped over heads. One or two were just staring into space.

The hardest part for a coach in that moment is that you feel so inadequate. There was nothing I could say or do that was going to erase their hurt. It was so painful to look at those guys and know that I couldn't help a group who had done so much to help me. I told them how proud I was of them. I apologized to them because I was so disappointed about how we played in the first half and blamed myself. I told them to remember how badly they were feeling and to use it as fuel for the next season when we could be an even better team.

I thought about how we had overcome so many things together; the Wears, Will Graves, Larry Drew, the tough start when nobody could ever have imagined an ACC championship or 29 wins. The depth of my appreciation for what they had done as a team made the pain of my inadequacy even sharper. Finally, I thanked them, and even that felt empty, knowing that there was no way those young men could ever truly understand how much they'd done for this old coach. There was no way I could ever thank them enough for that.

Roy Williams
April 2011

ACKNOWLEDGMENTS

THERE ARE SO MANY PEOPLE I need to thank in my everyday life, specifically when it relates to their help with my career and this book.

I have been extremely fortunate with the administrative assistants I've had, and even more fortunate that I've had so few. When I first got to Kansas my personal assistant was Suzanne Bangert, and she was sensational. Then Debbie Walker came and stayed with me for seven years and was off the charts. Joanie Stevens took over and was with me for seven more years and took excellent care of me. Other people in my office were Susan Bragg, Carole Dickey, and Tami Hoffman, and they all did a great job. I know my 15 years at Kansas were made so much simpler because of those individuals. When I arrived at UNC, Jennifer Holbrook took up where the others left off and was just unbelievable. Nadia Lynch is now my assistant and has some big shoes to fill, but I feel strongly that she is going to do it. I have also been helped in Chapel Hill by Kaye Chase, Emily Cozart, Armin Dastur, Cynthia Stone, and Kay Thomas, who have been outstanding as well.

I'd also like to thank Eric Hoots, who has been a wonderful video coordinator; Wayne Walden, who was the most impressive academic adviser I have ever been around—I was lucky to have him for 21 years—and Jonas Sahratian, who is the most talented strength and conditioning coach in the whole world. I also have been very fortunate to have worked with three great trainers: Mark Cairns at Kansas and Marc Davis and Chris Hirth at UNC.

The fans at Kansas and North Carolina have been unbelievably good to me. Your overwhelming support, from the opening of Late Night with Roy in 1988 at Kansas to the moment I walked up to the stage of the Smith Center after our second national championship has always given me chills. I know that I will never be the best to a lot of people, but so many of you have made me feel that way. I thank all of you so much. There is no way I could have had such a great life and been involved in so many memorable accomplishments without my staff. Joe, Steve, Jerod, C.B.—you all are definitely "foxhole buddies" as well.

Tim and I would also like to thank Steve Kirschner, Matt Bowers, and Terry Kermit Roberts from the UNC Athletic Communications department for their extraordinary help with this project. Chris Theisen, Mitch Germann, Doug Vance, and Gary Bedore from Kansas were also incredibly accommodating as we asked them to dig through their archives. Thanks also to Jeffrey Camarati, Rich Clarkson, Mike Dickson, Jeff Jacobsen, J.D. Lyon, and Jack Morton for their help with the photography that brings many of the stories in this book to life. Joe Mustian and Jack Wooten also played indispensable roles in making this project complete.

At Algonquin Books, we would like to thank our extraordinarily skillful and patient editor, Kathy Pories, as well as Brunson Hoole, Anne Winslow, Laura Williams, Craig Popelars, Michael Taeckens, Ina Stern, Elisabeth Scharlatt, and Peter Workman.

We also appreciate all the work done by Chris Parris-Lamb and David Gernert at the Gernert Company.

A special thank-you to John Grisham for lending his brilliant words to the foreword and to Wanda Williams for inspiring and enhancing so many of the stories in this book.

TIM WOULD LIKE to thank his wife, Dana, and his kids, Atticus and Sawyer, for understanding why they haven't seen much of him for a while.

Appendix A

COACH ROY WILLIAMS' PLAYERS

UNIVERSITY OF KANSAS

Name	Years	Name	Years
Todd Alexander	1990	Jelani Janisse	1998–1999
Sean Alvarado	1989	David Johanning	1990–1992
Luke Axtell	2000 2001	Ashante Johnson	1999–2000
Brett Ballard	2001–2002	Adonis Jordan	1990–1993
Scooter Barry	1989	Brad Kampschroeder	1989
Jeff Boschee	1999–2002	Todd Kappelmann	2000–2002
Nick Bradford	1997–2000	Mario Kinsey	2001
Joel Branstrom	1995–1997	Raef LaFrentz	1995–1998
Terry Brown	1990–1991	Keith Langford	2002–2003
Rick Calloway	1989–1990	Michael Lee	2002–2003
Jeff Carey	1998–2002	Marlon London	1999–2000
Eric Chenowith	1998–2001	Mike Maddox	1989–1991
Nick Collison	2000–2003	Pekka Markkanen	1990
John Crider	1999–2000	Chris Martin	1998–1999
Lane Czaplinski	1990–1992	C.B. McGrath	1995–1998
Ben Davis	1992	Aaron Miles	2002–2003
Lester Earl	1998–2000	Lincoln Minor	1989
Doug Elstun	1989–1991	Christian Moody	2002–2003
Drew Gooden	2000–2002	Bryant Nash	2001–2003
Jeff Graves	2003–2004	Macolm Nash	1989–1992
Kenny Gregory	1998–2001	Milt Newton	1989
Jeff Gueldner	1989–1990	Moulaye Niang	2002–2003
Greg Gurley	1992–1995	Terry Nooner	1997–2000
Jerod Haase	1994–1997	Scott Novosel	1994–1995
Darrin Hancock	1993	Brett Olson	2003
Lewis Harrison	2001–2002	Greg Ostertag	1992–1995
Jeff Hawkins	2003–2003	Eric Pauley	1992–1993
Kirk Hinrich	2000–2003	Sean Pearson	1992–1996
Alonzo Jamison	1989–1992	Paul Pierce	1996–1998

UNIVERSITY OF KANSAS (*continued*)

Name	Years	Name	Years
Scot Pollard	1994–1997	Sean Tunstall	1989–1991
Kevin Pritchard	1989	Jacque Vaughn	1994–1997
Nick Proud	1994	Stephen Vinson	2002–2003
T.J. Pugh	1996–1999	Kirk Wagner	1990–1991
Mark Randall	1989–1991	Rex Walters	1991–1993
Steve Ransom	1995–1997	Blake Weichbrodt	1992–1994
Calvin Rayford	1992–1996	Freeman West	1989–1990
Patrick Richey	1991–1994	T.J. Whatley	1993–1996
Ryan Robertson	1996–1999	B.J. Williams	1994–1997
Richard Scott	1991–1994	Travis Williams	1996–1997
Wayne Simien	2001–2002	Steve Woodberry	1991–1994
Billy Thomas	1995–1998	Chris Zerbe	2001–2002

UNIVERSITY OF NORTH CAROLINA

Name	Years	Name	Years
Harrison Barnes	2011	Kendall Marshall	2011
Justin Bohlander	2004	Sean May	2004–2005
Daniel Bolick	2011	Rashad McCants	2004–2005
Reggie Bullock	2011	Leslie McDonald	2010–2011
Dewey Burke	2006–2007	Phillip McLamb	2002–2004
Marc Campbell	2007–2010	Jonathan Miller	2003–2004
Stewart Cooper	2011	Wes Miller	2004–2007
Mike Copeland	2006–2009	Patrick Moody	2008–2009
Patrick Crouch	2011	David Noel	2004–2006
Ed Davis	2009–2010	Terrence Petree	2010
Larry Drew II	2009–2011	Damien Price	2004
David Dupont	2011	Will Robinson	2006
Wayne Ellington	2007–2009	Byron Sanders	2004–2006
Charlie Everett	2005	Melvin Scott	2004–2005
Raymond Felton	2004–2005	Alex Stepheson	2007–2008
Brooks Foster	2005	Dexter Strickland	2010–2011
Bobby Frasor	2006–2009	J.B. Tanner	2008–2009
James Gallagher	2010	Reyshawn Terry	2004–2007
Marcus Ginyard	2006–2010	Quentin Thomas	2005–2008
Damion Grant	2004–2005	Deon Thompson	2007–2010
Will Graves	2007–2010	Thomas Thornton	2010
Danny Green	2006–2009	Justin Watts	2009–2011
Tyler Hansbrough	2006–2009	David Wear	2010
Van Hatchell	2011	Travis Wear	2010
John Henson	2010–2011	Thomas Wilkins	2006
Jesse Holley	2004–2005	Jawad Williams	2004–2005
C.J. Hooker	2004–2005	Marvin Williams	2005
D.J. Johnston	2011	Surry Wood	2006–2008
Justin Knox	2011	Jack Wooten	2008–2009
Ty Lawson	2007–2009	Brandan Wright	2007
Greg Little	2008	Tyler Zeller	2009–2011
Jackie Manuel	2004–2005		

COACH ROY WILLIAMS' CAREER

643–163 record in 23 seasons

Two NCAA championships, 2005 and 2009

Naismith Hall of Fame Inductee, 2007

Seven-time National Coach of the Year

Seven Final Fours

Ranks first in the country in winning percentage among active
coaches (79.8)

Fourth all-time in winning percentage

Fourth all-time with seven Final Fours

Third all-time with 58 NCAA Tournament wins

Second all-time with nine No. 1 seeds in the NCAA Tournament

Second all-time with 20 consecutive NCAA Tournament
appearances

Third all-time with 77 NCAA Tournament games coached

Only coach to win an NCAA Tournament game in 20 consecutive
seasons

One of 13 coaches to win multiple NCAA Championships

14 regular season conference titles

Reached 500 wins in fewer seasons than any coach in history

Has won more games than any coach after 8, 9, 10, 11, 12, 13, 14, 15,
16, 17, 18, 19, 20, 21, 22 and 23 seasons

Second all-time with nine 30-win seasons

Has coached teams ranked No. 1 in the nation in 10 seasons

Has coached four National Players of the Year, 13 first-team
All-Americas, eight conference Players of the Year

Has coached 20 first-round NBA draft picks

NCAA TOURNAMENT FINAL, 2005

Official Basketball Box Score—GAME TOTALS—FINAL STATISTICS

North Carolina vs. Illinois

04/04/05 8:21 p.m. at Edward Jones Dome, St. Louis, MO

North Carolina 33-4

##	Player		TOT-FG FG-FGA	3-PT FG-FGA	FT-FTA	OFF	DEF	TOT	PF	TP	A	TO	BLK	S	MIN
21	Williams, Jawad	f	3-6	3-4	0-0	1	4	5	1	9	0	0	1	1	22
32	McCants, Rashad	f	6-15	2-5	0-0	1	1	2	0	14	1	2	0	1	31
42	May, Sean	c	10-11	0-0	6-8	2	8	10	1	26	2	1	1	0	34
02	Felton, Raymond	g	4-9	4-5	5-6	0	3	3	4	17	7	2	0	2	35
05	Manuel, Jackie	g	0-1	0-0	0-2	0	3	3	4	0	2	2	0	0	18
01	Scott, Melvin		0-2	0-1	0-0	0	2	2	0	0	0	0	0	0	13
03	Terry, Reyshawn		0-0	0-0	0-0	0	0	0	0	0	0	0	0	0	2
11	Thomas, Quentin		0-0	0-0	0-0	0	1	1	1	0	0	1	0	0	1
24	Williams, Marvin		4-8	0-1	0-1	3	2	5	2	8	0	2	0	0	24
34	Noel, David		0-0	0-0	1-2	1	2	3	0	1	0	0	0	0	20
	Team														
	Totals		27-52	9-16	12-19	8	26	34	13	75	12	10	2	4	200

FG%	1st Half: 16-29	55.2%	2nd Half: 11-23	47.8%	Game: 51.9%	Deadball
3-Pt. FG%	1st Half: 6-11	54.5%	2nd Half: 3-5	60.0%	Game: 56.3%	Rebounds
FT %	1st Half: 2-2	100.0%	2nd Half: 10-17	58.8%	Game: 63.2%	2, 1

Illinois, 37-2

##	Player		TOT-FG FG-FGA	3-PT FG-FGA	FT-FTA	OFF	DEF	TOT	PF	TP	A	TO	BLK	S	MIN
40	Augustine, James	f	0-3	0-0	0-0	1	1	2	5	0	0	1	0	0	9
43	Powell Jr., Roger	f	4-10	1-2	0-0	0	6	14	2	8	1	2	0	1	38
04	Head, Luther	g	8-21	5-16	0-0	1	4	5	1	21	3	4	1	2	37
05	Williams, Deron	g	7-16	3-10	0-2	0	4	4	4	17	7	1	0	1	40
11	Brown, Dee	g	4-10	2-8	2-2	0	4	4	1	12	7	0	0	3	38
33	McBride, Richard		0-0	0-0	0-0	0	0	0	0	0	0	0	0	0	2
41	Carter, Warren		0-1	0-1	0-0	1	0	1	1	0	0	0	0	1	5
45	Smith, Nick		0-0	0-0	0-0	0	0	0	0	0	0	0	0	0	1
50	Ingram, Jack		4-9	1-3	2-2	5	2	7	4	11	0	0	0	0	30
	Team					1	1	2							
	Totals		27-70	12-40	4-6	17	22	39	18	70	18	8	1	8	200

FG%	1st Half: 10-37	27.0%	2nd Half: 17-33	51.5%	Game: 38.6%	Deadball
3-Pt. FG%	1st Half: 5-19	26.3%	2nd Half: 7-21	33.3%	Game: 30.0%	Rebounds
FT %	1st Half: 2-4	50.0%	2nd Half: 2-2	100.0%	Game: 66.7%	1

Officials: Ed Corbett, John Cahill, Verne Harris
Technical fouls: North Carolina-None. Illinois-None.
Attendance: 47262

Score by Periods	1st	2nd	Total
North Carolina	40	35	75
Illinois	27	43	70

NCAA TOURNAMENT FINAL, 2009

Official Basketball Box Score—GAME TOTALS—FINAL STATISTICS

Michigan State vs. North Carolina

4/6/09 9:21 p.m. at Ford Field, Detroit, MI

North Carolina, 34-4

##	Player		TOT-FG FG-FGA	3-PT FG-FGA	FT-FTA	OFF	DEF	TOT	PF	TP	A	TO	BLK	S	MIN
21	Thompson, Deon	f	3-8	0-0	3-4	0	3	3	4	9	0	2	0	0	23
50	Hansbrough, Tyler	f	6-14	0-2	6-10	1	6	7	3	18	2	2	0	0	34
05	Lawson, Ty	g	3-10	0-3	15-18	0	4	4	0	21	6	1	0	8	37
14	Green, Danny	g	2-4	2-3	0-0	2	1	3	5	6	4	2	0	1	24
22	Ellington, Wayne	g	7-12	3-3	2-2	2	2	4	2	19	0	0	0	0	35
02	Campbell, Marc		0-1	0-0	0-0	0	1	1	0	0	0	0	0	0	1
04	Frasor, Bobby		1-2	0-1	0-0	1	0	1	3	2	1	0	0	0	23
11	Drew II, Larry		0-1	0-0	0-0	0	0	0	0	0	0	0	0	0	4
15	Tanner, J.B.		0-0	0-0	0-0	0	0	0	0	0	0	0	0	0	1
24	Watts, Justin		1-2	0-0	0-0	1	0	1	0	2	0	0	0	0	1
32	Davis, Ed		5-7	0-0	1-4	2	6	8	4	11	0	0	0	0	14
35	Moody, Patrick		0-0	0-0	0-0	0	0	0	0	0	0	0	0	0	1
40	Copeland, Mike		0-0	0-0	0-0	0	0	0	0	0	0	0	0	0	1
44	Zeller, Tyler		0-0	0-0	1-2	0	1	1	1	1	0	0	0	0	1
	Team					2	0	2							
	Totals		28-61	5-12	28-40	11	24	35	22	89	13	7	0	9	200

FG%	1st Half: 18-34	52.9%	2nd Half: 10-27	37.0%	Game: 45.9%	Deadball
3-Pt. FG%	1st Half: 4-9	44.4%	2nd Half: 1-3	33.3%	Game: 41.7%	Rebounds
FT %	1st Half: 15-19	78.9%	2nd Half: 13-21	61.9%	Game: 70.0%	5

Michigan State, 31-7

##	Player		TOT-FG FG-FGA	3-PT FG-FGA	FT-FTA	REBOUNDS OFF	DEF	TOT	PF	TP	A	TO	BLK	S	MIN
02	Morgan, Haymar	f	1-2	0-0	2-2	1	0	1	5	4	0	1	0	0	19
10	Roe, Delvon	f	1-1	0-0	0-1	2	6	8	3	2	0	1	1	0	17
14	Suton, Goran	c	7-10	3-4	0-0	3	8	11	3	17	0	3	2	0	31
01	Lucas, Kalin	g	4-12	0-1	6-8	0	0	0	2	14	7	6	0	0	35
05	Walton, Travis	g	0-2	0-0	2-2	0	1	1	3	2	3	4	0	0	24
00	Ibok, Idong		0-0	0-0	0-0	0	1	1	0	0	0	0	0	0	1
03	Allen, Chris		0-8	0-7	3-5	1	0	1	2	3	1	0	0	0	17
13	Thornton, Austin		0-1	0-0	2-2	0	3	3	1	2	0	0	0	0	3
15	Summers, Durrell		4-10	2-6	3-4	2	3	5	1	13	2	2	1	0	21
22	Dahlman, Isaiah		1-1	0-0	0-0	1	0	1	0	2	0	0	0	0	1
23	Green, Draymond		2-2	0-0	3-5	2	5	7	3	7	0	2	0	1	12
25	Crandell, Jon		0-0	0-0	0-0	0	0	0	0	0	0	0	0	0	1
34	Lucious, Korie		2-5	2-5	0-0	0	0	0	3	6	0	2	0	0	14
40	Herzog, Tom		0-0	0-0	0-0	0	0	0	0	0	0	0	1	0	1
41	Gray, Marquise		0-1	0-0	0-0	1	0	1	2	0	0	0	0	0	3
	Team					0	2	2							
	Totals		22-55	7-23	21-29	13	29	42	28	72	13	21	5	1	200

FG%	1st Half: 12-27	44.4%	2nd Half: 10-28	35.7%	Game: 40.0%	Deadball
3-Pt. FG%	1st Half: 4-10	40.0%	2nd Half: 3-13	23.1%	Game: 30.4%	Rebounds
FT %	1st Half: 6-9	66.7%	2nd Half: 15-20	75.0%	Game: 72.4%	4

Officials: Tom O'Neill, Curtis Shaw, Tony Greene
Technical fouls: Michigan State-None. North Carolina-None.
Attendance: 72922
Ty Lawson—8 steals most ever in championship game

Score by Periods	1st	2nd	Total
Michigan State	34	38	72
North Carolina	55	34	89

Index

Tim Crothers was for many years a senior writer at *Sports Illustrated*. He is the author of *The Man Watching*, a biography of Anson Dorrance, the legendary coach of the UNC women's soccer team. He lives in Chapel Hill, North Carolina, with his wife, Dana, his son, Atticus, and his daughter, Sawyer.